# The Lusty Life of
# LOON LAKE
# LLOYD

# The Lusty Life of Loon Lake Lloyd

*World War II Marine,
Logger and
Resort Owner*

## His True Life Stories
Chronicled and Illustrated
by Ellen Keeland

 **Binford & Mort Publishing**
Portland, Oregon

# The Lusty Life of Loon Lake Lloyd

## True Life Western Tales

by
Logger and Resort Owner
Lloyd Keeland

Chronicled and Illustrated
by
Ellen Keeland

Published
in the Year Two Thousand
in compliment to
Loon Lake Lodge's
Y2K and Autograph Party

by
Binford & Mort Publishing

Dedicated to the many customers and friends
whose escapades gave us a lot of laughs,
the material for this book,
and a good life.

"Had some rough times, and good ones. Always laughed
at them the same; that's the main thing."

*Lloyd T. Keeland*

# Acknowledgment

To Nancy Brown, for typing this book on her "re-puter."

For a year and a half, back and forth the stories went from our house to hers, in manila envelopes; including revisions as small as a comma, all delivered by "E-mail"—Earl, the rural mail carrier.

With two other secretarial jobs, the typing of this book kept Nancy burning the midnight oil. A lone light often shone long after all the other houses were darkened.

In the fall of 1999, as the fruit ripened on the trees, Lloyd brought her bags and bags of apples so she could make pies for her husband and mother, when time permitted.

We knew our typist was getting a little overworked when Lloyd asked her one night over the phone, "Do you have the apple pie ready yet?"

After a pause, a long breath and a sigh, she replied in a restrained yet forceful voice, "We will have pie tomorrow!"

She got the book done too.

Thanks for a splendid job, Nancy.

# OF CONTENTS

*Duckett's Resort—1960*

## Duckett's Resort

They came from all over
from near and from far,
and the word was
to come as you are.

They came in their work clothes
including Ol' Lloyd,
from driving his Cat
through the fog and the void.

They came in play clothes
on a week-long spree,
to the lapping of the lake
where the winds blow free.

At night they listened,
and talked galore,
they howled, and hooted,
and danced o'er the floor.

Their spirits were flung
in a neighborly mode,
no matter what work
or row they hoed.

So an evening was spent
so cozy and warm,
'til retiring to camps
or retiring to farm.

IF YOU FEEL WE ARE NEGLECTING ANY
SERVICE, TELL US SO WE CAN MAKE THIS
AND YOUR NEXT VISIT MORE ENJOYABLE.

"One thing about it, when I was a deputy sheriff, I never
had to worry about Loon Lake with Keeland up there."

Bob Migas, *Migas Automotive Service*

## Lloyd Keeland

He wasn't a sheriff
He wasn't a king,
But he owned a resort
Where us yahoos could sing.
He ran his logging crew
During the day,
And his store at night
Where the campers could play.
He lived a life
Of reckless abandon,
And traipsed these woods
From hilltop to canyon.
He knew about trees,
And timber and such,
And of the people who lived here,
*We were all in his clutch.*

It could be said of Lloyd Keeland as it
was of Andrew Jackson, that he was,
"Fervid to his country, faithful to his
friends, indifferent to other rewards."

# Introduction

Hearing these anecdotes and experiences of Lloyd's life, I was inspired by the ruggedness, the humor and animation in them.

As a wife I thought, "These are good, this is life!"

Over the years, I started bringing out a notebook and scribble stick and hastily jotting them down.

Lately, over a span of two years, I got them down in a more complete form, having him retell them slowly. The words were always much the same whether he told them years ago or now. Sometimes he told them to a group of guests exchanging stories, and sometimes just me. I tried to keep them in Lloyd's own words and unique style. A few names have been left out or changed for respect of others, and many of the expletives have been changed or toned down for delicate ears. Other than that, these true life stories are pretty much as Lloyd told them.

I followed him with my pencil and clipboard. Being interviewed did not bother him. Nor did he mind answering questions, being woken up in the middle of the night, while he was eating his meals or working in his shop. Ever cooperative and informative, he always had something to say. With a clear and deliberate enunciation, happy and positive tone, his words were from the heart, plain and simple.

Six foot two inches tall, 230 pounds, Lloyd is never weak-voiced, but has good lungs and volume, being heard all of his life over equipment, weather, and hubbub.

He has an excellent memory and can remember exact places and names from many years before.

"Lloyd Keeland!" called out a woman from a sidewalk in Drain, Oregon, "Your name shines up in my memory like a silver dollar in a mud hole! Do you know who I am?"

"Well, Harriett, I'd know your old hide in a tannery anywhere."

Another time in Reedsport a middle-aged fellow accosted him, "You don't remember me, do you?"

He replied, "Galen McDonald, I'd know your mug in a police lineup anywhere, you old spruce knot."

Later Galen told me, "You know, Lloyd WAS a big man. If he told you that you had enough to drink, you didn't argue with him. He was strong as an ox. When I was a kid, I thought it was the greatest place in Oregon, around Lloyd's place, fishing and the lake. When my kids were little, I used to take them there. I never heard anyone say anything bad about Lloyd. I haven't had a drink in twenty-five years, thanks partly to him."

At seventy-nine years old, just like an elephant, Lloyd is big, thick-skinned, and has a good memory. He has no pretense of morality or covering up of actual events for nicety's sake. He hates a phony, or false-fronted individual, feeling that fine, plausible words are not so good as straight-forward conduct. He feels a man whose deeds are enlightened by virtue—that of true feeling for and dedication to one's fellow man—need not be nice about his expressions.

He is not one of your good careful men of the town, but a rough and rugged American protecting his country and his community. Being successful at many things, he shares his principles with people, and being only human, he lives out his failures alone.

At an early age, he learned right conduct, self-reliance and the benefit of work. By age thirteen, a man's frame came upon him, and he found he could do the work of a man. At that point he lost all interest in school, graduated from the eighth grade, and went to work for his father. During these formative years, he gained a basic trust in the nature of vitality. Over his lifetime, he has used that vitality in the highest way—that of helping others. His goodness is part of himself, not put on. Putting on airs is not his way, there is nothing stilted about Lloyd, and definitely no inhibited behavior.

His greatest quality is that of being a helper of men to right living. Even if a man be bad, how can it be right to cast him off?

His life has been highlighted by heavy interaction with people, tribulations with the elements, trials with the odds of nature—and "everything," as he puts it.

His language is straight-forward and sincere, colorful and whimsical, as is that of many loggers. A refined but tough element, these men spend their lives working and gambling with the forces of nature. They have strength, and great reserves of it! Of their own volition and choosing, in winter rain, storms or snow, they work singly, in pairs or in teams performing dangerous work in rugged, steep terrain. They move tons of weight, logs and cables in great expanses of nature with few men in between. Their hollers can be heard as they communicate across the sides of mountain slopes. They pull practical jokes, drink, laugh and rough house together. They have not much sense of inner isolation due to any persistent guarding of an ego. Muddy and wet, they are one with the elements and their fellow man. Their work has made them tough and capable, yet gentle, with plenty of ego, and Lloyd, like them, embraces all things. Incorporating modern phrases, he once commented, "I guess I am a little muncho."

Like other bunglers of this big-hearted breed, he is generous to a fault, willing to give anyone the shirt off his back. Not a day goes by but somebody calls on him for something. He also informs me, amazingly, that "One thing we have plenty of—is time."

Famous for the loaning of his time, labor, know-how, equipment and tools, there is hardly a piece of land in the area that he has not worked on, cleared or improved.

I thought the stories of this well-loved and respected man, who has helped every one of us in this community, should be preserved. He has led an intensely interesting life. Of those who came his way, we won't say how he helped or embraced them or what the results were, but he loved people, their problems and all.

In my notebook were the anecdotes of a few others, so I put them in to paint a fuller picture of yesteryear. Some of the customers' accounts of their camping experiences are in the book, too. Together these stories portray a remarkable way of life led by the people of the Pacific Northwest.

# Early Days

*My father and mother, Joseph Eli and Martha Keeland in 1955. They were both from the old school. Dad loved to sing—hymns, about all they had in those days. You could hear him two blocks away, singing at the top of his lungs. Mom loved to cook and always raised a good garden. He helped, too. He was a hell of a good gardener.*

# The Cherry Highgrader

Mother and us kids were camped at the berry fields, picking berries to make money for our school clothes. Mrs. Lyons had a cherry tree on the domestic berry farm and gave Mom some of the cherries to take home. So Leonard and I were picking them for Mom when an older boy came along and was trying to take our pails of cherries from us. He was going to get his without working for them. He got his all right. I was nine or ten, Leonard fifteen, and he was about eighteen or nineteen years old, a big Portland bully. By God, he went back to Portland with some bruises and cuts.

Leonard came down out of the cherry tree and started boxing with him. The big bully couldn't handle that and got Leonard in a clinch and got him down. Next to the cherry tree was a fenced-in garden where Mrs. Lyons had been working. A hoe was leaning up next to the gate. I grabbed it and clomped him in the head and wherever I could hit the freeloader. After being on the receiving end of that hoe, he didn't want them cherries, he just thought he did. He left without the cherries, anyway.

Nothing became of it. We told Mom. I imagine she told Dad when we all gathered at home again on the weekend. He was in the logging camp during the week. Back then we had to earn our school clothes in the berry or hop fields. If some of these jokers would have to earn what they got, it would straighten them right out instead of highjacking other people's stuff. They would appreciate what they got instead of having it handed to them. I know whatever we wanted we had to work to get it.

# Climbing For Dad

After graduating from the eighth grade I went to work logging with my father. Maynard, my brother, was driving truck for him and Leonard, my other brother, was working in a logging camp—C & H, there in Vernonia—Callow and Hitchman. We lived just a couple of miles from where we were working, east of Estacada, in an area of woods known as the Squaw Mountain District. I set chokers and was a "go fer" mostly at first. Dad got out mostly pulpwood—hemlock—cut in four foot lengths and peeled and had to be brought out where the truck could get it. Also pilings. We had an old stripped-down Model A truck; it would go in amongst the stumps where we could load it up.

In the same country where we were working, Dad bought a section, 640 acres, of timber from a man named Crane, who was either the Police Chief or Fire Chief in Portland. We had to make a mile-long road through the Mt. Hood National Forest to get to it. They paid no attention to things like this in those days, they were happy to see it. They had more sense, it was just more roads for fire protection. We got cedar poles and pilings out of the section plus pulpwood where we made the road.

Before we made the road we had to survey across a mile of timber to find the section corners between Crane and Wooster and Crane and Noreen, all old, old homesteads. Except for a rough one on the backside of Noreen, there were no roads in there; but it had been surveyed years ago and there were corners. Dad was good at surveying and went right to the corner mark! We had an old rope, if I remember right, for a chain for our distance. Kept notes on that. Squaw Mountain Timber Company, owned by Mr. Lawsman, had logged up to an established corner and we took off from there. We started running our compass course

2

right through the woods. I'd go out ahead and mark or blaze a tree or slash some brush and stay until he got up for the next sighting.

After going on like this for a mile, he said, "It's got to be right around here." So we just started walking around in a little circle and pretty soon, "Aha! Here it is!" We found the witness tree with the blaze on it and numbers carved into it and we knew we were close. Then we found the corner, a post with rocks piled all around it. That's how they did it in those days, 'way back in the 1800s, just fell a yew wood tree, squared it up and put that up there.

From here we headed down Dad's section line a mile to the other corner. But that was easy, trees had been blazed to show the boundary line. Wasn't much underbrush in those days—Indians kept the infernal stuff burnt off. People run cattle back in those hills and with that new growth coming up, those White Face would just get rolling fat. The limbs were way up there on that type of timber— beautiful timber. Once we found the two corners and slashed a line between them, we built our road right to the middle of that section line of Dad's 640 acres.

I was fourteen or fifteen by then, could do most everything and a good climber. To clear the road we pulled the trees out, roots and all. That was cheaper than blasting the stumps. Dad would point out a tree to put the choker and line in and I'd run over there, climb it, get it set up, then he'd point out another one across the clearing and I'd run over and climb that one. I'd get the choker and line way up in them—no limbs 'til high up. Dad would get it choked with the Cat and start to pulling, put the clutch in and let the Cat slip back a little ways and then hit it again and get the tree a-shaking and pretty soon she'd come over.

Wherever the road was going, Dad would point out trees for me to climb—"We'll take that one, 'n take that one, and that one goes," and we'd pull them suckers over. That little ol' thing had a dozer on it, a blade, you could scratch and maybe cut a root on one side or other. If I remember right, those trees we pulled over probably went to the mill. That little ol' Cat—God Almighty—that little ol' thing didn't have enough poop to move those root wads after they were cut off the logs, so we just put enough rigging on other blocks and lines and rolled 'em out of the way. Shoot, nowadays, they'd just run right up against one of them trees with a big Cat and they'd be history.

Dad had a little ol' tie mill, too, cutting China ties—that's where they went. They went to China. Little ol' six by what the heck? Ain't that awful? I can't remember the size but they were a lot smaller than ours.

I know who it was that helped us—Isaac Luce! They were a family that lived in there—they hauled the old man away. Let's see, there was Isaac, Minnie, Gwyn, Mary, and Dean, he was the oldest, and another little girl and a red-headed boy. They had no mother and I guess it was Gwyn had told our teacher the old man had been molesting her and they hauled his ass away.

Isaac got married and took care of the whole family and moved them to Lewiston, Idaho, after that shameful mess.

Some years later I was in the Physician's and Surgeon's Hospital in Portland with my eye when a nurse came in and said someone over in ward so and so heard my name and wanted me to come over and talk to him. I couldn't walk for a long time, they had me sand bagged in, trying to dissolve the blood clot alongside my head. As soon as I could, I went over to see him and it was Dean Luce.

I said, "What are you doing here?"

He said, "I fell out of a spar tree, darned the bad luck." I forget how it happened—all broke up. That's when I found out where the rest of the family went. You know, it wasn't too long ago, in 1977, when we got telephones I called in over there to information in Lewiston and asked for Isaac Luce or Dean or any of them.

She said, "Well, we have [Somebody] Luce." By God, it was that little boy from forty years before, he was the postmaster of that town. We had a nice talk. But back to that section of timber, by golly, Dad had relinquished his contract right before the end of the war. When I got out of the service I thought, man, I'd get some equipment and start logging it. Dad and us had only taken out the piling, cedar poles and pulpwood. I went up to our old section and there was a logging outfit right in the middle of it, going right ahead on 'er. I looked at the guy and I said,

"Well, gol dang, Abner, what are you doing here?" Abner Eaton. Him and I were in the service together. He was out of Washington. He was melting babbitt, chunks of steel, and getting ready to pour some "D" 's on the end of the line, to make some high lead straps.

"Oh," he says, "We got the logging job from. . . ." He told me who got the timber.

I wished him luck 'cause that ol' place fed us for a long time.

# Blasting with Airedales

This ol' Pollock, Mike Mattalooski, had Leonard and I blow some stumps for him. He was the neighbor on one side of my folks' place. My dad and us boys were always clearing the stumps off our place. We were nothing but kids. I was fifteen or sixteen. We were making the holes and loading them with dynamite. And then when they were blowed we had to take a darned ol' team of horses and get 'em into a pile. We put a chain around them and drug them together. He had a block in a tree with a line run through so that when the horses pulled they lifted the stumps into a pile around the base of that tree. He had another block on a stump with a line run through it so the first line wouldn't pull the horses' harness up in the air. For little stumps and pieces, he had a sled. We picked them up and put them on that for the horses to pull over to the pile and we'd unload them.

To make the holes we had a bar and a sledge hammer. We pounded the bar in the dirt and turned it with a pipe wrench sometimes to keep it free. You wiggled the bar around so it would make a bigger hole and come out.

You put half a stick of dynamite in the hole to blow a pocket down under the stump, then, depending upon how big the stump is, put that many sticks of stumping powder in there, one stick per inch. If it's thirty inches across at the stump, you'd put in thirty sticks. That way it blows it in pretty small pieces; blows it clear out of the ground, too.

Albert and Fred Adalin, the neighbors on our other side, and Leonard and myself—we had a whole bunch of the holes in the stumps loaded up with dynamite. We were blowing a whole bunch of them at once.

Well, Mike Mattalooski had about a dozen Airedale dogs. Ol' Skeezics was the father of all of them. When that first fuse started smoking, the whole works of dogs ran up and started digging. They had seen the smoke of those fuses. We didn't use electric caps in those days, but fuses that smoked, and that's what attracted the whole pack of Airedales. When they started blowing, we had dogs in the air along with the root wads. Dogs end over end and twirling and every other way, up in the air.

He was hollering, "Oh, oh, oh, there's so and so," and "there's so and so," he was naming them off. One was named Felix, he went sky high, too.

Finally, with the last one he hollered, "There's Ol' Skeezics! There goes my Skeezics!"

That's when he started bawling.

"Boo Hoo Hoo Hoo. . .," he was crying out loud, just bellering.

We had to bury all those dogs—they weren't blown to pieces, they were still whole—but hell, that wasn't much of a job, we put them in some of those ol' stump holes.

# The Blow-Downs at Never Still

You talk about trees blowing down. Dad and I were on the cutting crew for Russell & Sons out of Yamhill.

We had went to work. I don't think we'd even got out of the rig. We sat there in the crummy and watched them tree tops whippin' back and forth and uh uh! We'd decided against it—too windy to fall timber that day.

We got down the road about a mile from close to where we was working and, man, the limbs was a-flying and BOOM a tree went down right in front of us. Backed up. Figured we'd get out of that area; just a-hittin' in that one spot hard. Then pretty quick there was one behind us and shoot—we'd better move out of there! It just kept doing that until we was—I mean hemmed in. We couldn't drive backwards or forwards, our vehicle was totally blocked. We got out of the crummy and got where some of the timber that was falling had crossed up double—trees crisscrossed on top of each other. We crawled up under some of them root wads where we was pretty well protected. There we waited 'til she quit blowing. When the storm died down, we hiked out half a mile over and under these logs until we were on the main logging road.

I don't remember if it was that same day or the next day. The boss, Ol' George Russell, brought the old D-7 down there and as the buckers with their crosscut saws bucked them root wads off the windfalls, George cold-decked the whole works in tree length. In them days you didn't have any portable loaders or anything.

Well, they had it named right—"Never Still." Actually, it's kind of a flat in through there. That's where the Forest Grove water supply is now.

8

# Sawdust Delivery

I had gotten accustomed to big trucks while still young, about sixteen years old. I drove a cabover Ford log truck hauling logs to the mill for my father's logging company. Then I made my living hauling and delivering sawdust and hog fuel to customers around Portland in an International truck and trailer. You have to realize most people in those days heated their offices and homes with sawdust. They had big bins in their basements to store the sawdust in. The furnaces burned it, heating the water for hot water radiators around the building. For homes they just blew the hot air through air ducts. So I delivered hog fuel or sawdust in a huge truck.

One time I had a load of sawdust from Wulf Fuel Co. and delivered it to the address they told me. I got to this address and they just had a new cement driveway poured. It looked awful soft to me.

So I stayed out on the street and went and asked the man, "Where are we going to put that sawdust?"

And he says, "Just back it in and put it in front of the garage."

I says "I don't think that cement will hold up this load, it looks awful green to me." Oh well, he just kept insisting, oh, shoot, he got mad and so I just put 'er in reverse and back in there I went. This truck had a bed sixteen foot long and at least eight foot tall on dual axles. She got back in there about half way to the house and she just, "Errumpp!" And there I set broken through. So I called the boss, the owner.

He says, "Dump it and I'll send a wrecker and get you out of there!"

So that's what happened. The home owner was screaming and yelling. That particular truck was called a push-out, both back doors opened up fully to the sides and the front of the box moved all the way out towards the back, pushing the whole load out as it moved. There was a nice big mountain of sawdust on his soft cement with the man still jumping up and down next to it. He wanted me to put it in the basement; which was never part of the delivery.

"No thank you," I told him, "I don't get paid for that."

All the customers wheeled their own sawdust to their hoppers themselves; sometimes I even dumped it out on the street. It seemed this guy was a big wheel with International Paper, Mr. Wulf had told me, and that's probably why he didn't want to wheel it himself.

Pretty soon a wrecker came along and, staying on the good hard cement of the street, pulled me out. It took quite a pull because the rear end of the truck, the "differential" they call it, was sitting lower than the broken pieces of the cement. I had broken through with my wheels to real soft mud. They must have poured that on a new fill.

The wrecker driver said, "What are you doing out on that?"

"Talk to that man over there," I told him.

Not too long after that is when the damned war broke out. Our boss, Mr. Wulf, comes along and told all of us, "Now don't get any ideas about quitting, you're froze."

That's when I told him, "I'm thawing out, right now, I'm gone." And I grabbed my lunch box and left. Anybody with that attitude, the hell with them. I went to driving log truck; I could make more money hauling logs. Three months later I joined the Marines.

# World War II

# Eye Witness at Pearl Harbor

## Told by Ron Weikum, Resident of Ash Valley

My father, Henry Weikum, was seventeen years old and in the Army at Pearl Harbor before the Japanese attacked. What had happened, evidently, was that the night before there was some special occasion and all the men of the company got drunk. He and the Surgeon General were the only two that survived out of the whole company.

When you'd ask Dad about the war, it was the main thing he talked about. To him, it was like nothing else happened during the whole war. He'd get so worked up about it, for him it was like a crazed passion or mania. I've heard this story many times when someone had asked him about the war, he'd go nuts.

Dad didn't drink. That morning he and the Surgeon General were the only ones that showed up for reveille. They saw the bombs coming down the beach. They ran back in and threw buckets of cold water on the guys' faces. None of them would wake up.

About all they could get out of them was, "Go away, leave me alone." They must have still been drunk, you know.

Finally, he and the Surgeon General ran outside and that's when the bombs started hitting the barracks. Six or so bombs hit. They went back in and it was just blood and guts, the blood was up over their ankles. They got out the ones that looked like they might survive and operated on them.

Dad became a medic for a few months after that. Later, on one of the South Pacific islands, he ran into that Surgeon General and got assigned to help him. They wrote and exchanged Christmas cards for many, many years until Dad died.

Dad also told about a time a bullet went right through his hat and killed his good friend behind him, but in no way did that compare to how he talked about Pearl Harbor.

# The CB in New Guinea
## Told by Jack Kelley

We were in the CB's (Navy Construction Battalion) in World War II. We had our own definition of the meaning of "CB's," such as the Confused Bastards or Cuddle Bunnies.

We were in a bombed-out village called Halandia in New Guinea for two years. It was so bombed out there was nothing left. Not even a stick left standing up. The first thing we did was build a PT boat dock for our supplies and logging business. That was the nice thing about the CB's, we had everything we needed to do these jobs. Everything was brought in to the dock we built. We logged, built a mill and made lumber. Then we proceeded to drill a well. There wasn't any good drinking water, and the natives really appreciated that when we got done. They really liked that clean water! We were there for two years and made a lot of improvements.

The natives were dressed from the waist down. The Japanese had been there and had slashed and mutilated them. All the women's breasts and everywhere else on them had been cut open and healed up. Those Japanese Samurai swords made just terrible slashes that, after a year of healing, were just horrible to look at.

We were six months on K-rations—no fresh food. No leaves for two years.

I did take a three-day pass when things were slow to go up the river and see an untouched village, which was twenty miles distant. The Japs had stormed through and taken over every other village, but they hadn't gotten to this one. Two other guys accompanied me on foot. Everybody else just wanted to go home.

The village was built on stilts over the river. Everything was very neat. We walked slowly down the line of huts, fearful of lurking Japs. The jungles were infested with them still. At the end of the row was the largest hut. There lived the leader

13

of the village, a large, tall Indonesian chap from Java who spoke some English with a heavy British accent. All of his villagers were woolly-headed little dark natives otherwise. He told me he had been there ten years and had a wife and two children.

All of them were gone, I couldn't understand how, from the conversation, when the Japs came to their village. They must have got the news that the Japs were coming, so the whole village went out and hid in the jungle. They were lucky to get away. We enjoyed the visit and hiked back to our camp satisfied of finding this untouched village.

One night a little later back at camp, two guys a few tents down started screaming and yelling real loud. They were running around waving their arms. Some died right off, others died a little later—hootch did it. Bad hootch. Either bad homemade stuff or Jap booze they left behind. They would put poison in it.

From New Guinea we went to the island of Mendoro in the Philippines. There one of the CB's took a pet monkey. It was a small, frisky little thing. He wasn't allowed to bring it with him when he left, so he sold it to one of my tent mates. I made a box for it to ride on the front of my bicycle I rigged up—even the bicycle was rigged up out of parts. For about a month we rode all around together. A lot of fun being with that monkey, but he wasn't so much fun when one day we were all out of tent. The monkey got loose from his tie at the center stake and really made a mess of things. He had watched us shave and fix ourselves up for quite a while. He got into the shaving cream and talcum powder and everything. We cleaned the tent up and got rid of him.

I went on another exploration trip to a remote valley in the Philippines, like I did in New Guinea with a pass and some other CB's. We took two jeeps and one weapons carrier. Five small rivers had to be crossed by winching the jeeps over with the weapons carrier. The weapons carrier was tall. It could drive across, but the water was up over the seats as we pulled the low jeeps across. Reaching the village we noticed something was going on. There were decorations tied up all over the place and a lot of excitement. I talked with someone who was raised in Manila and knew a little English. He told me they were celebrating the funeral of an old beloved and revered individual. A lot of wild hog carcasses were hanging covered with flies, and one bore hog was being roasted in a pit in the ground. We spent two nights there and got back home the same way by fording the rivers and being drenched in downpours of tropical rainstorms.

Shortly thereafter the war was over, and I went back home and was released from the CB's. It wasn't long before I was called back in for the Korean War.

*Jack Kelley in 1945. He now manages the Coast to Coast Hardware store in Veneta, Oregon, and occasionally finds time to vacation at Loon Lake.*

# Gay Navy Chief

The first gay guy I ever met was on a troop train. We were Marine recruits heading for San Diego. I don't know where that big bald-headed Navy chief was going, but at nighttime he was feeling up a bunch of guys in their berths. I thought it was Al Jungling, the guy under me.

"What are you doing?!"

"What are yooouuu doing?" came a very singsong sweet reply from the phony drone clod as he was fondling me finer parts.

That's when all hell broke loose. I just swung around out of that bunk and kicked him with both feet straight out. I knocked him clear across the aisle against the other bunks. All the guys came alive out of their slumber. Al Jungling was hollering, "I didn't do nothing!"

None of them wanted to admit it, I guess, that he'd been feeling around on them until we got to talking to each other.

There were a bunch of Army guards on the train; we told them they had a queer there, but they didn't do anything. Nothing. Everybody knows this is a court martial offense.

The Navy chief was back and forth through there all night—up and down the train. They had Navy, Army, and Marine recruits all separated on that troop train—everyone in different cars. He was still loose and seeing who he could fondle.

The train stopped at Mt. Shasta and as it was pulling out, here shows up that thus and such again. We got a couple of hammer locks on him and got him out to the platform between the cars and told him, "You bastard, you've molested the last guy on this trip, you're making a stop here!" and threw him off the moving train. Never did see him again.

He was a lot older than the rest of us; we didn't know why he was there. He might have been supervising those Navy troops; they probably didn't miss him either.

# Machine Gun Platoon
# I Company, 3rd Battalion, 23rd Regiment, 4th Marine Division

In Maui, training, we had an officer who said, "Well, we'll go on a little march today."

We had those big heavy machine guns to carry besides our backpacks. You're supposed to take a break every once in a while. It was too much trouble to unload everything— ah, shoot, we were just wearing him out, really. All he had was either a .45 or a carbine and a little bitty pack, maybe! So, we never stopped all day. He was pretty tired, the bumming son-of-a-bitch; half the time he'd bum a little smoke, cigarette from somebody. We just wore him out by not stopping all day.

We even did this to a sergeant. We were at our boot camp training in Camp Pendleton, California. This crazy gosh-darned sergeant had us, in Tent Camp Two, go on a march. Just as quick as we got out of camp he shouts, "All right, do a little double time!"

It didn't take long until he wasn't there doing double time; he was hollering, "Halt! Stop! Ah, you son-of-a-bitches!"

We ran off and hid in the hills. We come back about time for evening chow. God, he had us there at attention, cussin' and a-raring!

"Tomorrow," he says, "We're going to do that again. But this time I'm going to be in a jeep. Then we'll see how fast and far you can run."

Never saw him again. The Captain walked up and told him, "Sergeant, I want to see you in the company office."

He had done that starting-out-running the day before— shoot, we had heavy packs, weapons.

It was a good thing we were in good shape and young because when we hit the beach on Iwo Jima and all over the island, that sand was hot and so coarse you sunk in 'way past your ankles. It would be just like trying to climb a dad-gum hill in, say, something like wheat—you didn't get anywheres very fast.

*Lloyd with his sister, Hatti*

# Iwo Jima

We'd been on board ship a long time by the time we had sailed from Hawaii to Iwo Jima, an island seven hundred miles south of Japan. The day was just breaking when our huge convoy of hundreds of ships arrived.

For days B-29 airplanes had been dropping bombs, and battleships and destroyers had bombarded the five-mile long volcanic island with sixteen-inch guns trying to hit Japanese pillboxes, bunkers and strongholds for the initial landing.

It didn't do much good because all the 22,000 Japanese were securely dug in down in the bowels of the earth. They had dug twenty-six miles of tunnels and converted the old sulphur mines and natural caves into living quarters. For ten months General Kuribayashi worked his men around the clock, sometimes all but four hours a day to fortify the airstrips and island. The small Japanese village had been evacuated and buildings dismantled. With the help of hundreds of captured Korean laborers an oak forest on the island was felled and used to shore up the tunnels. Cement entranceways and ceilings were poured from six inches to ten feet thick. All entrances were angled at ninety degrees a few feet inside for protection against flame-throwers, artillery and demolition charges. Some tunnels were a hundred feet below ground, with huge hundred by forty foot rooms. Bunks were carved into the sides and all the walls were plastered. Steam and electricity and water were piped in. The water was from a well and a seawater distilling plant. Air vents were cleverly put in everywhere and so were the holes from which they fired rifles, machine guns, mortars, artillery and rocket launchers. They even had tanks buried with just their big guns sticking out.

There I was in the third landing wave. I had a backpack on my back, a gas mask hanging around my neck, an M-1 rifle, and a cartridge belt around my waist, from which hung a bayonet and a canteen.

Over the ship's edge we went down a cargo net. We climbed down that to a landing craft that's a-bouncing up and down. You try to time it just right to turn loose of the net and you're in. The sea was rough.

We looked out on our way in and saw landing craft being blown up, bodies and metal flying everywhere, the sea turning red. Rifle shells were hitting the side of the craft and we stayed hunkered down there waiting for the higgins boat to hit the beach. There she hit. When the ramp went down if you're on the right you're supposed to head towards the right a little bit, and if you're on the left you run out there to the left, and if you're in the center you work out there straight ahead. But shit all you did is run out to a bunch of people piled up there on the beach. So much crossfire no way anyone could move. Shells, bullets, shrapnel, everything flying—so much metal in the air I don't know how anyone survived.

Our squad, packing machine guns, tripods and ammo boxes, was moving right along zigzagging up the steep, soft sand dune, looking for a break in the heavy firing to get through. I got hit with shrapnel in the knee, and the corpsman who was running right with us told me to go back to the ship. I hobbled back past a lot of men lying on the beach begging me to take them with me. We had been instructed to let the stretcher bearers carry off the wounded so I boarded a higgins boat full of wounded and returned to the ship. There a ship's corpsman stapled up my knee and bandaged it and I went and sat on the deck. There all around me were men blown to hell moaning and hollering. Some had no arms, no legs, and I thought, who the hell wants to sit and listen to that? Not me. I caught another landing craft to the beach. Only this time the Navy coxswain must have been a new guy. He was one scared boy. The first thing he did was go under the bow of the ship. That was his first boo-boo. "Big Mo," the big sixteen-inch gun aboard ship was touched off, deafening all of us in the boat below. That boom impaired the hearing in my right ear the rest of my life, I never could hear anything out of it very much. I imagine the rest of those guys were the same way. We got turned around and we were getting in pretty close to the beach when a mortar shell hit right in front of us. The Navy ensign, scared shitless, stopped the boat. The Marine lieutenant jumped up and put a .45 pistol to the kid's head and said, "You'll go forward and put these men ashore."

I imagine the Navy kid was even scareder when the .45 was against his head so we went forward and pretty soon we were scraping sand. The ramp flopped down and the Marines never hesitated, but leapt out full force. Then the kid must have gotten excited again because all of a sudden the ramp closed again, piling men down on top of one another as they were trying to get out. Some were hanging on the top of it, some were half-way over, when the kid must have realized his mistake and opened the ramp again. I was still in the boat but got off with the rest of them this time. My outfit wasn't hard to find, they hadn't went much, over close to the airstrip.

We were a machine gun outfit and here's how we ran along. The head gunner, the guy running the machine gun, he packed the gun and one belt of ammunition. The assistant gunner carried the tripod and the ammunition carrier. I was an assistant gunner. It wasn't but a few days that I was a head gunner, replacing the other gunners killed and wounded.

After a few days of hard fighting, we took the airstrip and those other jokers raised the flag.

We had numbers stencilled on our back, which represented where we were from. On our dungaree shirt jackets was something that looked like this:

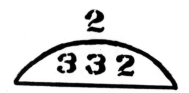

The half a circle shape signified the Fourth Marine Division. The first "three" meant the Twenty-Third Regiment, the second "three" was for the Third Battalion, the "two" inside the shape was for I Company, and the "two" on top was for my rank as a corporal. This stenciled emblem was right in the middle of the back, made a good target. The coded numbers were to throw the Japs off in case they got a hold of us. We were supposed to tell them nothing, only our name and our rank. The numbers were also to identify us on the battlefield. We removed all our other rank and unit insignias and left them in Maui.

The black sulphur-smelling sand was so hard to get around in that the tanks and Cats and other equipment on the beach had a hard time moving inland. They put down woven steel mats of different sizes, some fifty by a hundred foot long. You could see those mats flipping through the air like playing cards, so many bombs were hitting.

Sneaking around all these Japs in their hidey holes you knew they were close when you could hear "Clap, clap!" the sound of the Jap soldiers breaking open their hand grenades on their helmets. Then they'd drop back in their tunnels. The bombs never stopped. Oh hell, no, ol' "Washing Machine Charlie" just kept them dropping all night long, day and night, steady as a washing machine. I took some shrapnel in my arm, which is still there. Some of the shrapnel in my knee worked out years later.

Oh, God, this Walt Berry, he had a machine gun platoon. And we had a machine gun platoon. The lieutenant brought an Italian cook up there and put him in Berry's squad. Most of our whole company was Italian—out of New York and New Jersey. Berry was always in awful rough places. This time he was up on a rock cliff. We had our machine gun set up right below him. He was next to us, up high. They passed the word down for everybody to hold fire. Never did know what that was all about. Sergeant Ayers was in the foxhole right next to us. He stood up and that crazy ding-a-ling replacement cook cut him right in half with a machine gun. He killed one hell of a fine guy. I liked that guy. The cook was screaming and bawling—he was making more noise than the Japs were. It didn't take the corpsmen long to come and get that cook out of there. They gave him some kind of a shot and got a stretcher and packed him out. Then they packed Ayers out.

The Japanese were banzaiing. That night from our fox-holes we had heard a big group of Japs below us drinking their sake and getting primed for the attack. It just sounded like they were going nuts, chanting and yelling. We were up above in rocks and crags, and they were down below. They weren't sure where we were and we had orders to stay quiet. We let them get coming good, howling and screaming and then shot a parachute flair along with a mortar, which lit things up real good, just like daylight. We didn't need orders to start firing. When that ol' flair went up and popped, that's when all hell broke loose.

Walt Berry and I threw hand grenades during that banzai attack until our arms got sore. The Japanese couldn't tell where hand grenades were coming from. When you fire that .30 caliber machine gun, they know right where you're at. This is because every fifth round, or bullet, is a tracer, just a ball of fire so you can see where it goes; you can see what you're hitting. We picked them off just like shooting ducks, but they kept right on a-coming. We mowed them down right and left. None of the banzaiing Japs got through to us, none of them in that bunch.

Boy, we had a pile of those slant-eyed son-of-a-guns out there the next morning. That's where we ran into those Imperial Guard Marines—yes, Japs had big, tall Marines wrapped in cheese cloth—bullet would go right through them and they'd keep on coming.

We were in the same place five or six days. We finally moved forward and looked around for a place to dig in for the night. The guys were starting to shovel. In lots of places the sand was too hot to lay down on, kind of a black, ground up volcanic rock. About that time we saw huge metal doors open and a framework came up on railroad tracks out of the ground. An explosive charge was set with a deafening "BOOM!" releasing a huge garbage can-shaped projectile. We had been hearing this screaming "Tokyo Express" bomb, as we called it, but never knew where it was coming from. The noise it made was like an air-borne locomotive "wo-op, wo-op, wo-op," lobbing end over end in every damn direction. It screamed like nothing you've ever heard before and it would scare you because you didn't know where it was going to go. It never did any damage but sailed clear over the island, landing in the ocean. We radioed in its position and next morning the Marine Corsair planes dropped napalm on it; enough that the demolitions men could run in there and throw satchel charges of TNT dynamite in the hole. The enemy wouldn't be using that one for a while until they dug the boulders and dirt out of it.

In the Marine Corps we had been issued a solid brass emblem—you know it's the world with an anchor and an eagle—this one was about an inch and a half across—a little heavy thing. One guy had been shot and fallen on his face. The corpsman came to pick him up and I was there and helped. We took off his backpack and his clothes; we were trying to find out where he'd been hit. We couldn't find any wound or blood anywhere; we looked everywhere. We even looked in his hair. Then we noticed that Jap bullet had hit him square in the back and stuck right there in that brass emblem. He was carrying the Marine Corps emblem in his backpack. The concussion had just knocked the wind out of him. That Marine Corps emblem had saved his life. His name was PFC Neal Markley. He had a trucking business in Oakdale, California. Fifty-five years later I found him through the Fourth Marine Division Association, and we have talked over the phone.

Anyway, he was there in that mixup; we had advanced right up to this. . .like a big bluff in front of us. That's where we got pinned down in a hole about the size of a living room. As we were deciding where to set up the machine guns, Tim Shay and I were standing there talking to one another, and he says, "God Bless, you got hit there, too?"

I was limping, and I says, "No, that was opening day." As we talked, "Boom" he dropped to the ground. A sniper's bullet hit him right between the eyes. I called for a corpsman and he was hit dead center. Packed him out of there. That was a shame, that was one fine fellow. I dug in right there, and tried to draw fire. It was the front line. Some of the other guys saw the yellow smoke from that sniper; they tore right after him. We had overrun that sniper. He was in back of us. He was up on a twenty-foot-high hill a bulldozer had made. Frank Kallinger shot him. The shot tumbled him right out of there.

"Ha, ha, ha. Got him," Frank said.

We were there a long time from morning to must have been evening when they made a big smoke screen and we were able to get out of there. With the smoke screen the Japs couldn't see anything. I think the artillery laid 'em back in there, too, kept them in their holes long enough for us to get out. The stretcher bearers were able to come in and get PFC Markley out.

We had the machine guns set up, but there was nothing to shoot at; we were picking them off with the rifles. Then that one Jap committed hari kari. He must have been hit or thought he'd get it anyway. He looked up toward the sun, took that knife and stuck it right in the middle of his belly and that was the end of him, he tumbled off of the bank.

One night Frank Kallinger and I were in a big bomb hole—which made a good foxhole—there were plenty of them around, tailor-made. A Jap might be in the one next to you, though, so you'd better look around.

We weren't supposed to fire that night in a no-fire restriction. I had done my watch and I woke Frank up. It was his turn, so he was on watch and I went to sleep. A little later, I woke up with the clanging of a sword hitting a rifle barrel, "Clack, clack, clack, clack!" Frank must have dozed off because a Japanese man was at the edge of our bomb crater trying to hit him with a three foot long samurai sword.

Frank was fending him off with his rifle barrel. His hand was cut. He must have grabbed the sword because all his tendons were cut on his right hand. I finally got awake enough to see what was going on, it don't take you very damn long, either. I got the Jap by the ankles and jerked him down in the shell hole with us, then had to do him in the best way we could figure out to do 'er. Couldn't shoot, no firing that night. Frank had a hand he had the rest of his life—it stayed curled up, he couldn't even get his fingers all the way open. Bea, his wife, called them his "bird claws" when she'd get mad at him. Lucky he had any fingers.

I passed the word to the guy next to us in *his* shell hole thirty feet away, "Need a corpsman." The word was passed down the line.

Then the word was passed back, "A corpsman's coming," so you wouldn't shoot *him*. Well, you couldn't shoot. . .we were expecting a banzai attack; we wanted to surprise them. So, I guess, the idea was to wait until they made their big charge, then dump it on them. But no charge happened, the enemy stayed put.

We weren't supposed to take any souvenirs home, but I brought that Samurai sword back with me after the war.

One time we dug in; that was about all the time. They passed up along the line some rations. One guy Hartman, from Oklahoma, was complaining about the rations.

I said, "Well, hell, if you don't like that, cut a steak off of one of those burning blank-blank's there."

Those burning Japs were laying all over the place. He left us and went 'way out by himself in his own little hole.

We thought we were damned lucky to get anything to eat.

Then there was King, who was a replacement from the field music outfit. He must have been straight off the ship because he sat around there and kept saying, "Oh, if Daddy could only see me now. If Daddy could only see me now."

We were on the move and we stopped in one of those gosh-darned shell craters and them bastards were up above us. We were pinned down again, which was nothing new. We were in the low ground, they were in the high ground. So we had the machine gun set up there watching for when they'd fire; there'd be a little yellow smoke or something—we'd machine gun the hell out of that. This Japanese joker came up out of a hole, a hundred feet right in front of us, we didn't even know there was a cave there.

I threw the rifle up to my shoulder and King knocked it down, saying, "Hey, don't shoot, he's a human being!"

Boy, it's a lucky thing somebody else boresighted that bastard 'cause he was loaded to blow us all up. I don't know what happened to King, he disappeared, too. They probably got him to packing out dead or back on the beach in supplies. I doubt his Daddy would have been very proud of him to pull a stunt like that.

The Japs had the Nambu machine gun. We were using ones out of WWI. Shoot, all ours would put out is about 550 rounds a minute. The Japs were putting out about a thousand rounds a minute. We had the light machine gun, a .30 caliber. The heavy one was water-cooled, but we converted it and used it on a light machine gun tripod—that way we didn't pack that infernal water tank around with us.

Why in the hell did they do away with that old faithful M-1? Oh, they "needed more fire-power, needed more fire-power!" You could drag that rifle through sand, mud, dirt, whatever, and that ol' baby would still fire. I never did see one of them jam. Never. If it did, it was faulty ammunition. I hated to turn mine in. They took our M-1's and issued us .30 caliber carbines and .45 pistols, although some rifle platoons were able to keep their M-1's. The .30 caliber carbine was short, only made for jungle fighting. It would shoot just a little further than the .45 pistol. Neither shot as far as the M-1. One well-placed shot is all that is needed and that's exactly what the M-1 could deliver. They don't need to tell us that was a new type of jungle warfare. More political B.S.— someone paid someone off and told Uncle Sam they needed a new weapon. That M-1 was a damn accurate, faithful and long-shooting rifle. It had them all beat. The Japs had three different caliber of rifles— a .31, a 6.65 and 7.7, all good weapons.

Many years later, Frank Kallinger, the marine who had the tendons of his hand cut by grabbing the Samurai sword, found out where I lived through one of my customers. The man used to come up here to get this real fancy maple and myrtle. He used it in making furniture. I got to visiting with him one evening and we got to fighting the war again and I told him about Frank. I hadn't seen him since the corpsman took him away. I think he got hit again, down on the beach, waiting to be evacuated, because he had a big scar on his shoulder and shrapnel all in his chest. I told this guy when Frank joined the service he lived in Whittier and wrote to his wife there.

He said, "If he's still in California, I'll find him!"

Boy, about a week, ten days, the ol' phone was a-ringing—in those days all we had was the old radio phone. It was Frank.

"Boy, I'm coming up there!" And boy, he was here. He had a month or two to go to retire from U.S. Steel and he bought a house on Hinder Road in Elkton before he left here from that first visit. He moved up and together we had many a happy hunting and fishing trip. One year he developed pneumonia and passed away. The Sergeant Major upstairs called him to his final reward.

Another morning we had been dug in all night. It was almost daylight when we saw four Japs hotfooting along a trail there—all of a sudden these bastards stop.

"Ah, they went into a hole," I said, seeing them go into a shell crater where a bomb had dropped. They had come out of some caves nearby and went into that hole in the ground.

We passed the word down the line, "Don't shoot." We took some .30 caliber rifles and machine guns and snuck up to the edge of the hole. They were dug in there chattering away. I don't know what they were saying, but it must have been something to the effect that—what they thought they'd do is wait 'til about daylight and pick a few of us off. We weren't close enough to the edge yet to see them, but we could hear them. Three of us circled it and started lobbing hand grenades in it. Then we ran up there and finished them off; they were hurt. We got hell for that by that goofy-assed lieutenant who we had only for a day with the rifle platoon. I think what made him mad was that we were banzaiing the Japs. But we never saw him anymore, he left the rifle platoon. Us machine gunners never did have any lieutenant. By God, they wouldn't stay with us at all. All our outfit was so rough we couldn't keep an officer, they'd go over to mortars—transfer out of machine guns. So we just ran on Iwo without one. Actually, by the eighteenth of March, the end of the battle, there wasn't much of I Company left. Out of the 350 men that landed, there was only thirteen men of the company left. It was about the same with all the companies. After twenty-eight days of battle, there were 6,000 American men killed and 20,000 wounded. The Japs sustained 21,000 killed, and one thousand were taken prisoner; so few because most of them, when cornered or trapped, would commit hari kari rather than surrender. I was one of the few men who could say they landed on D-Day and made it all the way through the battle of Iwo Jima.

# Shifting Gears

Driving our 1942 International dump truck, my wife had trouble finding the gears. I drew the gear pattern for her, which looks like this:

1      2      5 (Overdrive)

R     3    4

You can see why she would grind gears, the gear pattern is a little unusual. She appreciated that but never used it much as she just stayed in the lower gears anyway. It was very seldom she drove the dump truck, just started it up and drove it around the yard or delivered it a half mile to the ranch. A year later, as she and I delivered some fill dirt to our neighbor up the valley, Pete Stingley, Jr., I told her this story while we rumbled up the county road.

You know we had these confounded things in the service. After the war, I was in Guam assigned to Motor Transport. I drove a deuce-n-a-half International lowboy, the same gear pattern as this, our 1942 dump truck. Our lieutenant, Pete Camerano, couldn't shift one of these things. Neither could a lot of the guys.

He was a great lieutenant, by the way, oh man, he was a good one. He was a first lieutenant; what they called a "mustang." He'd come up through the ranks. The little rascal didn't even know he was a lieutenant most of the time—he was just like another enlisted man.

The whole company was hauling lumber and materials. We were tearing apart a base is what we were doing, a little military base, a transit center where troops come in and are detained before being sent to their outfits—just come and go. Most everything we hauled out and just dumped. Actually, all this building material was unloaded by the guys from the brig—they had them out there working. A guy with a rifle was watching them. The brig guys were burning it all up, a terrible waste.

On one big trip Lieutenant Pete, as we called him when the other officers weren't around, was riding with me in the low-boy. We were taking a load of something he was giving away to the natives. We were 'way back in the boonies, too, on a dirt road. We were going around a corner rather fast. Another guy, in the truck ahead of us, was grinding gears; you could hear them back where we were. I shifted from overdrive back down to fourth without using the clutch. You don't hurt anything. You just have the motor going the correct speed and the gears just slip right in there. I told him, "Lieutenant, I can shift one of these things without the clutch better than he can with it."

He said, "You do that again and I'll court-martial you."

That's how they talk, you know, when they don't know something, and it threatens them.

You don't always have to put the clutch down to shift. A lot of times you must, but not always. To shift without the clutch, you just have to catch it at a free moment to pull it out of gear and keep your RPM's up to match with everything and it slips right in without any grinding. The gears mesh without any problem.

Guess Pete didn't know about that.

It was the same lieutenant who wanted us to cut the tops off the fifty-five gallon drums with the torch. He wanted them for planters for small palm trees to beautify the area. The drums were empty aviation fuel drums. Well, he handed me the torch and told me to do it. You know you'll get yourself killed that way. I wouldn't do it. He told Zoomie, the welder, to do it.

"Oh, no, Sir, it'll blow up," Ol' Zoomie told him.

The lieutenant got mad and took the torch and said, "Well, I'll do it myself!"

He had to straddle the barrel to cut it and when the hot tip of the torch cut through the metal lid and the fumes lit, "Boom!" just like a bomb, that fifty-five gallon drum became a torpedo. It shot away and smacked into a coconut tree. It just, "Boof!" stuck right there, wrapped around that tree about 150 feet away. The lieutenant wasn't hurt and left out of there real quick. Real quick; the torch was still a-burning where he dropped it.

By God, *we* got the hell out of there before he even started.

# White Shirt Saves Life

There was a car wreck right out of Carlton on that bad, bad turn. Mr. Black, of Ron's Oil in Coquille, at that time, World War II, lived in Carlton. He was going too fast to make the turn. No other vehicles were involved. It was just his car he crashed and got his guts all torn open and was bleeding to death.

It was Saturday, and my brother, Leonard, was on his day off from the woods. He just came from the dry cleaners and he had his white shirts all done up—starched and ironed. Coming upon the accident, he saw the driver in a dire condition and stuffed one of his white shirts in where Black was torn open—doctors said that's all that saved him.

He was saved by the clean shirt from the laundry; a fella couldn't have found a much better bandage.

# After the War

## Back
## to logging

That's me
topping a
spar tree.

# Dad Comes to the Rescue

I had a trap line near Yamhill. My brother Leonard and I were walking it. It was snowing heavily, and we were a mile from any house. We were at a trap, either checking it for animals or resetting it, when all of a sudden this big voice bellows out at us, "Hold it right there; just hold it!"

It was the game warden. He had seen our tracks in the snow and had followed us in.

"What are you doing?" he demanded.

"We're setting a trap. We're trapping here," I said.

"What's in your knapsack?"

I showed it to him, and he checked all the traps for brands; that was okay. We had some mink; only a few furs since we were just at the third trap. As the warden started to leave, he turned around and, touching my chest with his forefinger, asks, "What's under your jacket right here?"

"Oh, my pistol."

I'd stuck that pistol in the front of my overalls. It had a shoulder holster, but I didn't use it. Being so snowy, I'd buttoned up my jacket over it. I used it to kill the coon and the mink in the traps.

"You've got a concealed weapon," the cop said gloatingly, "I knew I didn't walk all the way out here for nothing."

I had to go with the cop. Leaving, I told Leonard, "You'd better walk back and take the jeep pickup home and get Dad."

Yeah, big crime they had on me. Never mind about the coon and mink in the traps.

So that game warden took me back to town and took me before the judge.

The judge asked, "How do you plead?"

I told him, "Well, it *was* covered up."

The judge told the clerk to write up a commitment to send me to jail.

Off I went with that bastard warden but as we came to the top of the stairs leading down to the street, we met and passed Leonard and Father. Dad went and talked to the judge. Whatever he said, it must have been pretty strong and quick because when the warden and I were on the street, the judge came to the head of the stairs and yelled down, "Hey, hey, bring him back up here!"

Once the warden and I got back up there, the judge handed me back my gun and said, "Go on home."

Once down on the street again, I passed the game warden and told him, "You know, I got paid sixty-six dollars a month to kill Japs. I don't know what they'd pay to get rid of someone like you!"

I ran that game warden ragged the next few years. Joe Fore was his name. That son-of-a-gun was about seven feet tall; he was a big man—big ol' fat, ornery guy out of Idaho.

I never will know what Dad said to that judge. I said to Dad, "You didn't pay him, did you?"

"Nope, I never give him nothing."

Dad had the power. He sure saved me that day.

You know, that trap line paid off. I took those raccoons and skinned and gutted them and took them up to Portland to the Chinaman. He had the Golden Dragon Restaurant down by the river and would pay seventy-five cents a pound for them. I suppose they'd put them in some Chinese dish and pass them off as pork. I was making more off the raccoon meat than I was for the pelts.

# Joe Fore

Joe Fore, the game warden, was nearly shot by Dick Aust. Dick had just shot a big buck during the first part of the season. He and I had it drug up on the side of the road. We thought we'd celebrate by having a drink of whiskey.

The game warden came along. Dick hadn't put his deer tag on it yet, and the warden says, "Well, I guess I'll have to take this one!"

"You'll take that one. . . ." Dick cranked a round into the .30/.40 Kraig rifle he had, pointed it at him and said, "After I get done emptying this."

"Oh, oh, oh, oh! You'd better get a tag on him. . . ."

Dick didn't give a damn; he'd just gotten out of a prison camp—forty-two months or three and a half years in the jungles of Burma somewheres. He was on the U.S.S. Houston, flagship of the fleet, when it went down in the Java Sea. It was sunk by the Japs and they picked him up. That's why he'd spent the war in the Japanese prison camp.

Dick and I had gone to school together since the first grade and both he and I were in the Marines in World War II.

The game warden thought it was all right, after Dick threatened to shoot him, for us to keep the deer as long as Dick put his tag on it.

I never did put a tag on a deer while dragging it out of the woods; it might come off and get lost; don't make sense.

# The Pot Shotter

I had been out of the Marine Corps for two years. It was the second hunting season after the war. You can ask Harold Cushing. We went hunting together up above Estacada and were down there in the bushes when, "Pop!"

Some hunter took a pot shot at us, right above our heads. We hollered and stuck our red hats up in the air on our rifle barrels, but he didn't quit.

"Pop!"

Here came another round out our way.

We got to looking around. Oh, there he was, the son-of-a-gun sitting on a stump. Who knows what some of them drunken bastards out there are doing?

I had a .32 Special then, lever-action, and I just gave him a taste of his own medicine.

"Pop!" I rolled him right off that stump. I thought I'd get him right in the leg. Must have missed and hit right into the stump. The pot shotter rolled off kind of sideways, then went off running as fast as he could run.

Harold Cushing and I met in the service in Oceanside, California, when we got out of boot camp and went out there to Advanced Training. We were together most of the war then he got hit bad at Iwo Jima and they shipped him out to Guam. We have been friends ever since, all of our lives. Now he lives up in Lincoln City retired from the Newport School District. This really did happen, you can ask him.

We never did know who that pot shotter was, but he quit shooting at us.

# The Misery Whip

After WWII was over Ol' Red Williams was looking for a second faller (falling partner). His own son wouldn't even work with him. I looked him up and went to work. They had to rub me down with a liniment in the evenings, my muscles were so tired.

That first day Red said, "Now, I've always been top faller on the scale (top faller on the crew). We are going to keep 'er that way!"

I picked up the two-man cross-cut saw, the sack with wedges, my axe, and oil bottle. He carried his axe and the springboards and oil bottle, and we headed for the tree.

These oil bottles each have a hook on them, and they hook right on to the bark of the tree. This kerosene oil is to keep the pitch and rosin off the blade, off the teeth of the saw, so you can pull it; otherwise it wouldn't budge, being like honey on the blade.

I handed the saw to him with the teeth toward the tree.

He comes just roaring over and says, "Now! We're going to get things straight here right from the start. After this, when you pick the saw up and hand it to me, the teeth are going to be away from the tree! We'll oil that side, then we'll flip it and start cutting, and we'll be oiling that side."

Boy, we got that straight real quick. That shows how gung ho he was about time. It takes, what, about a split second to turn it over. Of course, you make that double turn, and you lose a lot of oil off the saw, that'd be another thing. He was right. Talk about a high-baller. You got to squirt that oil right while you're sawing, "squirt, squirt. . . ."

After about two weeks I got my muscles loosened up, and I worked him into the ground. He liked working with me.

When the chain saws first came out, Red and I were able to out-cut them. They were two-man, and they were broken down all the time. Sometimes they'd crank an hour, an hour and a half, to get them going. By that time we'd have some trees on the ground!

Or you'd hear them fire it up. Then a big silence. Next thing you'd see them hauling it out of the woods. We'd just keep whettin' away.

"Now we're logging," we'd tell 'em. "You, Whistle Britches, over there, better get on the ball!"

We were laid off a while, and Red got sick. Seemed like the old guy got appendicitis. He didn't finish the job, and I got Howard Boyd for my partner—he wasn't much poop.

Next was Joe Gieberson. He and I finished that unit. Ol' Joe—I had to bring him sandwiches 'cause his wife gave him carrots and peanuts—he called the meat in the sandwiches "forbidden fruit." She was a very religious Seventh Day Adventist and vegetarian. He's the man that got me to come to Loon Lake.

After Joe and I got through with that job, Joe went to running log dump, and I think he was scaling for a little ol' gypo mill and a damned load of logs fell on him, busted him all up. Then the state rehabilitated him, and he was a scaler for the state. He was down scaling for this mill up Soup Creek at Loon Lake, came home to Yamhill and told me they needed a logger and that's what got me to come to Loon Lake.

# Honey in the Snags

After those famous forest fires, I never saw the likes of honey that was in those old snags in the Tillamook Burn. The bees came in after that Indian Paintbrush and Wild Vetch that sprung up. Man, with those thousands of acres of flowers, they had something to make wild honey with up there.

I was working on the rigging and my good friend, Everett Smith, was falling timber. I don't know how many times we robbed bee hives. We'd burn some sulfur in one of those burners and run the bees out of the hive and take comb, honey and all in wash tubs.

Everett fell one old snag that gave us three tub fulls, it was a hollow-butted old growth that was full of comb and honey for about twelve feet up. Some of it was new honey, and some of it was old honey. They'd just kept building and building. We took it home and the women had one heck of a time getting the honey out of the combs. They were mad because we got some sawdust and dirt in the honey.

These trees were salvaged from after the fire, and fell for logs and they were going to the mill. The bees would make a new nest somewhere else. Plenty of flowers for them in the land that was known as "the Tillamook Burn."

# Topping Trees in the Tillamook Burn

I worked in the Tillamook Burn before and after the war. We built logging roads before the war when I worked for Verle Russell and Sons and I logged and topped trees for Heissler & Son after the war. The Tillamook Burn was a forest fire started over by Gale's Creek, west of Forest Grove. It was a real hot day in August of 1933, the woods were shut down and all the crews came in. Bill Lyda & Son kept logging to get that one more last turn—that's always the one that does it—when two logs rubbed, you know dragging a turn of logs over a cedar and it just exploded into a fire. That's one of those old Indian tricks: rubbing two sticks together to start a fire. It burnt 2,500 square miles or 311,000 acres. Then, like the old saying goes, it burnt every six years—first in 1933, then 1939, 1945 and 1951.

From the first and second burns all the railroad ties and trestles were burnt up and we were making railroad grades into logging roads and bypassing the old trestle crossings. I run dump truck, sometimes I'd be up there on the Cat, sometimes I'd even be on the little shovel loading trucks. We all traded off just to break the monotony.

After the war I logged and blew the tops out of those old growth to make spar trees. A spar tree is one that has been topped and rigged to yard logs to the landing and also carries the rigging to load the log trucks. Once I was at the top of the tree, I'd decide where I was going to cut it off, then drive railroad spikes in the tree to keep the bark from slipping and coming down on me. That's from the trees being burned that the bark was that loose. Those spikes I drove were right above the line where I was going to cut. I would saw in or chop in a groove all the way around in which to lay the dynamite. This notch was about six inches deep and a couple of inches wide, plenty high for sticks of dynamite to be laced in butt to butt and just pile them in on one another, and you want to have a fuse in one of them. I always liked to stretch an old inner tube around to make it airtight, gunny sacks, anything; she'll cut 'er right off just like it'd been sawed.

So I'd get it ready like this and touch 'er off by lighting the fuse. I went down those trees fast. I gave myself ten minutes to get down. I slid down. I'd go about fifteen, twenty feet a shot that way. Here's how I'd do that. With the shoulder against the tree, you'd let the spurs just kind of skin the bark to slow yourself down, then kick them in to stop. You'd throw the slack of the climbing rope 'way down the tree and slide down to it. There was a little knack to doing this.

By the time you got down, you'd be pretty black from the burned trees, and then you'd get to sweatin' and it'd stick right to you—about all you'd see is eyeballs.

The trees were good and sound, though, just the limbs burned and bark loosened and black. Thousands of acres of black trees. They salvaged all that timber and sent it to market before it rotted.

# A Neighbor That Wouldn't Cooperate

A big Douglas fir tree stood on the boundary line of Clyde Cook's and his neighbor's yard. It was leaning right over Clyde Cook's house. It was dying up there in the top—dead limbs. It was probably diseased from some root fungus. There was a good chance of the top breaking out in a storm and threatening life and limb inside Clyde's or other neighbors' homes by dropping through their roofs.

Clyde, who had done about everything, including logging, offered to take it out of there. He knew enough about timber to know what would happen in a windstorm to that dead top up there, but he couldn't convince his neighbor it was a hazard to everyone under it. Clyde even offered to have it topped. It was about thirty inches across breast high; Clyde and I measured it. Actually the trunk was more on the neighbor than on Clyde.

The neighbor didn't want it cut. His own house wasn't threatened by the dying and leaning old fir, so he wasn't interested—didn't want to think of it.

Clyde says, "I got a remedy for neighbors that won't cooperate."

He went down to the store and bought some copper nails. He just pounded them into the bottom of the tree about five inches apart, all the way around the base of that old fir tree. He fixed it.

Within a year all the other needles started wilting off the branches, dying, turning red—killed it deader than a doornail.

Mr. "Not Interested" pooped in his own packsack because Clyde was going to take that tree out originally. After it died he made that feller take it out at his own expense, which cost him a bunch.

This was in the city limits of Dayton, Oregon. All the neighbors on Clyde's side of the leaning old tree were relieved.

Yes, fir trees are beautiful, but not under certain conditions. Back then they all weren't nutty, just that one.

# Driving Without Lights

I was living in Yamhill and drove to Carlton to work to my job driving log truck. My brother, Leonard, drove to work in just the opposite direction. He was living in Carlton and drove to Yamhill to catch the crew crummy to work in the woods.

I had to leave home early in the morning when it was still dark. I was driving along when my lights went out. So I thought I'll just crowd the yellow line until I get there, I could make it. You know you can just barely make out that yellow center line in the dark.

Leonard was out driving to work and his lights went out. It was at the north edge of Carlton right at the city limit sign—there used to be a tin shack and now they sell tractors there. Just a great big crash; I came to a sudden stop. Next thing I knew I was out on the road and Leonard was there.

I said, "Where'd you come from? How'd you get here?"

He says, "Somebody run into me and hit me."

"Somebody hit me, too."

We were both crowding the yellow line and hit each other. Now if that isn't a coincidence!

Both cars were damaged and we had a hell of a time collecting the insurance.

# Scorching the Rats

You talk about rats—there was eighty acres of walnut orchard set right there between my house and the city dump. They took a bulldozer in there and covered up the dump. Those rats left out of that dump when they started filling it. They had a trail beat right down in that orchard coming through to our house—beat down in the dirt about an inch deep—that many of the damned things. Some of them were ending up in my basement. I was trapping them but couldn't keep up with them. I had three traps set and I was assured of three rats every day. Every time I checked them, I had rats. I was even shooting them.

My neighbor, Clyde Cook, worked with me cutting timber. I told Clyde, I says, "Jesus Christ, I'm trapping them right and left but I'm just infested with them!"

He says, "Well, we'll run the traps this evening when we get home from working and I'll show you how to get rid of them forever."

When we got to my basement, there were three rats in the three traps I had set. So he just poured gas on one and set it afire and let it loose out of the trap, and it took off through the basement door, which we had left open. That singed rat was smoking and stinking and ran as hard as his legs could carry him right down through the walnut orchard. He was going back where the dump used to be.

We set another one loose from his trap. He joined the others that smelled the rat afire and they started running in all directions, leaving the country. Clyde poured gas on the last one and set it afire. He put his foot on the spring and turned it loose and it was gone! It went under the front porch through a cubbyhole—it was back under there burning and stinking.

We called the fire department because we didn't know if the rat would set the house on fire. They came out and didn't do anything, just stood by. By that time we had that sucker out. I knew every one of them on the fire department. They got a hell of a charge out of that—scorching the rats.

The rats never did come back. That one that went back through the orchard must have given them the word. By gum, I don't know where they went. I never did see 'em again and that suited me.

# Teeth Inspect the Clay

Sam Whitney and his wife, Clare, owned the Newberg Airport and had hired me to make a dam for irrigation. I dammed up a creek and made a pond about 300 feet long.

With my D-6 Cat I cleaned off the sides, then made a core trench, a little wider than the Cat blade, ten feet wide and four feet deep. This goes right under the middle of where the dam's going to be. You have to pack it full of clay so the lower current of water won't wash the dam out; and there can't be any sand in this clay.

The inspector was out of Texas, and he was pretty damned strict. I was surprised to see him put some of the clay into his mouth and chew on it. He said you can't fool teeth, your teeth will tell you if it's got any sand in it. I imagine if the government found out how he was checking the clay, they'd make him test it some other way.

Well, my core trench clay passed the inspection and that dam and pond are still there today, forty-five years later. Sam's son-in-law now runs the airport and says they have maintained it through many winter floods and it is still a great pond.

# Moving the Cat Legally

After I finished the dam, I needed to move my D-6 Caterpillar tractor from that job at the Newberg Airport. I was going twenty miles away to a little logging job west of Carlton. Kenny Whitlow's brother, Clifford, told me he could move my Cat "legal."

"Oh, yeah! I can move your Cat legal."

Shoot, all he had was a little ol' single-axle trailer. I drove the Cat up on the trailer and away we went. He was pulling that along and I was ahead of him in the crummy.

We were going down the road and the weighmaster was out at the scales by Dundee. He and his helper were weighing all the trucks and measuring for width and length—including us when we came through. We had already scraped all the mud off my Caterpillar to make it lighter.

The weighmaster told Clifford, "Park it over there until you legalize it."

I guess they figured we would come and take the blade off or something. He was 'way overloaded. Of course the weighmaster gave him a ticket—that went with it naturally.

I forgot who I got—we just backed up to Clifford's trailer one night, might have been the same night, and just run it off of that son-of-a-gun and on to another one. I think I got O.C. Yokim. And then Clifford Whitlow could deal with them—all what was left was his trailer sitting there empty at the scales. I never told him, let him figure it out, just went on to my next job. He could deal with the overload ticket, it wasn't my responsibility. I paid him for the trip as far as he got me.

# Saving the Seats at the Wrestling Match

My wife and I arrived early to my sister and her husband's fiftieth wedding anniversary. It was January 28, 1995. We were by ourselves standing in a light drizzling rain under the diffused light from the lit-up sign of the American Legion Hall. This quonset-hut shaped building was one I helped to build right after the war. I didn't go there too much, but. . .this is how I told it to my wife, "One time, when I was married to my first wife, Mary, she and I and another woman went to see some wrestlers here at the American Legion Hall. Right when it was about to begin, Mary and the other woman had to go to the rest room. While they were gone I was sitting there with two empty seats beside me.

"Here came two guys—a big ol' German named Charlie Ziegler and another big ol' loot.

"I said, 'These seats are taken.'

"Ol' Ziegler says, 'Yeah, I know, I'm taking them. . . .'

"And I replied, 'Well, when those women come back, you guys are out of here one way or another.'

"When Mary and her friend returned, the two big men wouldn't get up. So I just lifted the German up by the head and knocked him right in the snoot.

"One of the wrestlers came over thinking he was going to break up the fight, and I knocked him one, too.

"The wrestler—was known quite well because he tied in a boxing match with a famous boxer, so and so (ain't that awful, can't remember his name). Anyway, the wrestler said, 'You've got quite a punch there.'

"I said, 'Yeah, well, I ain't boxing with so and so.'

"He went back to his wrestling match, and we enjoyed the show."

# The Chow Dog and the Back Door

When I was first married, I drove truck hauling hog fuel to the mill. You're low man on the totem pole when you're hauling that irregular waste product of a lumber mill. You have to dig it out by hand with a special darned hoe-like rake. Hog fuel is the scrap from making lumber, waste run through the "hog." It is all kinds of things—it is bark, twelve foot ribbons, chips, slivers, slabs, and sawdust—that comes off the conveyor. The conveyor dumps it into bunkers. You backed right up underneath them and pulled the lever. That was supposed to open up a trap door there in the bottom. Then you got underneath there and got to work.

I raked it on by hand from Carlton Manufacturing and L, H & L, also in Carlton. Then I took the load either to the paper mill in Newberg or the one in Salem. Same thing there. You raked it with the hoe into troughs. They used it to fire the steam engines that ran the paper mills.

One day I got home early. I had a full-blooded Chow dog. I was talking to the dog as I came up to the porch. You'd think he'd known my voice, but he bit me. I grabbed the axe and was going to kill that dog, chasing him around the house on the porch.

The wife was in bed, she woke up, and let the dog in the back door and locked the door. I worked the door over with the axe. The wife and the dog went about their business inside; and by the time I got in by stepping over where the door used to be, she put that dog out the front door. What she wanted to save it for, I don't know, after it bit me.

Later we gave the Chow away to an older couple who thought the world of it. Just adored it. It never bit them, I guess, when they came home tired from shoveling hog fuel.

# Clyde Cook Cures a Wood Thief

The Oklahoma family moved into a house behind ours in Carlton. We had a wood heater in the living room and a combination trash burner/electric stove in the kitchen. But boy, cold mornings I'd light the trash burner, warmed things up good. Had lots of wood split up, stove size. Someone was stealing these and it was easy to track where our stove wood was going—they had tramped a path in the tall grass. I told Clyde Cook, "Those Okies are stealing my wood."

He said, "We'll fix 'em."

He came with a coffee can of black powder and took a piece of stove wood into the basement. He bored a hole in the butt end of the wood and poured black powder into it. Then he made a plug out of the same wood and put it in there over the black powder to conceal it. Then he took a handsaw, sawed off the end of the plug. Heck, you could never tell there'd been a plug drove in that thing.

We laid it back crossways on the woodpile right in the area where they had been getting wood from. That was to make sure *we* wouldn't pick it up.

They must have gotten it in the first load that went to their stove because the next day or two the mother of the two Okie boys told our other neighbors, Ida and Bob Simmonson, that, "My stewers blew clear to the ceiling."

Her "stewers" must have been an old-fashioned name for her pots, heavy little cast iron pots with lids for stewing. I bet those stove lids blew to the ceiling, too. She must not have known her boys were stealing wood but after that things changed. She and her boys must have figured that gunpowder got into the stove. We never had any more trouble out of any of them stealing our wood.

# Ruby Creek, Idaho, and the Mink Farm

My first wife, Mary, had asthma and the doctors recommended a dry climate. There was some logging going on in Idaho I'd heard; all of Oregon was shut down because of the economy so we moved to first Parma, then Atlanta and then Ruby Creek, above Boise. That's where I got hurt.

Mary and I lived in the basement of a nice couple's log home. I was working for wages for Builder's and Producer's Supply, out of Boise. Lawrence Hettenger and I were up in those woods logging just above Ruby Creek.

Camped on up Ruby Creek there were two horse loggers. One was named King and the other one was a little basco guy and his wife—boy, they were nice people. They were working for B & P Supply, same outfit I was working for. At this logging show all the yarding was done by horses. We were falling the timber and King and the basco were yarding them out. 'Bout all the Cat did was build roads for the log trucks.

This horse logger, King, was taking his horses up the road one morning. A huge, big ol' six-point bull elk came off the bank and hit the horse right in the guts. His rack ripped him right open. Mr. King had to shoot him.

This guy, Ole Nelson, owned the ranch we were taking the timber off of. He had a Jersey bull he run with the Herefords—just on account of it—meanest thing there was. He could whip those bull elk. Those little Jersey bulls are quicker and meaner than any Hereford or elk ever thought of being.

While working we didn't live on Ole's ranch, but we lived near by. Our landlord was still building his log home while Mary and I rented the basement. He worked on his place and also had a mink farm. The mink farm was right close to the house—hundreds of them in hutches. One night I had to do some repair to my chain saw. So I cleaned the filters all up and put in a new plug—got that all done. I was going to crank it up and adjust the carburetor, so I did. I fired it up, "Rrrooomm!" The man came out running and waving his hands signalling me to shut it off; he was really in a dither and a frenzy.

"Oh, God," he said, "I should have told you! Any loud noise like that will make those mink eat their babies!"

We ran out to the hutches—those mink were grabbing their babies and just killing them! We started sticking sticks through the wire to keep the mamas out of the little hole to the nests where their babies were lying. The mamas had already killed half of their babies or more. They're biting sons-of-a-guns and they were killing the little ones right and left just as fast as they could bite them. They really weren't eating them, just killing them. You couldn't reach in there and hold the mamas back from the nest hole, they'd bite you to death.

We were all out there—the landlord and his wife, and me and Bob, my partner. The mink seemed to quiet down after a little bit. I guess quick as we got the noise stopped. The guy was sure nice about it; I never knew any sudden or unusual noise made them go off like that. He apologized, said he should have told us. (I wish I could remember their names. Her brother was a bow hunter named Fred Bear, who had just got back from Africa when we were there and had shot an elephant and everything with a bow.) The wife and the mink farmer sure treated us good and told us we were welcome to stay as long as we wanted, provided I didn't start up any more chain saws.

We came in there with an International panel—it had a straight pipe coming up the side of it. A good ol' rig. It's a wonder *it* didn't scare the mink when I'd start it up. I often wondered about that when I was working. Boy, that chain saw sure put them on a killing spree.

You know, there were thousands of those blasted hawks up there. It was just thick with them, I don't know how they got so populated. Bob and I would go out of an evening and, shoot I don't know how many of them; there was a bounty on them. They bothered everything—chickens, ducks, geese, fish in the creeks, wild birds and eggs—anything that don't eat them.

One of those treacherous hawks wasn't quite dead and he got Bob's spaniel right by the nose. I mean he was locked in—those talons on the bird's feet wouldn't let go. The spaniel was howling and screaming and bawling. We had to cut the hawk's leg off to get him loose.

Ole paid us for the squirrel tails, ten cents a tail. They were just tearing the alfalfa he had planted in the little creek bottoms all to hell. They were little rodent-like things; I guess the closest you could come to describing them is that they were like a woodchuck. I'd never seen anything like them—something like our grey digger squirrel, they weren't though. They were a little ground squirrel of some kind; they would just destroy a crop. After the day's work—shoot, it was daylight way up 'til way late in the evening—Bob and I would shoot them with .22's. We stayed along the edge of the alfalfa field—there were hundreds of them. Once you shot one, the rest of them became long distance shooting. Ole would give us the shells.

He was glad to have us, and I guess we were glad to be there, too. We fell some big pine trees, made a little money and met some fine people in Ruby Creek, Idaho.

# Splicing the Mainline

In Idaho I was on a "log-cutting" crew. Here in Oregon we would call it a crew of timber fallers. We were cutting timber for Lawrence Hettinger, and they were loading out trucks and we rode back and forth with the loading crew. They broke the eye in that damned loading line. They said they were going to go home.

I said, "Hell, we can tie a knot in it."

"Naw, you can't tie a knot in it, sometimes we got to run it through the shieve up on top of the shovel."

The shovel is a crane-like piece of equipment that runs on top of double axles with rubber tires; it has a boom for loading logs on trucks.

So I says, "Well, hell, I'll put an eye in it, anything from having to go in, first damned thing in the morning."

I used the phillip's screwdriver and a hammer, that's all they had. I finally got an eye in the damned line. They didn't know how, probably. That Idaho loading crew had never seen it done.

Now here's how it's supposed to be done:

An eye is a loop on the end of a heavy steel cable or line. You first cut out the frayed end of the line clean off with an hydraulic line cutter or old wire axe. The wire axe is like a double-bitted axe; you put one end of it in a stump, then you lay your line to be cut across the other bit (sharp edge of the axe), and hit it with a sledge hammer. It is not recommended for beginners—you can lose an eye awful easy because pieces of that axe fly. So you cut it clean with no frays, then you get three railroad spikes out and get the (right-handed) Lang Lay line formed as a loop on the top of a stump or butt of a log with the short end on the left and drive the railroad spikes in to hold it in shape. Then you have to know how to splice, of course, and you open up the lay of the line with the marlin spike (a long, tapered punch with a sharp point). Then you weave the short end of the cable in and make a loop. So there you've made an eye in this big, heavy line with the right tools.

You can imagine how determined I was to do this with only a phillips screwdriver and a hammer.

That loading crew started loading and yarding, us "log-cutters" started cutting, the log truck drivers started hauling them out; everybody was happy. We got in a full day's work and came back home with that loading crew.

# The Fruit Tramp

I got in a fight with one of those lettuce workers. This was in Parma, Idaho. I was kind of a little guy then, only 192 lbs. working every day falling timber in the woods. I guess you wonder where in hell there was any timber around Parma, Idaho. It was where we were logging—sixty, seventy miles above Boise. We'd just come home to Parma on weekends.

This guy was a professional fruit tramp. You know they started 'way down in Arizona and they traveled all the way through, clear to the end of the harvest—thought they were tough characters.

He was a big guy. They had slot machines there at Halley's Place. He had been playing it and walked away. Mary, my wife, was kind of nuts about those machines. She asked him if he was through with it. He said yes. She went up to the machine—they were a quarter—and "Bang, bang, bang," she hit bars—the jackpot.

He called her a dirty bitch.

I told him, "Hey, that's my wife you're talking to like that."

He says, "Well, what are you going to do about it?"

I busted him in the jaw.

"You can't get away with that," he snarled.

"Well, let's step outside and we'll see if I can get away with that," I declared and outside we went along with all those cotton pickin' ol' lettuce tramps—that's about all there was in there—and also a retired dentist.

The dentist was watching on when we were fighting and it didn't last very darned long. I hit him a few licks in the gut and then in the head—I had good reflexes then. He'd start to swing, and I'd just beat him to the punch. He had had enough. His ol' eyes were starting to swell shut; he wouldn't have known where he was pretty soon.

The Doc says, "Where'd you learn to fight like that?"

"I didn't," I told him, but later I suppose I related back to him I'd done some fighting in the Marine Corps and ever since I was a kid.

Dad taught my brother and I to box. We had a ring set up in the barn and we practiced there. Leonard and I boxed other guys in regular boxing matches in the hop yards—little "Smokers" they called them. We made more money doing that than we did picking hops—about all you made in a day was two dollars and a half. They'd throw in pennies, nickels and dimes. Get a real good one, he'd throw in a quarter. The ring deck would just be covered with change. The referees to these matches judged everything pretty much as a draw. That way the money was split fifty-fifty, even though you knew you beat the guy or he beat you.

That doctor, he had been a prominent fight manager at Madison Square Garden and everything. He had managed John Henry Lewis, the light heavy-weight world title holder for four years—Lewis was beaten by Malio Bettina in 1939.

I think the dentist's name was Dr. Gasper. He had a little, what they called "screw-tailed" bull dog in those days and had made him some gold teeth. He'd sit there and smile and show off those gold teeth—you know those ones on a bulldog that always shine up there.

I saw the lettuce worker after that. He didn't speak and I didn't either. He kept his foul mouth shut anyway, calling people names. I got that accomplished.

# Mormons

I'll tell you about some Mormons out of Parma, Idaho.

Shoot, I was topping trees for one and the next morning I come there, his barn had burnt down. I mean down, cattle and all burnt up.

Next thing you know, here comes a Cat and a backhoe, dug a trench and buried all those cows. Then they cleaned up the mess.

The next thing a barn started going up. Then here comes cows, some from here and then a little later a few from there. That went on and in a week's time he was milking cows again.

They put him right back in business. Not a cent was charged or anything. Now that's what you call brotherly love.

I didn't feel sorry for him, though. I bid the job for so much and I kept him to his word.

# "Only Trying To Scare Ya"

When we were logging in Idaho, it was kind of a select logging—taking trees that they marked and the tree in particular was right over the bank from where they were loading logs. It had been scarred up from another tree that had got felled into it. The Forest Service guy come along and he says, "Well, no need in leaving that one there, just go ahead and cut it."

So they were loading logs out right there, right above it and I told the shovel operator, "Don't throw nothing in there, we're going to fall that tree!"

I'd got the face in it and just started to back it up; had an Ol' McCulloch with the handle bars for a saw. I got started backing it up and boy, next thing I know, log hit the handle bars and had me squashed there. I was kind of in between the damned handle bars the way we'd got knocked around there. One of them was against the tree and the other one was against the log. They were both broken and twisted up and I was in the middle.

Well, Ol' Bob Pierce helped me up out of there 'n he was a-hollering and a-yelling, so was I. The son-of-a-bitch threw that log down in there. I thought maybe something happened that one of the logs got away from him.

I told the shovel operator, "I'd kill ya if I could. You don't screw around with people like that, you gosh-darned half wit. What were you doing?"

He said, "I was only trying to scare ya."

That was it—no work—they x-rayed my hip there in the Catholic hospital in Boise, Idaho. I was laid up, couldn't work. Since our move to Idaho, we had rented our home out in Carlton, Oregon, not getting much for it. I told Mary, well, we'll just go back and see what's going on.

I got into Portland, walking down the street there, when my leg went out from under me. Then they found it—cracked pelvis. I just had to lay there for a while and let that thing knit back together.

I never heard anything more about that shovel operator. I never went back to that outfit. Hope he didn't kill somebody else.

# Hank Larsen

Working for Heisler and Son, I done part of the climbing and pulled rigging. Heisler had a guy from California working for him and he was setting chokers. He was a pretty good worker but everything was "California this" and "California that." You heard about how they did things differently in California every time you started to do something. Every time we ate lunch, we had to hear about it.

One time while we were eating our lunches, the guy was going on about California. Finally, Hank Larsen had enough of it and jumped up and threw his tin hat on the ground and said, "All I ever seen come out of California is hot rodders and (blank) suckers and you don't have a hot rod!"

They were putting in a long splice and the Californian thought he knew all about it and he let his marlin spike slip. It hit Ol' Hank right between the eyes. That would have hurt a normal man but I don't think that bothered Hank. The Californian's talk sure got under his skin, but a five pound marlin spike hitting him in the head didn't phase him. He was tougher than a spruce knot. Here's the kind of man Hank Larsen was. When he was sixty-five years old, Manley Watson wanted a man.

Manley said, "I'll give you a try."

And the first day on the job none of the crew showed up. And that first day Hank and Manley and the Cat skinner got out twenty-two loads of logs. Hank knew how to get out logs.

Tough, oh God he was tough. He got up there in Portland and one of those damned Volkswagens—the bug type—ran across the street and hit him. It demolished the Volkswagen; Ol' Hank got up a-cussin'. Broke his leg, I think, when it hit him; broke something, laid him up good. I think he died from that later.

I quit Ol' Heisler, right in the middle of the day. Oh he come up there just a-raisin' hell, right there on the riggin'. I don't know what he was thinking about—I told him that.

In this Tillamook burn, we were on a flat, hooking up logs and there was a big steep rock face right below us. I had been working on the landing doing the loading, but a few months before, Hank quit and that's how come me to be in the brush. I took over his job and was pulling rigging. I spotted the chokers when they came back, gave signals and was in charge of the choker setters. The whistle punk was working right with us. I yelled to him and he used the bug to get the signals to the yarder. The bug was a hand-held electric tooter with an electric line running all the way to the yarder on the landing.

The hillside had been felled and bucked. We were yarding the logs downhill off that steep rock bluff. The tailhold was on a stump where we were, on the flat above the rock. The line was sawing into the rock bluff back and forth. As the logs were pulled over the top of that rock, the chokers would get slack, the logs would get to rolling, change end for end, come out of the chokers and end up down there in a hole. We were losing them off that bluff—the haulback line wouldn't hold 'em. Those were big big logs in that burn—all old growths—lot of one log loads.

That was a poor lay-out. Ordinarily that was my job, but Heisler's son, Rich, was side rod and all over the place. That's the way he laid it out; shoot you don't argue with the boss. I don't know why he wouldn't change his mind.

I said, "My God, Rich, let's leave these logs and get them from above." When we made a whole new layout uphill, it would be easy to get them then. The next spar tree was going to be right above, about five, six hundred feet. Shoot, it was going to be duck soup logging, 'cause where we were, we were out twelve hundred feet.

The Old Man come up there and he says, "We got trucks down there waiting for logs and no logs coming in. What's the matter?"

I says, "I'm not going to chase them sons of bitches."

"What are we going to do?"

"Well, when we get this top cleared off here, we'll go back and pick them up."

"Well, that ain't getting them up to the landing."

"You know I'm not chasin' each individual log down there in that heap of yours to hook them back up." What I had planned was to wait 'til we got where we were working all cleared off then go get the logs all together—the ones that had rolled, slid, and came out of their chokers.

The logs *were* coming in to the landing, but what was making him mad was that I wasn't down in there chasing the strays. When they'd come out, I'd just whistle the chokers on back up the hill and hook up some more.

He come to the house one time, shortly after that; he wanted me to come back to work for him. He said Leonard (who had quit him for more pay somewhere else) and I were the most experienced loggers he had. Leonard had given him notice and quit him a couple of weeks before to go to another logging show with more pay. Jack Graham and Bob Nelson were working for him and I asked Bob, "What'd the old bastard do after I left?"

"Same thing as you was doing. He wasn't going to chase them logs, either."

That old fart also came to see me after I was logging with my own logging company down here at Loon Lake.

# The Goose That Flew with the Car

I met Mr. Yarty, pronounced "Why-arty," in a hospital room in the Physicians and Surgeons Hospital, 19th and Lovejoy, Portland, Oregon. It was a two-bed hospital room and this Basque gentleman and I were both having our eyes doctored.

Mr. Yarty had some old black powder he was going to dispose of. He threw it in a fire and it exploded on him. It got both of his eyes. I think he lost the sight of one, but I don't remember. At that time they were trying to save mine, but they weren't able to. I had poked it with a climbing spur.

After out of the hospital, I stopped in to see Mr. Yarty. He lived way over next to and adjoining the BLM, son-of-a-bitches, by Burns, in French Glen. The BLM was always cutting his fences and letting his cattle out. They accused him of shooting on their sanctuary. It was a reserve for wildlife. Both Mr. and Mrs. Yarty said the BLM gave them a lot of grief and misery. He and her wrote the song, the "Shifting, Whispering Sands." It was quite a hit, a good country and western tune about a miner who lost his life. All the jute boxes carried it, including ours.

They had a tame Canadian goose; had it since a gosling. Whenever a car would go down the driveway, the goose would go, too. Their driveway was about a quarter of a mile long, a real long one. When the wife drove to town that goose would fly right along with the car about level with the windows.

At the end of the driveway the goose would stay while the wife went on to town, hours and hours the goose would stay down there waiting for the wife to come back. There was plenty of grass and the goose could feed.

When the car came, then she'd fly home with it. If it got dark, the goose would fly home by herself.

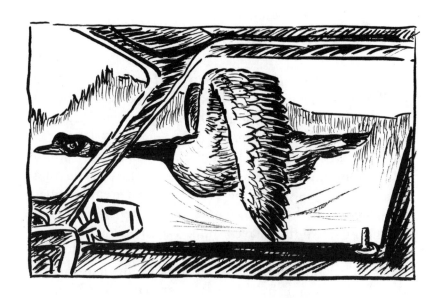

*"Can you see out of it?"*
*"Only the colored funnies."*

73

# Mad Otter in the Boat

Ol' Clyde Cook was with me when I lost my eye, come to think of it, just him and I. God, we trapped together, did a lot of things together, nobody else could get along with the ornery ol' son-of-a-gun.

We had a five, six mile long trap line on the Yamhill River. One time as we were drifting down the river in a boat, we pulled up a set there, and it had a great big boar otter in it. The otter must have just gotten in that trap by sliding down the beaver slide. We had caught him in a drowning set, so he was down at the bottom under the water. That otter must have just gotten in that trap by the time we came by. My pet otter, Humpy,—I timed him once—it was seven minutes under water before he came back up. So we couldn't have come by much later than that.

We pulled up the trap and otter from the bottom of the river and got them in the boat. He looked like he was dead. Clyde was resetting the trap, that took some time, and the otter just stayed in the boat. All of a sudden the otter came alive. With "Ca, ca, ca, ca, ca, ca," and "Yak, yak, yak!" he was mad. That baby was after whoever he could get ahold of.

Ol' Clyde was hollering, "Do something. Do something!"

I said, "He's up there in your end, you do something."

He picked up a hatchet—cruiser axe is what it was—and took a swing at the otter, missed him and knocked a hole in the bottom of the boat; water just poured in.

He repeated, "Do something!"

I kicked the otter the first time he came at me and after that got a paddle to keep him off. Boy, things were hot in that boat. Finally, Clyde got smart and turned the axe sideways and got him with the flat part of the axe.

74

We were stuffing rags and stuff in the hole. The ol' potlicker was screaming and hollering, "We're sinking!"

We went on down the river, after pulling the boat up on the bank to get the water out of it. I tore up my sweatshirt and stuffed that in the hole; then we finished our trap line that day, checking our traps on the banks. We had a long ways to go back to McMinnville, and we sailed on down the river just as happy as if we had good sense.

# Mrs. Cook's Weimaraner

Clyde Cook got tangled up in the berry vines so badly one time when we were trapping. He got so mad he just bit the vine in two.

He had a little bitty dog and I had Jeep dog, also a little dog. And then he had one of those Weimaraners. The wino dog, he didn't last long, first trip out in the woods. His wife had paid quite a price for it—it was registered and everything. She was a madam from Alaska; she had lots of money and thought a lot of this dog.

We were walking down the river banks way out in the woods looking for maple burls and the two little dogs ran out a whole family of coons—six of them. The raccoons had beautiful pelts and were nice prime fur. They ran up a big maple and out on a limb. Clyde was shooting them off with his .22 woodsman pistol and I had a Ruger. We plucked them off of the limb, and they'd fall down on the ground and weren't dead yet and, naturally, the little dogs went right after them. Each one of the little dogs had one of those coons trying to kill it, shaking them and hanging right on, and I was trying to finish them off. Coons are hard to kill with one shot unless they're hit in a vital spot.

Some of them had climbed down. They were all on the ground by now. I'll never forget that—the Weimaraner run on over there and stuck his nose out to see what was going on—not interested a bit you know—one of the raccoons wasn't quite dead and got ahold of the big dog with both paws around his neck, bit him in the ear and hung on. That dog was so dumb it just sat down and howled.

The coons were squalling and carrying on and the little dogs were yapping and biting them.

Clyde says, "Look at that, the two little bitty dogs are killing the coons, doing all the work, that thing just sitting there howling—big enough to eat both them coons."

Then, "Pow!" he shot the Weimaraner.

"God," I says, "What are you going to tell the wife?"

Clyde announces, "I'll just tell her it drowned."

I don't know what he ever told her, probably just that. She never mentioned it and neither did I. That wasn't something we were going to talk about.

Another one of Mr. Clyde's great capers.

# How Umca Got Its Name

I was running a logging show for a guy named Morgan, a Cadillac car salesman in Portland. He came to me and said he had some timber he bought by Dundee. He wanted me to log it. He had a Cat and everything and we agreed on a wage. It was too wet to Cat log yet, so I and my worker, Tommy Archibald, just went to cutting it.

Morgan came out there one day and he says, "I've got a good friend; he was born in Sweden and now a merchant marine. I'm going to send him out here to keep you guys company." I don't know what that was all about because I wasn't working by the hour, I was doing everything by the thousand anyway, the cutting, the yarding, the whole works. So one day Steve Nelson showed up and after that he would come out, off 'n on, off 'n on.

One day I says, "This guy paying you?"

"Yeah, he's supposed to be paying me."

I says, "Yeah, he's supposed to be paying me, too, and so far I haven't seen any money."

Steve says, "Foxy (Mr. Morgan) owes everybody in the country. Why don't you and I form a partnership and we'll buy a Cat."

So far Foxy's Cat was tied up in the repair shop and they wouldn't let him have it until he had some money.

I said, "We'll have to talk to the man who owns this timber and see if we can buy it the same way Ol' Foxy was buying it." That ended up a mess—it wasn't even his timber. But I says to Steve Nelson, not knowing anything about the mess yet, "I'll talk to the owner and see what he says. And how will I get in touch with you?"

That's when he said he was staying at the Umca Hotel in Portland.

I says, "I never heard of that. How do you spell it?"

"Oh," he says, "That's easy. You know the Y.M.C.A. on Third Avenue, the Umca Hotel!"

I think that was just one of his Swedish jokes because his wife was working with Foxy's wife at the Aeroclub, a club where you had to own an airplane to be a member. They must have been in the country long enough to have their own place by then.

Well, we found the owner of the timber, a Mr. "Harmless" Hall, who said, "I don't give a damn who logs it, as long as I get my money." Turned out Hall didn't own it either, there was an old lady in Dundee who owned it. She had a filbert orchard she was trusting Harmless to oversee. He was supposed to harvest it, and so he thought he'd just harvest her timber, too. Well, anyway, one day here comes a great big tall Irishman. It was the old lady's son, Elmo Shannihan, an insurance man in Portland.

"Aha! Who gave you permission to be doing this logging?"

"The man up on the hill, Harmless Hall."

Well, he told us, go ahead, but he wanted a copy of all the paperwork for the logs and everything that we'd sold.

I told him, "That'd be no problem," he'd get that from the bookkeeper. So the Irishman, Mr. Shannihan, the real owner's son, sued Mr. Hall, the filbert overseer. Oh, yeah, Steve and I were tangled up there in court a few days over that Harmless Hall; that's what he called himself and how his name appeared on his card. Shannihan made a believer out of Harmless, he got his mother's timber money from him.

We made some money there. With only three miles to the log dump, we kept two log trucks just a-humming. After that, we logged around Dundee, then Wilsonville, Willamina, McMinnville and Carlton. That Swede and I had a great time from 1952 to 1955. Then I bought him out and moved to Loon Lake. The people here thought I was mispronouncing the name of the Umca Logging Co. Many of the stores and businesses have Umpqua as part of their name, being so close to the Umpqua River.

"What did you say the name of your logging company was?"

"Umca."

"Umca. You mean Umpqua?"

"No, Umca."

"How do you spell it?"

"UMCA."

# "Yam and Yelly"

Steve Nelson, my logging partner, was a Swedish merchant marine. He landed in Chicago. He went to night school there to learn our lingo; he said he used to leave his overshoes out on the porch or entranceway there, and he'd come back from class and they'd be gone. He lost quite a few pairs before he got wise. That's the custom there in Sweden.

Steve said, "Another thing, it took me three years in this country to learn to say 'yam,' and then they changes it and calls it 'yelly.'"

# Mad Hornets in the Caterpillar Tractor

Oh, that son-of-a-bitch, my partner! He was on the Cat making a Cat road—no, hell, we were logging. Anyway, he got out there and he stirred up a hornet's nest; those big ol' round nests that hang off the limb. Only this nest was in some brush. The Cat bent down the brush and shook the nest up good. The hornets got right in the Cat and Ol' Barney had to leave it.

He got down and left the Cat there. I went over to it and them S.O.B.'s—I mean they were mad! I did reach in there and get the compression lever threw from start to no compression—that got the thing stopped. I went back to where he was and said, "Well, in the morning we'll get rid of them suckers. We'll take out an open can of gasoline and I'll just slap my hand over the bottom of the nest so they can't get out and you cut the limb off and we'll put it in the bucket of gasoline. That'll fix 'em."

"All right," he says.

We got there about daybreak the next morning, and it was a chilly one; the hornets were probably all still in there. They enter and depart, you know, through the little hole in the bottom about the size of a fifty-cent piece.

By the time I got my hand over the bottom of the nest so they couldn't get out, one of them buzzed around Barney's head, and he left off down the Cat road; he was gone. He had the knife, so there I was stuck holding my hand over the exit hole of the hornet's nest. By the time Barney got going down the road good, the choker setter had come to work and seen what the hell we were up to there. He came and cut the limb off. I had them stirred up good; they were mad they couldn't get out. The whole nest was just rumbling there—"BUZZZZ, ZZZZZZ, BUZZZZ, ZZZZZZ." The whole nest went down in the gas can. Actually, you don't have to get the whole thing in there, just the hole. That nest is just like paper or a cardboard-like stuff; acts just like a wick.

I didn't think any of those hornets were out of the nest yet that early in the morning. It could be Ol' Barney just thought he heard one buzzing around his head.

Out of Yamhill, up by Pike, on the Jack Sheppard place is where this took place. Dad and Jack had a sawmill there—they'd taken out smaller stuff. We were taking out the old growth they had left. Their mill was too small for the old growth; shoot, that stuff was six, seven foot through.

# Clyde Cook and Chain Saw Trouble

One time we were making horse jumps for the Menefee Chicken Farm, two miles out of Carlton, due west. Two brothers owned this outfit. P. L. Menefee was the chicken man and L. B. Menefee was the turkey guy. They developed those bronze-breasted turkeys—I always thought they did, anyway.

They also had jumping horses. L. B. had laid out a course for the horses to run. He had me making those jumps for the horses; I was running the Cat. Clyde Cook, about six foot three inches and he wasn't a skinny guy either, fell the timber and cut the logs twelve, maybe sixteen foot in length for the jumps. We'd stack them two on the bottom and one on the top, then cover them with dirt.

Clyde was cutting away—"yerom, yeom, yeom." The saw would not cut. I had seen him filing down the riders—too much. Then he stuck it in a log, and I heard it go "runt." The motor would quit. He tried it a few more times. Then he got mad because it kept grabbing into the wood and dying. He grabbed that saw right by the bar (part that the chain runs around on in a circle), and he ran just as hard as he could go and hit it right on top of a stump—"kersmack!" Just broke it to pieces. The pieces just flew. The motor broke off. He still had it by the bar. He ran out to his jeep and got a can of gas and matches, and back he come! I didn't know what he was getting them for. Scared Ol' Mennefee, I think, who didn't know what Clyde was doing. Then he poured gas all over the saw and set it afire. Shoot, the rest of us didn't dare laugh. Then he got in that jeep and out of there he went and bought another saw. When he came back he said, "By God, I got one now that'll cut."

Had him a new Homelight. Those McCulloughs were cantankerous son-of-a-guns, especially when the riders were filed down too much. Clyde was working for me at the time.

God, you look back on that—I was working a D-6 Cat and myself for thirteen dollars an hour—that was the going wage then. That was probably '53, '54.

# Freak Wind

Once we got to that job west of Carlton, we were taking out some trees that were leaning back towards a power line. I had bought these fir trees—nice ones—and we logged them. Les Cox, Junior Barker and Ed Kirk worked for me and Les Stabler was the independent trucker taking them to the mill.

I was climbing the trees, setting a small choker in them and a light cable to pull them back away from the power line. Ed would tighten them up with the Cat, Ol' Pappy Cox would fall them and Junior would gather up lines to help me set up another one.

A peculiar thing happened. We were all sitting there eating our lunches one day when all at once a wind blew up to beat hell I mean and blew the trees back over the way we wanted them. Three of us jumped up, grabbed chain saws and started falling trees. We had to just hope we didn't get a lull in the wind. Junior was running around pounding wedges in all of our back cuts just to make sure they didn't set down on the stump. We got about a half dozen felled there before the wind died down.

# Denailing With Dynamite

Once I saw a home get torn down in McMinnville. The men who did this used some old-fashioned know-how. They really harnessed the power. They sealed off all the windows with plastic real tight. Then a stick of dynamite was hung upside down from a rafter in the middle of the house. When they touched her off, it loosened every nail in the place. With the house sealed off, the concussion just popped those boards out an inch or so—really neat. That way the lumber wasn't cracked and ripped up by the crowbars and was able to be salvaged a lot neater, board by board.

# Ironing On the Stove Pipe

Ol' Mae Gandy used to iron her clothes on the stove pipe of her wood stove. She'd clean the stove pipe off real good until it was down to black, clean metal and kind of pull the clothes back and forth around it. The pipe was real hot and made a good iron. She'd do her husband Sam's work shirts that way.

# Morning-Style Eggs

Ol' Barney Hurt used to say when a waitress asked him, "How do you like your eggs?"

He'd say, "Morning-style."

"Morning style? What does that mean?"

"Just like I am in the morning, straight up and about half hard."

86

# Coming to
# Loon Lake

# Brooks' Mill

When Joe Gieberson, my old misery whip partner, became a scaler for the timber coming off the state lands, he worked at Brooks' mill up Soup Creek at Loon Lake.

He went home to Yamhill and said, "How's the logging?"

"I've just got one little ol' job, finished up that other one and got a land clearing job for about one day, that's all I have," I told him.

"Well, come on down to Loon Lake, they need a logger."

I came down and saw Stan Brooks. He took me up on a hill and showed me some ground. He said he had to go. I looked around and told him I'd meet him back at the mill. I scrutinized the slope and timber and found him at the mill.

He said he'd pay $28 a thousand. I said that was too cheap for what it was—rough-assed ground. It might not have been for Sam Hughes and them, but it was for us.

I wish I would have said $36. I said $34.

He said, "How 'bout $32?"

"Well, I guess we have to compromise."

At the first pay period, he said, "Hey, come in here. I want to show you something. You got more log scale in here than all the rest put together with your drunks."

That's what they called them.

The "rest" of the loggers were Sam Hughes and Merle Moore, Shorty Harrison, Marvin Haskell, Bud Parker, Louis La Mar, and Henry Hendricksen. Hell, we stayed right up there on the job. Hughes was helping run Duckett's Resort; Merle lived in back of Duckett's in an old filing shack and came to work with Hughes; and Shorty, Marvin and Bud all had farms and cows to milk besides the logging. We'd have all the time one load, sometimes two, already to the mill by the time they'd come to work. I think Mervin Boast, the log truck driver who hauled my logs in, put in twelve loads one day. The La Mars crew, George and Ray, now that's the ones they should have called the drunks. They spent more time down there at Duckett's—every night they were down there whooping it up.

# Brooks Come Into the Country as Timber Fallers

Stan and Gene Brooks came into Ash Valley and E. K. Woods put them to work falling timber with the old cross cuts, the misery whips. They were from Minnesota or Wisconsin, somewheres. They were cutting that hill right behind the school. This was about 1942 to 1946—during the war the logging companies just had to take what they could get.

When they first started coming into this country you could spot every one of them—they wore those old railroad caps. Talking to an old guy in a rigging shed down there in Sheridan, he said, "There goes another one of those dust bowlers—got one of those catch-me-dittle-me-quick caps on." They were new in the country whether they were from the dust bowl or Minnesota and their work showed it.

Their stumps were still pretty fresh when I come into the country in '55. They'd have a face in there ("V" cut or notch in the tree that aims the tree in the direction you want it to fall) 'bout the size of a springboard hole—just a little tiny hole—shallow and narrow. It's a wonder they didn't get killed. Pulled roots right out of the ground when the tree fell. Shoot, with those big trees you want to go 'way in there—big face. Yeah, it's a wonder them Brooks didn't get killed or ride one of those root wads down the hill.

Carl Collins was bucking behind them. I forgot to ask Carl who cut the roots off the butt cut—by God, I wouldn't have—you don't get paid for that, you'd have to fall it twice. I understood you couldn't hardly get a bucker to go behind them.

Yes, I saw a fight right in the crummy over that.

A bucker (man who cuts the fallen trees into lengths) told the faller, "You make any more of them cougar traps (big entanglements of trees one on top of the other all whichways, crossed up, and dangerous to buck up) and you'll be down there bucking them yourself."

The faller told him, "We don't make any cougar traps around here!"

"The hell you don't!" the bucker retorted.

The faller came back with, "You calling me a liar?" and the fight was on! The bucker kicked the faller right in the gut! That was Ol' Johnnie Dushane, the bucker, and the timber faller was Ole Johnson. Johnnie laid it on him and that pretty much ended the argument.

Stan and Gene Brooks may not have been timber fallers to start with, but they soon started a very successful mill, which cut millions of board feet of lumber. The Brooks mill on Soup Creek Road needed more logs and that's what brought me into this country.

# Case of the Eye Watching the Teeth

My crew and I had only been down in this country a week or so. It was in August, hot and dusty. We used to go down after work and clean up in the lake. Some of them guys that could swim would go out in the lake and swim. Old Pappy Cox and I would stay close to shore and wash up. Felt good.

We decided we'd stop in the Duckett's Resort and that was a memorable first visit.

A big ol' Indian was getting after an old man, pestering him. He was ruffing him up and shoving him around. They worked together, by the sounds of it, over at Ernie Lee and McCloud's sawmill across the lake, and were having a dispute over something that happened at the job. The old man was old enough to be the Indian's grandfather.

Pierce Duckett, the owner, was sitting there doing nothing.

I kept thinking, "Man, ain't he going to stop that? Say something?"

Pappy Cox said, "God, doesn't look like that man's going to stop that."

Later we found out Pierce only had one leg, he didn't need to be over there wrestling around.

I told the Indian, "You shouldn't push him around."

"Oh, you think you want some, huh?"

He took out his false teeth, put them on the counter and said, "Stay right here."

I put my eye out on the counter and said, "Watch these for me."

Man, he came unglued. He made a charge at me and I caught him a good hit right in the nose and, man, blood just flew.

He put his head down, and I popped him four or five times in the ribs. Then I threw him out the door.

The Indian's name was Rich Hunt. We were friends after that. I pulled him out of the lake. Old George Montgomery got him off the bottom and I got him up the rest of the way. Later I got to know the old man, Bill Anderson. He was a happy-go-lucky guy, always laughing, and I liked that man.

# Ex-Pug

Pierce Duckett used to say, "If I had my leg, I'd show you something!"

"You couldn't show me anything if you had three legs," I'd say.

Finally, he hired an ex-pug from down the coast there some place to thump on me. It was the night before elk season. Leonard, Bob Simmonson and Oscar Payne were down there to hunt, all my crew was there, I never could figure why the guy was bugging me.

The crew pulled me off of him, said, "Hey, you're going to kill him." It wasn't 'til later Althea told me Pierce had hired that guy to beat me up.

Boy, I saw the fella the next day, his eyes were damned near swelled shut, his nose bent over. I said, "Well, do you want to try it again?" He didn't want nothing to do with me.

# Lloyd Comes Into the Valley (cont.)
### and
# Logging Across the River

That patch of timber I bid on and got was just a bunch of relog. E. K. Woods and Harold Dick had creamed it there during the war. Well, that's the way it was in those days, they just took the best, that's about all the mills would buy. Years ago, too, about all they did. Been lots of good money made just going behind and logging what they left. That's what everybody was doing here on this Brooks project.

After my crew and I got rained out up there, everybody went back up to Carlton—Yes, "Pappy" Cox and Mommie Cox—she ran the cookhouse—Junior Barker, Ed Kirk and the two truckers, Merlin Boast and Jones.

About then some outfit out of Philomath (some woman!) bought Brooks' mill out and the timber there, what little was left. That included our patch. We never finished that; we were rained out. There was just one little corner left up there, some pretty good stuff, too; I was wanting to get into that. Well, the new outfit sawed up the cold deck (we had a hell of a cold deck there) and then said there was more money in logging than running a sawmill. The logging didn't last long. They bought E. K. Woods' old holdings up in the Elliott— that was about gone there. The Brooks mill's cold deck was located where Bill English's place now stands. That's why his brush fire that got away in 1990 burnt so long in there and was hard to put out—it's just a deep pile of old rotten bark and duff.

After being rained and bought out I went 'way down there by Reedsport—right across from the dump road. Had to cross the river to get to it. The timber was on one steep slope! Steep as the back of God's head but, by God, Ol' Bud Ernest was working for me, and we showed 'em.

Douglas Electric had fell a whole big bunch of old growth trees—nice logs—to clear for the power lines to come through. There was quite an area, ten acres or so of it, and they'd been laying there three or four months. We never had to fall anything, just buck them up and get them out of there. I never knew that timber was for sale or I'd have bought it. Instead, Van Etten, the Ash Valley schoolteacher, bought it and hired me to log it.

There was a steep bluff where the power lines spanned the river. Douglas Electric must have had helicopters to bring the power poles in there. There was no log roads. Chain saw winch would be the only way, maybe, Ol' Frank Barth got the electric poles up there.

They kept saying, "You'll never get a road up there, you'll never get a road up there."

"Oh, yeah? We'll get a road up there unless we hit rock."

To get the Cat to that job, I low-boyed it up the Smith River Road and unloaded it at old Louie Seymore's place, which is now his son-in-law, Wade's. From Wade's place the Cat walked by itself the rest of the way. So you see, we went up the Smith River, logged the top of the mountain and skidded them down to the Umpqua River. I know I spent a few days gouging out a road up there. I just angled up to the ridge and once I got on the ridge, winched the Cat up backwards.

Ol' Bud Ernest and the schoolteacher, Van Etten, were pulling winch line for me behind the Cat and would hook me up to a stump or a tree, whatever, and I'd just let the winch line pull me up backwards; and the tracks—I had them going to help me. We'd make seventy-five feet or so at a time.

We got it backed up to the ridge where it was not so steep and from there it could go up by itself. After I got to the top, I could come on down, build road on the way down. Shoot, I had a road up there in a couple of days—just a Cat road to bring the logs down with, only road up there.

We were yarding the logs down the Cat road and tying them up in the river. When we finished the logging show and I come back out for good, I had the Umpqua barge to pick me up. By then we had a good road where we'd been taking the logs down to the river.

And down in the river is where someone opened up the raft and took a lot of logs. Boy, lost a lot of money there. Hell, they just opened up the chains—the rafts have a hole bored on the ends and the boomsticks have a toggle out at the end—hell, ain't nothing to opening them if you got a little slack.

I went down to the mill in East Gardiner—a little pecker wood outfit on the Smith River. By God, we found some of them there; I had branded some of them, and we got lapse on that and didn't have them all branded. Ol' Bert Freytag went with me to get them away from that thus and such, the owner. He didn't want to let them go. He changed his mind when Bert showed him who he was—a state policeman and game warden.

The old man that owned the property on the Umpqua River, I always wondered if he did it. We had to take the logs across the old man's property to get them to the river. That old guy was Katherine Parker's uncle; I liked that old guy.

The schoolteacher and the old man had quite a dispute—even went to court in Reedsport. A log got away and broke the old man's water line—he was pretty mad; he was milking cows. You can't milk twice a day without water you know. He had cows to wash, buckets, milking equipment and all that.

That big log was the last damned one we were bringing in for the day. I had it behind me and was pulling it downhill with the Cat. At one bad, bad turn, the Cat road was sloped to the outside downhill, and the log rolled over the side of the road, got going, and I turned it loose with the winch brake. I let the brake off and turned the Cat around real quick. It had the Cat rared 'way up there. I was turned around, the Cat standing on its back tracks, and I was hoping the log would kind of stop somewhere. It kept a-going, son-of-a-bitch—winch line and all—POW! It smashed into the swamp down there. I never knew it hit his water line or I would have fixed it that evening.

Boy, the next day I fixed that road so the logs couldn't roll off of that turn any more. I just tilted the blade and dug a big ditch so the logs, going around the bend, ran right to the inside and in that ditch. Logs from then on followed me in an orderly manner around the bend.

The judge decided Van Etten would pay the old man and fix his pipe. Van Etten brought him some—Ha!—old worn out pipe from the school, that really made the old man mad! The old man probably fixed it temporarily, and Van Etten's repair job was worse than the temporary fix.

I always figured the old man might have done it. Maybe not—probably some of them ol' thieving young scallywags-getting-logs done it. Probably so.

It was summer time and hot weather and the school-teacher, Van Etten, wouldn't bring no lunch—run around and eat blackberries 'til he dehydrated. That happened one day. He got dehydrated and cramped up all over so bad he couldn't move. I started to take him across the river and that damned ol' outboard motor he had wouldn't run, old antique thing that it was and outdated. I grabbed the oars and started pumping and rowing hard as I could. I ended up 'way down the river from where we usually landed. I helped Van up the bank and got him up on the road. We were nowhere near our cars. I lucked out though. A big "Wincoln" convertible came along. It was Kenny Whitlow. He stopped when he recognized me, backed up and hollered, "Hey, Lloyd, you got a man hurt?"

"Yeah," I said, "I don't know what's the matter with him; he's all cramped up."

Van Etten was laying on the ground kicking like a digger squirrel. I know it sounds funny now, but it wasn't then. Kenny picked us up and took us into a doctor in town.

The doctor said, "He's got to get some place where they can get some stuff back in him."

I borrowed Pete Stingley's car and took him on in to the North Bend hospital. They hooked him right up and got some juice back in him. How anybody eating blackberries could get dehydrated, I'm not sure.

I guess he had slim pickins that day.

# Duckett's Resort

In 1920 the county passed a levy to build a road from Allegany to the Umpqua River. From Allegany, in the hills above Coos Bay, this road was carved past Gold and Silver Falls, blasted through rock and hillside fourteen miles to the floor of Ash Valley, then four miles, including a covered and other wooden bridges, to Loon Lake. It continued three and a half miles around the lake's edge, then over a covered bridge spanning the gorge at the lake's torrential outlet, over another at Kelly Creek, then nine miles to the Umpqua, following Mill Creek. Mill Creek is a partly tidal body of water which carries the outflowing water from the lake and Camp Creek basins to the Umpqua River.

A crew of thirty convicts from the Roseburg jail, under the supervision of Mr. Lucksinger, horse rancher from across the lake, built the section from the river up. Eighteen local ranchers built from the valley down, then up to Allegany, all foremanned for the county by Luther Judy. High waters took out a large section of road along the tidewaters of Mill Creek that first winter, but the convicts rebuilt it the following year.

By 1928 two bridges had been completed, one a steel bridge spanning the Umpqua near Scottsburg and the other a covered wooden bridge paralleling the Umpqua and spanning the mouth of Mill Creek.

The old overland trail over the ridges from Scottsburg and Elkton down Tom Fool Creek on the Boak place was pretty much abandoned. Ranchers loved the new Loon Lake county road which was more accessible for all travelers, whether by way of foot, horse, wagon, light rig, motorized stage or automobile. Travelers plying their way up the narrow dirt and gravel road enjoyed viewing the spectacular scenery, bluffs, rock formations, wild flowers, waterfalls, and of course, the lake itself.

The new road was planked in places from the upper end of the lake where Tom Fool Creek and the old trail joined in, through Ash Valley and all the way to Allegany.

This road was built during the 1920s. During this time, David and Bessie Wakefield owned the old Upton homestead on Loon Lake. From the homestead and orchard on the ridge, a meadow spread to the lake between two hills. The new road, making a "U"-shaped curve, came down around one hill, across the meadow, over Upton Creek on a wooden bridge and up around the other hill. Wakefields started the first resort by towing the road crew's shacks onto this scenic spot near their lake front. The shacks of the convicts were built on skids and had been left over after the building of the road. A sign was put up in front of the road crew shacks which read, "House of Wakefield. Eat and Sleep or Both, Pop on Ice." Then the Wakefields traded this resort and the 155 acre Upton homestead to Bob and Edna Duckett, who owned twenty acres on the Umpqua River, just west of the Scottsburg bridge. A little cash was thrown in with the Umpqua River property and the swap was made. In the early 1930s Bob and Edna helped finance their son and daughter-in-law, Pierce and Althea Duckett, in the building of Duckett's Resort. A store and restaurant were built with an attached home. Then, eight cabins, a dock, a dockhouse and two "Honeymoon" floathouses were constructed. With good spring water, good hunting and fishing, a stone fireplace and hearty welcome in the store, Duckett's became a favorite stopping place or vacation spot to get away from it all.

Pierce Duckett was the only child of Bob and Edna Duckett and was raised at Scottsburg and Loon Lake. Although a good sized man, he was no match for his father. Falling timber with the ol' crosscut saw, his father would be on one end of the misery whip and Pierce on the other.

The dad would wear him down and then some other guy would take over and he'd work on him. Bob was just a little wiry fart, strong and good-natured. I know Althea really loved that old man. He died of leukemia after Pierce and Althea were married.

Pierce had an old Sixty Best, it was the forerunner of the Caterpillar and it was a Caterpillar. It had a big flywheel which stuck out there on the end of the motor. You stuck a big round bar in and turned the flywheel over, a quarter of a turn at a time, to get it started. If it kicked back, it sent the bar flying in the air about thirty feet. He used it to log the old growth off the hills of his Dad's places and off the Upton homestead, what he and Roy Waggoner could reach here. I think Ol' Roy Waggoner run the damned thing. They may have pulled those original road crew shacks here with that old Sixty Best.

Pierce and Althea met Frank Laird coming to the resort as a fisherman, a customer. Frank was the big bronze bushing for the Utah Construction Company, a Mormon outfit. He was building a road in California from the Coast Range to Fort Bragg, and hired Pierce as the bullbuck, lining out all the timber cutters. Pierce and Althea left the resort in the hands of Bob and Elaine Fullhart, with a lease to manage it for the duration of the job, less than a year. While Pierce was in the woods Althea and their two daughters, Faye and Jody, stayed in a company camp in Ukiah. It was in one of the logging camps that Pierce developed Burger's disease, which is blood clots in the leg. His big toe turned black. When they returned, Pierce started developing complications of the Burger's disease. They amputated his leg up in Portland. He had trouble with his prosthesis, a cork-like plastic false leg which went almost to the hip. It would come unattached and he'd fall flat on his face. He went back up to Portland in 1955 to get a new leg and that's when he had his heart attack and they found him deceased in a hotel room.

I married Pierce's widow, Althea Duckett, in 1956 and together we ran the resort. I would log during the day and run the store and tavern at night.

Edna Duckett, Pierce's mother, lived in Cabin Six for many years. She could never remember my name. She called me "That Feller." She was one hard-working lady and cleaned the cabins for us. We had a time with her being so senile. Some vacationers would just get moved into a cabin and here she would come with her cleaning equipment and start cleaning, washing the dishes, straightening things up, taking the sheets off the beds and moving their luggage out. The customers would walk down to the store to ask us why our cleaning lady was there when they were just moving in.

Althea would say, "Oh, God, she's done it again," and would remove Edna to another locality.


Our grocery wholesaler was in Coos Bay, and when we went in for groceries we'd ask Edna if she wanted to come along.

She'd say, "Oh, my, clean to Coos Bay? I'd better go get my suitcase packed."

We told her we'd be back the same day, Coos Bay being only an hour and a half away, but she still packed her toothbrush, gown and overnight things in her suitcase—you weren't going to get that away from her. She was thinking it was still an old plank road over the mountains to Allegheny and then a riverboat the rest of the way. No way you're going to do that in one day—the boat's fighting the tides—yep, she remembered that—"Clean to Coos Bay."

# Early Days in Scottsburg
## As Told by Jackson Beaman

I lived in Scottsburg until about in second grade. My folks had a confectionary—ice cream, candy, sandwiches, and a pool table. I really don't know what a confectionary was because I didn't spend much time in it. I spent more time outside. The sidewalk that ran past the confectionary went 'way up in the air five or six feet. It must have been on a second floor or something. Gus Mitchell lived in a white house next door; he was some kind of sailor that had roamed all over the world and retired there next to the confectionary.

My grandfather, Enoch William Beaman, ran and owned the ferry that took passengers, cows, horses, wagons, everything, I guess, across the Umpqua River. He pulled it across by hand. In my grandfather's day a cable was stretched clear across the river and on the Scottsburg side I know it was tied to a couple of stumps. On the Jimmy Creek side it was tied to a tree or rock or stump, I'm not sure. Anyway, the steel line held the ferry in place and this cable held the ferry from drifting upstream with the tide, or downstream with the current. Right where that ferry was, it was the head of tidewater, you know. Later, when I came back, they ran it with an outboard motor. Anyway Grandfather, pulling it across by hand, used to not like to pull Pierce Duckett across—just one passenger at a time like that. Pierce would stand there all by himself. I spent a lot of time with my grandparents—see, they lived down beneath a great big cherry tree there in Scottsburg.

I was living in Scottsburg when Hedden's store was robbed one night. The two robbers went up in Fisher's barn all day, while everybody looked all over town for them. Nobody looked in the barn. When one of the robbers tried to make his way down to the ferry landing, he was shot and killed.

Robbing stores was a federal offense and they wanted to stop people from doing that. Sonny McCline was Sheriff of Douglas County then. I came back later and he was Judge.

Enoch, my grandfather, had the biggest hands, I heard other people say, that anyone had seen in their lives—I don't know what that has to do with anything.

My mother's father had a store in Elkton and was named J. J. Hedden. We were not related to John and Fanny Hedden who owned the store in Scottsburg. All I'd ever heard was that two cousins came here from England and came across the plains. So I guess we don't claim them and they probably wouldn't want to claim us either.

Long before it was an automobile, the stage ran with horses. The mountain out of Elkton was long and steep, and wound around so much with so many switchbacks, the passengers used to get out and walk to help the horses. A lot of romances were started on those walks up that Elkton hill. Another place they walked was through the tunnel in later years when the motorized stage went over the hill. Passengers enjoyed walking through the tunnel while the stage took the longer route of the old road around the mountain, crossing Elk Creek twice. That same tunnel that we drive through today was going to be a railroad tunnel but the railroad never got west of Drain. That's what those cement piers are that you see on either side of various creeks, such as Elk Creek. They were the start of bridges for the railroad to go across the creeks. I have no idea where the money was from to build that railroad, or why it never went through.

The Campi Hotel was down near the ferry landing. Jerry Ruben owned it, and he had a son Howard, the one and only, who rowed a boat working around the bridge. They broke the mold when they made him—I guess! He kept the seal population stabilized. The hotel was a good sized building with a saloon, dining hall and six bedrooms. During prohibition there wasn't much cause for business in the saloon. There used to be a hooker down at the hotel, they called her "Wishbone" because she had such a prominent pelvis. There was no one other like this 'til you got to Drain. No road to Reedsport. The loggers who worked at Camp Creek would run to Scottsburg Saturday nights—the only place to go. There was nothing in Ash Valley.

I started school there with Nola Kent, she was the school marm at that time. She had been a schoolmate of my mother in Drain; they'd known each other for many years. She boarded with us, so you can imagine I didn't get away with much.

When I was in the third grade Dad went fishing down on the Rogue River and stayed camping out for quite a while. Imagine the adventures he must have had there! Later on Dad and Mother had a restaurant in Harrisburg. For quite a few years they worked so hard and almost worked themselves to death until finally we put Dad in the hospital and Mom on the train for Medford to treat her for asthma. My brother and I stayed with my grandparents on 12th Street in Salem. During our childhood we had chicken pox, red measles and scarlet fever. After a while the folks got better and ran an apartment house in Salem. That was right down from the Southern Pacific depot on 13th Street. There were a bunch of foreign girls there that knew a hell of a bunch more of life than I did. You ask me if I fooled around with those girls?

Put it the other way around. We sold newspapers there, the Something, and the Portland Telegram, which is no longer in business.

Then we moved to Raymond, Washington, where Dad worked in a mill. Working in a mill is the end of the world as far as I'm concerned. But he had a job in the back and burned up lumber that wouldn't sell, scrap lumber. He took it home since he always had a boat of some kind, he loaded it up with this lumber from the mill and took it back up to where we had a place on the Umpqua River and used it for wood in the stove.

Well, here I came, back to Scottsburg when I was in my teens. I hitchhiked my first time away from home, where my folks now had a restaurant in Raymond, Washington, in 1928. The Clackamas Construction Company out of Oregon City, or some town around there, was starting to build the Scottsburg bridge across the Umpqua. Phillip Hult and his partner, Al somebody, hired me. They didn't know how old I was, because I lied about my age. I was one week shy of sixteen years old. That wasn't so bad, I'd been lying for a long time.

Pierce Duckett, in his early twenties, was the only local man to work on the footings of the bridge; all the crew was from up around Oregon City, brought in with the construction company. I worked with him and later Howard Ruben and some others helped on the span part of the bridge.

We built coffer dams for the piers to go down into the water. The water is not very deep there, only six feet or eight feet, and the coffer dams, or frames for cement, were made out of two by eight or ten inch tongue and groove, which were tapered with snipes on the ends—more tapers.

Pierce kept the dams pumped out with a pump that ran from a belt off the PTO of the tractor on the bank. Pierce also did some hard-hat diving to build and secure the wooden frames of the coffer dams under water. His wife, Althea, manned the hand pump that gave him air. Pierce got tired of the diving and I tried it, too, while he supplied me with air.

I had done some dynamiting for my uncle up Salmon Creek, so I also worked on as a powder monkey. We had a gas-powered air compressor that set up on the coffer dams and ran a jack hammer. We drilled about three feet into the bedrock, and put six or eight single sticks of dynamite into the holes, lit the fuse on one, jumped into the boat and rowed like hell. I was the best rower of the group, all them Swedes sat in the boat and counted one, two, three, to my rowing strokes. We had so many counts before it blew, and we would be ashore by that time. A foot a minute that fuse burned. When the dynamite blew, rocks cascaded everywhere. Being surrounded by that eight by ten foot coffer dam, water and rocks went straight up for a while before it came down. We were blowing footing for the piers to have a solid base. The bases were concrete poured into the bedrock about three feet. We wondered if that was bedrock, but the engineer figured if that wasn't it was a huge boulder.

After helping build the piers, Pierce went back into Ash Valley, and I joined him and Althea later that winter and stayed with them milking cows. The construction of the actual metal bridge was done by Clackamas Construction crew. We just helped build the footings.

By the way, there's an old, old story in the olden days of whores—they didn't like people who ran jack hammers because with jigging up and down all the time, it made their balls hang down so far and they couldn't get them ejaculated.

Hitchhiking across the country, my idea of money in those days was a place to sleep. A baker in Columbia, Missouri, asked if I would work. I picked up a broom and started to sweep.

The baker said, "Okay, that's enough, I just wanted to see if you could work," and he gave me a sack of bread. I rode the trains at night and hitchhiked during the day. I got off the trains in the morning so those railroad bulls wouldn't get me, they were mean. I went all over the United States.

Pierce Duckett used to sharpen my pencils for me in school in Scottsburg, when he was in seventh or eighth grade and I was in first. We always liked each other, even back then. By the time he was married and living in Ash Valley, I spent a lot of time up there with him—he must have been about twenty-five and I was a teenager. At that time his parents, Bob and Edna Duckett, lived up the Carlson Road. Early one afternoon we were coming home from brush cutting the Bob Duckett place. We'd been cutting brush which was kind of taking over. We'd cut it and stack it to burn later. Well, we were walking home for lunch and passing the school, when we met up with an uncle or cousin of the Esselstroms who had brought up a couple of fruit jars of moonshine from town. We stopped and drank quite a little bit of it, it didn't take very much after working half the day and then that walk of a few miles. We kept on walking to Pierce's place and to get to his "shotgun" house we had to cross the one hundred foot span of roaring Lake Creek on a footbridge only two planks wide—all I can remember is crawling across that wooden bridge on my hands and knees. When we got there Althea was madder'n a wet hen of course. I don't know what she did with Pierce. I slept it off in the barn.

Pierce's mother, Edna, was a better milker than any machine ever invented I guess. She could get a cow milked by the time you even could get ready to sit down beside one. Bob Duckett had bad feet all his life. Edna was the toughest one of the bunch. She could milk seven or eight cows and bitch and whine and cry all night. There was some wild story about her and Caddy Knottage across the river from Well's Creek when the Ducketts lived in Scottsburg. Lots of gossip—Bob would go off to camp for weeks on end.

When I first came into Ash Valley I thought there'd be twenty killings before morning the way people talked about each other. Everybody made fun of what everybody else did—but nobody did anything. The Ash Valley people called the lake people "Swamp Nannies," and the lake people called the residents in the valley "Hootenannies" or something like that. This is not very big area—the lake being three miles long and the valley, four miles long, neither being more than a mile wide. In those days there was a lot of vitality and interaction between neighbors, which naturally led to some griping and complaining at times. They also worked together building homes and barns, logging, haying, hunting, fishing, quilting, and a miriad of other chores and self-sufficient work they did to live off the land.

I used to think that if Lloyd and Pierce would ever get into it Pierce would beat him. But over the years I realized he never would have beat Lloyd. Pierce was a stand up boxer. Lloyd was an arm breaker—he knew all the holds. He was trained that way.

I was a boxer, myself, from 122 lbs. to 160 lbs. as I grew. I ran an athletic club in Aberdeen, Washington.

Lloyd:  Old Dewey Abbott, Forest's brother, wasn't afraid of Pierce. He about beat him to death. Althea said they'd gone to a dance down in Lakeside, and Pierce, who had boxed a little bit in the Marine Corps and thought he knew everything about the manly art of fisticuffs, just kept picking and picking on Dewey. Dewey had a reputation of being a tough son-of-a-gun so Pierce had to test him. That would be a mistake. Dewey owned and operated the Tugboat *Welcome* and was known to be one tough man even after he was 'way up in years. Althea's sister, Little Mary, who was also Dewey's wife, agitated that one. I guess Dewey about done him in. A lot of guys about done him in.

Oh, heck, yeah, Bick's uncle cleaned him. Pierce was kind of a half-assed bullbuck, and the fight with Bick's uncle was probably over some scale or something. He probably adjusted the uncle's scale, then *he* got adjusted.

And that guy from Allegany, Harold Noah, cleaned his clock.

# Red Devil

In Scottsburg in the early 1900s, my father, Pearl Andrew Beaman, built a boat. He called it the *Red Devil*. That was a very bad word in those days. Rock Fryer helped him build it. Together they netted and sold a lot of salmon out of the Umpqua River. They had built a "false eddy" out of planks for the salmon to rest behind when they were running and resting there, and they would set off some dynamite caps in the water to scare the salmon and make them rush into their set nets. One time Rock and my father accidentally set off ninety-nine dynamite caps in the boat—there was a hundred caps in the round can—one went off and the jolt made them all go. The blast blew the stern out of the boat. It still floated, and simply drifted down and stuck on the wooden wall of the homemade false eddy. You would have thought that they would have gotten hurt with all that copper flying around—the caps were all made of copper in those days.

As soon as the boat was loaded with fish and they had them all cleaned they'd sell them to the pickup boat, an old "one-lunger" that came up the river from Reedsport. It came about every day or every other day and delivered the fish to the cannery in Gardiner. This was in the wintertime so the fish stayed nice and cold awaiting the pickup boat. After many years the price of salmon went up to ten cents a pound. One time Father made $100 in a day, enabling Mother to take a trip back to Elkton to see her parents.

# Butter and the Civet Cat

Beaman: Pierce Duckett was having heart trouble and went to Portland to stay, as long as he could of course. He had me house sit and watch things while he and Althea were gone. One night I heard a civet cat, a little, spotted relation to the skunk, scratching around on the back porch. Then I heard him walking with a "click, click, click." They make a lot of noise, walking, you know, and thump their feet, too. I went into the spring house on the back porch where the ice cold spring water ran through wooden troughs and kept everything cold. Milking cows, Pierce and Althea had a lot of milk, cream and butter in there. The butter was put down in cold water inside wooden troughs, and held down by weights. I had a pistol and a candle and went to investigate. There he was—about to get some butter! When I shot at the civet cat, the candle went out and everything got blacker than hell. I don't know how much butter was ruined that night with that civet cat smell.

I thought I was a pretty good house sitter before that.

# Carl Collins

Jackson Beaman: Carl Collins slept on the ground. Early one morning I was walking over there by the old McClay place, they'd had some kind of a party or something, and Carl was asleep on the ground. He got up, and just kind of shook himself like a dog and walked off. But you know as much as he drank he was always a gentleman. I don't know what the hell he drank or where he got it, there was no moonshine in Ash Valley in those days. Nobody could have a still because any time someone did have one, some stool pigeon would turn him in to the law.

Jane Kaiser, the Ash Valley school teacher, once asked Carl how he lost his eye. He told her,

"Well, Jane, it was a beautiful gal; she looked a lot like you." She blushed and everyone got a kick out of that. He got kicked by a horse, really.

Lloyd: He was up in years and Dick Hunt said, "You're my dad!"

"No," Carl remonstrated, "All your mother and I ever done was a handshake." Dick Hunt kept on and kept on and finally out behind the resort, by God, Ol' Carl whipped the guy. I watched and I thought I was going to have to break it up. I saw him punch him in the guts over and over; finally he hit him in the jaw and that was the end of him. He was an old man then but was doing all right.

He could have told Dick Hunt, "Well, your 'Dad' gave you a whippin'."

Carl wasn't really his dad, oh, hell, no. That Dick Hunt was always coming up with something. He was the crazy son-of-a-gun I had to overhaul, and then saved his life down in the lake; regular loony.

# Shotgun House

JB: "Louis Strommen—does that mean anything to you?"

Lloyd: "Oh, yeah, the Strommens used to come to the lake and visit Althea."

JB: "Bob and Edna Duckett made two or three thousand dollars one year selling cream—they talked about building a house for Pierce. Louis Strommen was a house builder—I mean a real carpenter! A real nice old man. He came down to the lake and built a lot of houses and barns in the valley. He built the Carlson house and dairy barn, Boak house and dairy barn, Parker house and dairy barn, and his own house towards the end of the valley, where he and his wife raised three girls. These are all big two- and three-story houses. You ask how those farmers could afford to have such nice homes built—in those days labor didn't cost very much. All the lumber was from old growth logs off their own places, milled right there from Baker's mill, up around the Newkirk place (behind Paul Coates').

"The shotgun house was built. I think this name was something they just made up. It looked like this:

| Living Room | Kitchen | Bedroom |
|---|---|---|

It was located straight across Lake Creek from the Soup Creek junction. Nels Fredericksen had a bridge there. About 1980 Dale Fredericksen burnt the shotgun home down and his father, Nels Fredericksen, burnt the bridge down when it got in disrepair and dangerous."

# By the Line

JB (Jackson Beaman): "Bill Esselstrom was standing on the log with my Uncle Claude when he got killed. They were working 'by the line.'"

Lloyd: "By that back line, I guess, be my guess."

JB: "Took Esselstrom's hat off. Hit Uncle in the head. They took the cook house door off and used it for a stretcher—took him to Scottsburg to bury him."

Lloyd: "Probably had a siwash in the line, around a stump or something—when it come loose—swooop! That was the end of him."

To define "by the line," that's the logging cable—it should be run straight, but it gets around a stump or log or anything when it is slacked down, and you think you're out of the way, but you're not. When it comes tight—kerthump! It gets straight again and hits what's ever in its way.

Lawrence Bloomquist got killed the first day he worked in the woods working "by the line."

Chester Beaman got his head cut off by the haulback. In those days a man got killed, the whole crew quit. Everybody'd go home for three, four days. That was out of respect. Nowadays they'd just go ahead on 'er.

# Mills Jackson Beaman Owned or Managed

I started out in the plywood business as a worker and stockholder in the Peninsula Mill in Port Angeles, Washington. We were the second mill to have stockholders and operate as a co-op, the first being the old Olympia Mill, owned by a bunch of Swedes. My first white collar job was as secretary on the Board of Directors of this co-op. "Shilli ham ne da," that means "excuse me," in Taiwanese, I knew exactly where it was in Tacoma, Washington, but I can't think of the name of it, the next mill. I bought it, owned it for a day and sold it the next day. That's when I sprung out on the world and started buying and selling mills.

I started and managed the Umpqua Plywood Mill in Roseburg. Then I went down to Grants Pass and was the sales manager and then general manager of the Southern Oregon Plywood Mill for twenty years.

I was the first president of the American Plywood Association, headquartered in Tacoma, Washington. Then Pacific Wood Products, headquartered in Los Angeles, hired me and sent me to Callenbougan, Philippines, as President of the Finley-Miller Timber Company. We built a mill, town, school, and a hospital for the workers, who were mainly Filipino. From there I went to work for Weyerhaeuser, International Division, and my title was President of the Far East—not bad for a ninth grade education! We exported logs from the Southern Philippines, North Borneo and Kallimatan, Indonesia, to Japan and Korea where they were made into plywood. I was in the Orient and all over the world for nine years, seven of which my wife and I had a home in Manila, Philippines.

Though my heart was always at Loon Lake, where I spent many happy times of my boyhood and where I also owned the Selburg cabin across the lake and the Boak ranch adjoining the lake, my wife preferred to live in Portland. We made that our home upon returning to the States. From there I ran an import and export business, exporting heavy mill machinery to the Orient and importing smaller logging equipment to the States.

In 1972 along with two other guys I bought the fiberboard part of a mill in Olympia, Washington, and made a lot of money upon selling my part. I subsequently lost it investing in land in Florida. In 1992 at age eighty-one we sold the Boak ranch to Lloyd and Ellen Keeland. I exported machinery until I was eighty-three or four.

*Jackson Beaman died at age eighty-seven on April 23, 1998, at his home in Portland.*
*Lamenting his death is his wife Irene, son Jackson Beaman, Jr., grandson Jackson Beaman III, granddaughter Alexa Rose, and friends all over the world.*

# Carl Collins Shoots the Bull

Carl Collins was asleep in his bed at the Everett McClay place in Ash Valley, still known as the Old McDonald Ranch. It was early morning when his neighbor, Vera Judy, burst into the house, out of breath from running.

She yelled, "Get your gun, the bull's going after Bill!"

Carl woke up. Then the sound of a man yelling and a bull bellering really woke him up! (If you've never heard the deep guttural bellering of an angry bull, you don't know what a soul-shaking, hair-raising sound that is. It is a very low, long, loud and rattling roar, threatening, and full of trouble. Add to it the sound of a man yelling and trying to scare the 1,000 lb. bovine off—you've really got trouble!) Carl knew the Judy's didn't have a gun so he grabbed his .30/.30 and ran over to where the commotion was coming from on the neighboring ranch.

He arrived on the scene to find his neighbor, Bill Judy, being attacked by his own Jersey bull. The bull had him down. Carl Collins had to shoot the bull in order to save Bill's life. (A perfectly calm bull can become a roaring, raving, berserk animal when aroused to anger. Dairymen, like Bill Judy, often see a bull angry and fit to be tied when the cows are let into the barn to be milked. The bull is separated from "his cows," often some of them in heat. He is not always agreeable to going in his bull pen.)

This rifle was an old model .94 Winchester with a hair trigger. It had an old crooked stock—it had been laid out in the weather too many times with Carl Collins. It had gotten warped. Heck, Carl would just go out in the woods and sleep under a windfall. He was catching cougars. He was making more money catching cougars than logging in those days. He took that Model .94 Winchester with him on his trapline to shoot cougars and other fur bearers in his traps. And that same gun, crooked stock and all, saved Bill Judy's life.

# Kenny Whitlow

After World War II, things were booming around Reedsport. There were seventeen gypo loggers, just small logging companies, bringing in logs for the E. K. Woods, Longbell, Hinsdale, and Reedsport mills. It was that way all over. Up in Carlton, I never got out of my uniform until I was offered two or three jobs. Everybody was wanting a man. The Whitlows, like me later, came down to the Umpqua River area because they heard the mills were looking for loggers.

A lot of the logging camps were big. It was said that one gypo in the Reedsport area had a camp with 300 men in it. The Whitlows built their camp here in the coastal mountain range and hired a crew of fifty whittling down to as few as ten in the winter. So there they were set up on the left-hand fork of Weatherly Creek. Jim, Old Man Whitlow, was logging with his two sons, Bob and Kenny. Jim's wife, Daisy, was cooking in the cookhouse along with the daughters-in-law, Mary and Gertie, and later granddaughter Pat. Bob and Gertie's three children, Sharon, Gloria and Bobby, and Kenny and Mary's three, Pat, Joe and Crystal all grew up in this logging camp on Weatherly Creek.

Kenny was the boss of this gypo logging outfit, but Old Man Whitlow gave him a lot of grief. One time they got in an argument over the jam at the table. Kenny said something disrespectful to his mother and the Old Man socked a knife right through Kenny's cheeks. He had a scar, pretty little dimples. That's why he talked the way he did—the knife cut through his tongue and gave him a lisp.

Kenny Whitlow was not a tall man, but he was a big logger— short and fat with a big belly sticking out there. A lot of people got fooled with that big fat belly of his, though. He was as rough and tough as the rest of them and a whole lot more so. He was so short and wide, he could climb a tree just about like a squirrel. He put on the spurs and belt and zoom—went right up there.

Over in Weatherly Creek I was logging with him, not for pay, just helping that old son-of-a-bitch out. Hell, we'd known each other for years and years since we were back in Yamhill together. I was driving a Cat for him. I don't know what he was doing; he had me swing a block up in a tree for him. I don't know what was wrong with him he couldn't do it himself. Hell, that's no job. You just ride the pass line up to the top of the spar tree and move the block over to the other side—he was going to yard some logs from that side.

Junior Lee was the head loader, loading the logs up on the log trucks with a heel boom—boom rigging off of a spar tree. He had a second loader unhooking the tongs from the logs from atop the truck. The ground and roads were steep and slick, and Doyle Murphy, the log truck driver, took off with a loaded log truck and slid down off the dirt road into a ditch. It shifted the load pretty bad. Kenny Whitlow blamed Junior Lee. He grabbed Ol' Junior and spun him around and kicked him in the ass a couple of times, just hollering,

"I've told ya and told ya, ya can't load them damned logs without saddles!"

It wasn't even Ol' Junior's fault. He had saddles, he had the load well-built. That was the days when they had cheese blocks not them damned hay rack stakes. Just chains held the logs on. I thought Junior was a pretty good loader; he did a good job; had a few riggin' fits. But the problem was the road was slick and the truck just slid off.

"Well," Kenny said, "I've got some 'wogs' hanging out in the chains, better get down there and straighten them up." So he went down there and pushed the load back on straight with the Cat. Junior got booted just because he was lower on the pecking order, I guess.

It seemed Old Man Jim was really the meanest one and flared up at Kenny quite often for some unknown reason. The loggers told the story of the Whitlows shooting at each other while they worked but it stems from a story that Kenny's daughter Pat tells:

A rifle was always kept in the crummy and sometimes in the rafters of the loading bitch or the yarder. One time Bob was on the yarder and Kenny on the Cat, both bringing logs to the landing.

The Old Man was chasing, unhooking chokers from the logs. He was unhooking a turn Bob had just brought in with the yarder, when Kenny on the Cat showed up with another load. It must have been too much for the Old Man because he yelled over the roar of the yarder and Cat motors, "Kenny, unhook those chokers!"

Kenny replied in a powerful voice from atop the Cat, "Do it yourself! You're the chaser!"

The Old Man said he wasn't going to do it and pulled a knife, running at his son. Kenny picked up a limb and around and around the Cat they went.

About then Bob grabbed the rifle down from the rafters and yelled down from the loader, "If you don't drop that infernal knife, Father, I'll shoot your hand off."

122

That got things smoothed out and the argument ended. Kenny took his own chokers off and wound the Cat back in the woods for more logs, the Old Man stomped around on the landing, disgruntled, with a peevee in his hand, Bob revved up the yarder and things went back to normal—until the next thrilling episode.

Kenny ran a tight, high-ball, hard-working show, and any hunting was done before or after work. A rifle was kept in the crummy for that reason. Occasionally a buck was brought up out of the canyon on the high lead during work hours. A choker was set around the antlers and it sailed overhead all the way to the landing. In the camp sometimes a game warden stopped by and had coffee as the cookhouse was a gathering place for everybody. Grandma, Daisy, figured it was better to talk to them; she never forgot how in earlier days in Yamhill, Jim Emlah, the game warden, used to warn them when the revenue men were coming. In those days they had a still.

But the land was wild and woolly yet and I'll tell you another thing, those men were so gosh darned mean, they had a cookhouse and they were living off the fat of the land. Althea and I, and Tom and Clara Stevensen went to see them, right there at meal time. Kenny came in right off the Cat. The women had all the food spread out there on the table. They had pies laid out and the first thing he did was dig into that. Then he stood up and tore a chunk right out of the roast—"Yeeow!" then he had a great big ol' fruit jar full of water. Took care of that. Then he disappeared. That's when he come back with his suit on and tie heading for town. Didn't look like he'd washed very much. We asked him where he was going.

"I'm getting in my 'Wincoln' and going to Reedsport to look for some 'wemon.'"

Probably scared them all off.

123

Kenny was a teetotaler, he didn't drink at all. He just went into the taverns to socialize and talk to the loggers. Sometimes he was looking for a man; that used to be the place where most of the hiring was done in those days—right out of the bars.

In one beer joint in Reedsport, two guys were playing shuffleboard and they got into an argument about the points and how to add them up. Kenny standing there said, "He's right."

The one guy said, "It's none of your business, why don't you get out of here?" Kenny just knocked the feller under the table. He saw no reason for getting out of there. He was a gypo logging boss and besides that, he might have known something about scoring shuffleboard points. And if he didn't, he wasn't going to take any guff.

Then he had to go to court. Ol' Ray McNight quit him and Kenny stopped his unemployment because he quit and they were having a hearing about it with the State. Ray got on the stand and they asked him a lot of questions and he says, "That guy's so damned mean you can't work for him. His own cow kicks him." Kenny kept milk cows right in camp. Most the loggers were laid off in the winter time and took their unemployment and started again in the spring when the weather got better. A lot of the loggers joked about the milk cows, which sometimes numbered ten, and when Junior Lee was asked what he was doing for Kenny Whitlow, he answered, "Well, I've got two jobs, I'm loading logs and milking three cows." Actually the women milked the cows.

At one time they had a shingle mill operating at the camp too, and Kenny ran two shifts a day. They were making shingles out of those big ol' cedars and shipping them to San Francisco. The shingle weavers were the ones who really were the characters. They were terrible drunks. On weekends they'd go to Eugene. They'd come back two or three at a time and you would think they would double up and get a cab together, but no, each one would hire a cab from Eugene up to camp. Kenny would be up all night long, paying the cabdrivers their fare. And the cabdrivers made good money. Sometimes it took as many as six hours to get there from Eugene—the shingle weavers must have had them stopping at bars along the way.

Another time Kenny was logging up Soup Creek and moved his whole camp up there.

"By the Eternal! I need a Cat skinner," he told me.

So I go up there and fire up a T D 24. The hill right up from the truck road, where the Cats were parked, was steep and muddy. The T D 24 wouldn't go up it.

"I'll give you a push," he says. "We'll get that ol' Cletrac started, and it'll 'cwime' right up there. She'll 'cwime' a tree if the bark don't slip."

He had an old, antique Cletrac, and that old thing was his favorite. He had me pour about a quart of starting fluid in the air cleaner filter and he got in it. I got behind it and pushed it with the 24 to get it started. It fired up and it was just great to see it going up that hill, smoke a-flying. He cleaned enough mud off that I was able to climb it, too, without any help. Well, from there we went loggin'! The old growth Douglas firs were already felled and bucked.

He was yarding the logs down to the main Cat road with the Cletrac and I was taking them to the landing. I could take a whole bunch at a time with the 24.

Our resort was a favorite with all the loggers. One day we were out front of the store all dressed up.

Kenny Whitlow comes by in his Lincoln convertible—his "Wincoln"—and says, "Where ya goin'?"

"Althea's nephew," I tell him, "Got to go to his funeral out there in Eugene."

"Take my 'Wincoln,'" he tells us, "That'll 'weally'

impress them!" His Lincoln convertible had a retractable top that went right down into the trunk and folded up.

"Oh, no, no, we've got a car. . . ."

"Oh, yeah, take my convertible. I want to use your jeep anyway today."

So we took the Lincoln. Come to find out, the S.O.B., and I don't mean "Sweet Ol' Bill," used my jeep up Soup Creek to get out three elk.

He did a lot of hunting and the Whitlow children also had pet deer, three different pet deer, and the deer never did like drinking. Well, a lot of the hired men liked to kick up their heels on the weekend and one time they heard this guy screaming and yelling out back. They couldn't figure out what was going on and ran out there to find that a buck deer had the hired man down in a ditch, just stomping him. He was more than a little drunk and couldn't get away from that pet's sharp pointed hooves. Don't know how he got down in the ditch but he probably gave the pet deer a lot wider berth after that.

There were horses around as Kenny had riding horses in the camp for his and his brother Bob's children and himself. He built a barn out of split logs and sawn shakes and made stanchions for the cows and stalls for the horses. He always loved horses and still rides today at the age of eighty-four at the Flying M Ranch out of Yamhill.

The children attended school in Reedsport and were driven by Kenny's wife, Mary, to the bus stop on the main highway every day. It was the same road the log trucks drove so of course it was very scenic. All the kids from town wanted to come out and spend the weekend at the logging camp and it seemed there was never a lack of excitement with all the kids around.

The shopping for the cookhouse was done in Eugene. The big freight trucks brought fruit and produce from California to Eugene and at one point E. K. Woods got

126

the trucks to deliver straight to the camp. On the return trip Kenny loaded them up with shingles to be delivered in Oakland, California.

"Hey, here they are! Here they come!" the Whitlow equestrians would holler as the big forty-foot freight trucks loomed up the logging road to camp. Finally the boss came one time and made the drivers quit taking the trucks up that rugged mud and dirt road. From then on they stayed at the bottom of the hill on the main road and Kenny would have his men truck the shingles down there and load them up. The boss must have been used to his asphalt jungle down south. He got to changing things—he's lucky he got out of there without a broken nose or something—Whitlow would work him over.

*Going over boat reservations with Bill Anderson.*

*Me and Kimo*

# *Resort Days*

*Ken Lender and the "kids," Humpy and Dumpy—1967*

# Beaver Talks

I was called to see what I could do. I don't know what they were thinking of, trapping at that time of year; it was the middle of summer. Anyway, I got in the boat and went across the lake to big Salander Creek, right where it comes out into the lake; and there, caught by his hind leg, was a big ol' beaver.

He'd gone around and around a stump and the chain was all tied up. He was just sitting there held by a Number Four long spring trap.

I got out and talked to him, "What in the hell are you doing here?"

I opened the trap, and he pulled his foot out and off he swam. Pretty soon he turned around and swam back and talked to me, "Grunt, grunt, grunt."

His head was way up high out of the water as he addressed me just like he was saying thank you or something.

Althea was there with me to verify that. Some people on the shore, too, saw him swim away and then come back to thank me. You can't tell me that animals don't talk.

# Underground Gas Tanks

Pouring cement in the driving rain for the footings of a new shed roof over my lumber mill, my wife asked, "Is this rain going to hurt the cement?"

I said, "We'll do what Ol' Bert did."

Years ago Ol' Bert Shipey helped me pour cement at Duckett's Resort to hold the gas tank under the ground. When I first come here they had gas barrels inside the building on the dock. They were stacked up on top of each other, just like logs. These fifty-five gallon drums were up on a heavy wooden stand and you'd draw gas out of the infernal things and measure it in a can. You'd pour it into their boat motor cans and mix two-cycle oil with it. People would piss and moan. Some of them hollered, "Aaaah, you're cheatin'!"

Others, "You're getting too much oil and not enough gas!" Half of them didn't have enough sense to mix their own. All they had enough sense to do was bitch.

I said, "I'm going to change this bullshit."

I dug the hole by the lake's edge with a shovel, down there with hip boots and the water way up. I had to go to town and rent a pump. Water would be running in there, and I'd be digging like a bastard.

I bought a new 750 gallon fiberglass gas tank. It was delivered to Bud Karcher's Union Oil dealership in Reedsport, and I picked it up from there, brought it home and when I put it in the hole, Bud had his truck right there to fill it. He filled it and it half-assed sunk. I ran the pump and it started sinking. It won't sink, you know, if it's floating in water even if it's clear full of gas. It finally sunk because I pumped almost all of the water out of the hole. I dug a sump hole at one end and kept pumping the water out as we poured gas in there. It was pouring rain. I had rented a cement mixer and after the sump hole was empty, we poured cement in there and all the way around and over the top of the tank. The rain was still pouring down. That's when Ol' Bert Shipey, our handyman, came down there and said, "Grruuurp. . ." kind of a grunt is mostly how he talked, never said very much. "Put some dirt on the wet cement. That'll keep the rain off. Water helps cure cement, but we just don't need it beating on it!"

So we put leaves, moss and twigs and all kinds of stuff on the wet cement right over it. It cured up great. The tank stayed in the ground, too. Had a vent pipe 'way up above in a tree. I went underground across to a tree and anchored the vent pipe against it, then continued it on up in the tree so when flood waters came in the winter, water wouldn't go down in the vent pipe into the gas tank. The vent pipe was shaped like a "T" at the top, too, so rain water couldn't get into the gas. So that new gas tank ended the damned bitchin' and a-gripin' about enough gas. If they wanted to they could mix their own, otherwise I'd put in the right amount of oil for them, and we didn't run out of gas, either.

The Empire Gas truck made regular deliveries and on a busy weekend he'd leave the truck for me. I could refill the tank right from his truck.

There was an existing gas pump and underground gas tank right in front of the store. The pump was cracked and needed replacing. They always went bad, so I bought a newer one. I got Larry Ross Petroleum from North Bend to hook up the pump to the tank—State wouldn't let you do that yourself. I also got out my shovel and dug up the tank by hand. It was the same thing as putting in the gas tank down by the dock—water everywhere. You don't have to go down that far before you hit water—bad as Florida.

I removed the old tank, got the water pump again and kept pumping while I was in hip boots digging. I put in a new 1,000 gallon tank and filled it full of gas to make it go down, sanded the sides and ends in and that held it until we got the cement poured on top of it. That night the temperature got down to almost zero degrees. We put some tarps and quilts on top of the cement to keep it from freezing but by the time the cold weather broke in a couple of days, the cement had froze and crumbled—almost like cottage cheese. So we had to dig it all out and do it again. That time the cement hardened up right.

They dug it out not so long ago, an outfit the current owner, Jim Brown, had to hire to get all the gas tanks out of here. With new State laws requiring double tanks, computerized, nothing but bullshit, nobody can afford to replace their tanks with the legal ones. The guy said seeing all that cement, "By Ned! I have never seen that before."

I said, "You ain't seen nothin' yet, wait until you see the one down by the lake. We didn't use sand, used cement all the way."

I bet they had quite a job of it to remove all that solid cement to get to those tanks and get them out of there. You know all the soil has to be hauled to special dumps—really nonsense—a lot of gas stations folded because of this law to remove underground tanks—darned shame.

# Husband and Wife Gypo Loggers

Old Elwin and Gertrude DeGnath weren't so dumb. They had everything paid for and they were making money. They had a little HD7 Alyss Chalmers, about like a D-6 Cat, that Elwin used to make roads and log with. Gertie worked right with him. They were logging the timber on the hill across from the school, just him and her.

With all the farm chores to do, they probably got a late start logging in the morning because they were still logging at night. It was many an evening I passed by the school after working all day in the woods myself. There on the hill I could see a lantern shining the way for the Cat to bring another turn of logs down to the landing. It was Gertie leading that Cat off the hill, walking in front shining a way for Elwin to see.

# Shorty's Barn

It was early summer when Shorty Harrison's barn burnt down with the cows in it. Another logger, George McClellan, brought a Cat down the hill and buried them ol' burnt cows in just kind of a low spot in the pasture. We were up on the hill logging, we'd logged all winter on gravel up there.

Shorty's wife, Shirley Ann, was working for us helping in the store. All the crew—they liked Shirley. They would gang up in there in the late afternoon for a cold one. One time she mentioned that Shorty was getting the lumber to get that barn built back and she didn't know how he was going to do it all alone. So the crew says, "My God when he gets ready, let's just go over there and build his gosh darned barn." So we told Shirley to tell him to be ready for the weekend, we'd be there. Saturday and Sunday we went over there; I think we finished it on Monday and we built that gosh darned barn for the bastard. Then he said Keeland and his drunks were the only ones that helped him. Nobody else in the community showed up. It was about sixteen feet tall and held sixty cows to be fed. We had it all framed in and most of the tin on it. Shorty could take over from there. Shoot, there was Ol' Bill McKenny, Frank Lewis, Nels Fredericksen, Bill Fisk, Donny Potts, and Barney Hirt, my partner.

That *was* a crew, all but Bill Fisk. Later on I finally had to let him go. As long as you were there he'd work, but as soon as you left—I also let another man go, who was nothing but a lazy house dog, to keep Bill company.

Back then I told Shorty, "Yeah, them guys drink, but by God, they work, too." Nels didn't drink, being a religious man.

# Smelt Dipping

One time all of us were dipping smelt in the Umpqua River
and a guy from out of state pulls up in a big, fancy new Cadillac.
He said he always wanted to dip some smelt.

We told him, "Well, here's a net, go right to it."

He waded right out there, about knee deep or a little
deeper. I remember his shiny shoes. He had on a suit, white
shirt and tie, the whole schmeal. He was so anxious to dip
some himself, he bailed right in.

I offered him a five-gallon bucket to take his smelt home
in. I was going to give it to him—he had one about full—but he
wouldn't take it. Instead, he opened up the trunk of his car
and poured them right in! There was no box or plastic or anything—just the empty trunk.

He was one pleased, well-contented man, I guess, as he
drove away in his Cadillac with a load of smelt.

You think that was something, I was in the crotch of a tree which was exposed because of low tide, it had blown down and was laying out in the river. Pappy (Clyde DeWitt) was in his waders standing in water clear up to his knees. The smelt were coming in with the incoming tide. The two guys above us weren't catching anything. I would dip and pass my full net to Pappy who was dumping them in wash tubs in the back of the pickup. The two guys came down and said, "Think you could pass us a couple of netfulls over here?"

"Hell, no. . ." Pappy started to say when they continued, "Think maybe you ought to think about quitting before McDonald shows up?"

Pappy says, "Oh, you know McDonald?"

McDonald was the state game warden working out of Reedsport.

"Oh, yes, we're from the Coos County Sheriff's Department."

We fixed them up where they were illegal.

They were hollering, "No, no, oh no, that's enough."

They had a couple of plastic bags. We made sure they had enough, then we went ahead with our smelt dipping.


It was usually pretty rainy when the smelt ran and a lot of people like to dip them and bring them home for the frying pan. They fry up real crispy so you don't have to bone them, and they're so small, sardine-like size, that some people don't even gut them. Most people wash them off real good, though, all except the old horse logger, Marvin Haskell. He would bring smelt home—hundreds of them—and pour them right into the freezer—sand, leaves, sticks and all.

# The Logging Citation

Barney Hurt and I had a logging contract in one area up there in the Elliott State Forest in 1962. Everything was laying on the ground from the Columbus Day Storm. It was all second growth Douglas fir and very little hemlock. There was no old growth, it had all been burnt up in the Great Coos Bay Fire of 1868. When the Columbus Day Storm came through, it just blew down timber in big patches and this was one area where fir, hemlock and the whole shiterie was on the ground.

We clear-logged the whole darned thing. Then they marked out some of this gol-derned thinning. Everything's so crowded you can't get around very good. The blade of the Cat hooked one of those damned exposed roots that's sticking out and tore a slab out of a tree eight or ten feet up. The Elliott State Forester in charge of the job came inspecting and said, "Oh, oh! A crime has been committed. I'll have to write you a citation."

I said, "Oh, come on now, this is no crime, anybody can do this; it just happens sometimes. That rip won't hurt the tree, it'll scar over. Anyone Catskinning is bound to do it once in a while; it's called 'slabbing a tree.'"

He responds, "Well, I don't know what you want to call it. I'm going to have to write you a citation anyway, and I'm going to guarantee you that!"

I said to him, "If you do, I'm going to bust you right in the nose and I can guarantee that!"

The forester got in the truck and wrote it in the truck. When he went to hand it to me through the window, I took it, then I grabbed his hand and pulled him towards me and popped him with a left. Laid him right back in the truck. Right over sideways.

He was out for a couple of minutes. Barney, my partner, said, "Jesus, Keeland, I think you killed him."

When the forester came to, he said, "Oh my, you struck me!"

I responded with, "Now get the hell out of here."

Gave his citation back to him, too! Threw it back in the seat.

The next day the Coos Bay boss comes out and says, "What happened between you and that forester yesterday?"

I told him, "Well, come on over and look at this and you can see for yourself what happened. It's no big thing." I showed him the slabbed tree. That scab won't hurt that tree. His scab may hurt, though. The nut! Where'd they get him, back hiding in some office someplace?

That was about the start of things way back then of the environmental whackos ordering a lot of nonsensical rules, citations and penalties to loggers. Those office people and college graduates are not familiar with the woods.

They got another man to supervise the job from then on and got no more citations from him either.

# The State Auditor Man

Gay Vaughn didn't mess with them.

It was Christmas Eve. One of those non-producers from the unemployment office came to Duckett's Resort and wanted to look at the books. I called our accountant, Gay Vaughn, at home, and he said go ahead, we have nothing to hide. So I showed the auditor the check book. There was some kind of problem, so I called Gay back.

Gay said, "Send the guy down to my office, and you come down, too."

I got there just in time to see Gay bodily throwing that guy out the door. Gay was right on him.

Gay told him, "Don't you ever mess with any of my clients' books after this without a court order!"

The auditor would have landed on the cement if it weren't for the hood of his car. There he hit pretty hard and splayed out. He just piled that briefcase back in his car and was gone. Ol' Gaylord! Gaylordie, he fixed him.

He was from the unemployment office trying to help Kemo Couteure. Kemo, our neighbor who was working for us, had turned in for unemployment benefits. Hell, he hadn't worked enough quarters to get it.

# Ed Seabloom—"Camp Push"

Ed Seabloom was a big shot for E. K. Woods Logging Company, the biggest boss in the camp, and also a log rafter.

On Pearl Harbor Day, December 7, 1997, one of my Iwo Jima survivor buddies, Allan Ansema, pronounced Ansemaw, came to visit. He is a Navy man, a Finlander and a native of Reedsport. He remembered this:

"I got to tell you a story about Ol' Ed. When he first came to Reedsport as woods boss for E. K. Woods, he wanted to get on the tugboat with Granvil Leach. He was taking over everything as Camp Push and wanted to see the log rafts. As he was boarding the tugboat, Granvil couldn't remember his name and so he said, 'Hello, Mr. Ocean Flower.'

"Ed Seabloom said to him, 'No, it's Seabloom.'

"Granvil laughed, 'Well, I knew it had something to do with the water and the flowers.' Ed Seabloom was escorted around to inspect the log rafts and soon became well loved and respected by all the men.

"We were rafting logs on the Umpqua up at Scottsburg. We had boomsticks that were all chained together except for the opening on the side where the logs were dumped. We walked around on the logs poking more in with pike poles. We poked them in just as tight as they'd go and got 'er full, and connected the last boomstick on the log raft— 'closing up the chute' they called that. Later a steel boat with an outboard motor on it that would turn 360°, called a log bronc, was used for rafting logs, with men and poles helping. But at that time we used the tide and its currents to push the logs in place. The logs were dumped right in the river. They took me off by myself to raft some down by the mouth of Mill Creek, off the Umpqua. Just me there and Ol' Ed. Ed was poking them out to me and I was rafting

142

them up. I just happened to look over and I saw Ol' Ed swimming. I just pretended I didn't see anything. I did watch to make sure he got out and was all right.

"Pretty soon he came over and yelled at me, 'Hey, Al, you got any cigarettes?'

"I replied as if I didn't know, 'Yeah, what the hell happened to yours?'

"'I went overboard and mine got wet,' he said.

"I didn't say anything more, and we worked out the day. That's all we had to say to each other. He was one heck of a fine man to work with and a fine boss.

"Then there was the time the two old maids thought he was a bear. He was rafting logs up at Loon Lake, and these two old-maid school marms lived in a little cabin across the lake. Jane Kaiser was home that day and Harriet Ward was teaching music at school when here swims Ed Seabloom over to check them out. All he had on was his black wool underwear. Jane said she thought it was a bear. So did the guys rafting until they saw him get out of the water."

"Nowadays some of these nuts probably would have shot him," I put in.

"That's right, but I don't think he was worried about that," Allan continued, "Ed was a married man and quite a character and I think he wanted to just impress these two old maids with his prowess and ability to swim across the lake. They thought he was a bear swimming along.

"Another thing—Ol' Ed was always a sucker for a guy who was a good B.S.'er. I don't know where he met that guy—in the tavern, I guess. Anyway, he hired this guy who was supposed to be a powder expert. He came to the job where we were logging up Vincent Creek. There was a culvert there that had the end blocked full of mud. We used to blow it out and keep it free.

"Duffy Lewis, the foreman, told me, 'Go down there and help him blow that culvert.'

"The guy started stuffing whole sticks of dynamite in there—ditching powder and real hot—whereas we used to use just parts of ones. When we did it we cut the sticks in halves or thirds. I knew what was going to happen, so I went and crawled under an old fuel tank trailer. Pretty soon I heard a big "Kawhoom!" and I stayed under there until all the rocks quit hitting off of everything. When I got up and looked, the whole end of the culvert was sticking straight up in the air—'bout ten feet of it, standing up through the road. Duffy came down there and laid into ME!

"He said, 'Why'd you let him do that?'

"I said, 'You couldn't tell him anything—he was an expert!'

"Hell, he didn't know any more about dynamite than the man in the moon."

# Who Has The Best Retriever?

Louis Pogue used to sell cars. He made a fifty dollar bet he had the best retriever. I took him up on it, and we decided to meet Saturday morning at the dock at Loon Lake.

He showed up with his Lab dog. He had one of those dummy things they throw out in the water. The ol' Lab would get it every time, bring it back to him or take it different places for him. Louie would direct him right by one whistle, left by two whistles.

"Whiiit, whiiit-whiiit. . . ."

Then it was my turn.

He says, "Where's your dog?"

I says, "I don't need a dog. There's mine."

The pet otter had been taking all that in. I just had me a good rock there, put a grease pencil mark on it and threw it out in the lake.

The ol' otter, he knew what he was going to do. He jumped in and first thing he done was, boom, he went out of sight. By golly, I didn't think he was ever going to come back up.

Pretty quick he surfaced and swam back over to the dock. We had a little ramp that extended from the end of the dock to about two feet into the water. It was for pulling boats up to drain the water out of them. Humpy just come up that ramp grunting and groaning, "Runt, runt, mmp, mmp." He was happy; he had that rock, too.

That's when Ol' Louie said, "Darn you, I ain't betting against no varmint!"

I said, "Send the Lab after the rock. You said a retriever."

Well, he had a good dog there, but, of course, he couldn't retrieve a rock in twenty-five feet of water.

The next time I was in town, I told Pete Stingley, who was holding the stakes, to give him back his money.

# The Columbus Day Storm

On Columbus Day, October 12, 1962, the winds hit 152 miles per hour. Some guys from the Charleston Navy Base were here. They'd been hunting with me the day before and, by God, we got three deer. That day before was pretty windy, too.

We were gathering our gear to go hunting, went into the store, heard a big, big, awful "ROAR" and here it come. Here came the rain, too—rain hitting the store front windows.

I said to the Navy men, "Get back, that's no place to be in a great blast like that!"

By golly, it *didn't* knock it out. I was surprised at that. You could just see the windows shaking after they were hit. Then. . .

"Oh, my God, there goes a boat. . . ."

"There goes a picnic table."

"Eeeooo, there goes the top out of two cedars. . . ."

"Yeah, by God," I said, "I'm going to have to get down there and tie the rest of those boats up."

We were outside looking up on the hill when I saw the wind twist off a big ol' old growth; and it wasn't blown, it was twisted off, about fifteen, twenty feet high off the ground—not just the top but the whole length of the tree! It sailed about 300 feet airborne off our property, clear over to BLM. Later I bid and logged that sale of timber on BLM and bought and logged my own tree.

I removed the limbs out of the road from those two cedars, went down through the campground tying up stuff.

I was crawling up the dock on my hands and knees.

The boats we had laying there were going flying up through the campground, smacking into trees. I had a whole stack of them there on top of each other and some others weren't stacked so good. It was a lucky thing I had this big ol' rope in the boathouse. I got it tied on one end of the dock, threw it over the boats and went over to the other end of the dock to tie the other end and secure the boats; and that's when I saw the whirligig.

It was like a funnel or some gosh darned thing. It just dropped down and sucked all the water up out of the bottom of the lake, about the size of our bedroom. I could see the mud where the water is usually about twenty to twenty-five feet deep. Here I am, at the edge of the dock. It's amazing it didn't suck ME up. The wind and gale slapped that water from the whirligig right up against the boathouse and broke boards and glass.

Well, I continued my tying. We had a pipe—one inch, one and a half inch—something like that, bolted to blocks. We used it to tie the boats up with. It had been put in with great big drift bolts. I figured they weren't going to pull out. So I run the back of the rope out, grabbed the bite of its own line and made one of those hay hauler knots. Cinched 'er up fiddle tight—that was the only way you were sure to hold anything down. Lot of the boats were ending up in the campground, but the rest of them stayed right there.

Across the lake Harriet Ward also saw the whirligig. She was the music teacher and authoress who lived for many, many years in a cabin she built. In front of her cabin that twister hit and pulled all the water out of the lake. She saw the mud at the bottom of the lake, too, and it scared her to death. She was in a panic. She hung on to a pillar of her porch and screamed and screamed even though there was no one to hear her. Seeing the bottom of the lake was quite an unusual thing. She probably thought that whirligig was going to take her cabin away airborne. I guess we all wondered if we'd have any houses left after the Columbus Day storm.

# The Peevee

Ol' Chisel Bit and I were getting logs out of the creek there at Wes's. We had a log that was kind of hung up on the bank at one end. I was a-rolling on it with the peevee and I heard the damned handle crack.

He said, "Man, what'd you quit for? Had it going!"

I said, "Handle's breaking."

He said, "Ah, hell, you can't break that handle."

He grabbed the peevee and socked it in the log and put his shoulder against it and I thought to myself, "Oh, oh, here goes nothin'."

Right out and over that log he went head first, right in the creek. We had a pike pole there, so I handed that out to him as he thrashed around in the water.

He got ahold of that pike pole and he said, "Yeah, you can break 'em, can't ya?"

As I pulled him on the bank, rain pants, caulk shoes and all, he said, "Well, go ahead and laugh, 'cause I'm only going to put on one show today."

That damned ol' tin hat—there was a little log jam down below there—it never did turn over, just bobbed along until it was down there against that log jam. Though it was pouring rain, we worked out the day and stayed there until we got all the logs floated down to where we could get them later with Caterpillar.

# Daffo-down-dillies

Ol' Frank, my Marine buddy, was a newcomer to Oregon in the Elkton area. He bought a home and I think that was five, six acres in there.

He told me, "Boy, that would be a beautiful pasture, but it has about a half dozen stumps that needs to be taken out." He was going to make it like a golf course.

Well, Ole Collander, who worked for Langfelt Logging & Construction Company, overheard the conversation.

He told Frank, "Ole come blow your stumps."

So they made a date. Ole got the fertilizer and dynamite off of Langfelt. He went over to Frank's and overloaded those stumps something fierce. Well, when they ignited it took out the power line and phone line and had rocks and sticks and pieces of stumps all over the daffodil field over the way. Chunks and debris lit all over a couple of acres of Benny and Sadie Knypstra's commercial daffo-down-dillies in bloom. I don't know how it missed, but the clods and roots went clear over Frank's house.

Frank says, "Jesus! Gosh darn, Ole!" I thought you knew what you were doing!"

Ole says, "You don't see any stumps, do you?"

Franks says, "No, but I see some holes it's going to take me months to fill up!"

The Douglas Electric Co-op came and put the power lines back up.

That's when Frank had nerve enough to ask them, "When am I going to get a phone?" I guess they put their application in when they first moved in there.

The guy told him, "When you quit knocking the phone line down and tearing things up, that's when you'll get a phone."

# Drowned Man Floats Around on the Bottom

One day down there at the boat dock, someone looked out the window, "Hey, you got a drowned guy floating around down on the bottom!"

"What?"

George Montgomery jumped in and pulled him up to the surface and I got ahold of him 'til George got back on the dock. Then he lifted up on the drowned guy, and I pulled on George.

We laid him on his belly and pushed on his back. We pumped and pumped and must have pumped two gallons of Copenhagen out of that guy, water and I don't know what all. We got him breathing again.

That was Dick Hunt; he had fallen out of a boat. He was living with his brother-in-law at the time, Ray Holliday, up in Ash Valley.

The funny thing was a county doctor was staying there in that float house and stepped right over him. He had to walk over him when we had him stretched out there across the dock. The doctor said later he might have been liable for a lawsuit if he'd have helped him, which is true the way everybody hopes to get money out of doctors for malpractice. Our liability insurance on the resort would have covered us, which we didn't have, come to find out.

Boy, George Montgomery and his wife Mikey were the best help we ever had. He ran the dock, and she was the cook in the store.

# Dick Hunt Backs Up

The drowned victim, Dick Hunt, was born over there on the Shorty Harrison place.

He was running around without a driver's license. He saw the sheriff parked in front of the resort and slammed on the brakes. Come to think of it, that was still a gravel road, too. He got stopped in the gravel about Cabin Seven, stuck it in reverse and just roared up the hill backwards. Back up around that hill he went, the front bumper of the car was the last thing we saw. The sheriff, who was a reserve—just a summer cop for the county, said, "Well, I guess I'd better go up and see what's the matter with THAT guy."

He left the store and drove up there to find him.

He gave him a ticket; oh, hell yeah, he didn't have a license or anything else. The cop said later, "Hell, if he'd just gone on about his business, everything would have been all right. . . .I wasn't going to bother him. Had no reason to bother him if he'd kept on coming down the road and past the resort, but he just roared up the hill backwards so fast, something was the matter."

Just stuck his own head in the noose is what he done.

# The Deputy Sheriff With the Flashlight

I had a pinball machine and a shuffleboard. The shuffle-board was in the back part of the store, being rather large and long, and the pinball machine was right by the front door.

A deputy sheriff came in and intoned, "These kids shouldn't be playing that pinball machine." I intoned right back, "Now that pinball machine is legal. We pay amusement taxes on it every year. If you'll just step outside we'll discuss this."

We go out to the cement at the front of the store, and I informed him further, "We pay a federal tax and get a stamp that goes right on the machine. We pay a state tax and I get a card that goes on the machine. We pay a county tax and get a card to stick on there, and if we were in the city, we'd pay a city tax and get some kind of rigmarole put on the machine, too. There is no law the kids can't play the pinball machine; it is for amusement only. Oh, they do get some free games if they hit it just right. Do you county cops think you have more authority than the federal and the state? Is that all you guys have to do is snoop around and watch some kid play a pinball machine?"

That's when he started preaching and thumping me on the chest with his long-celled flashlight. He was telling me this and telling me that.

I told him, "I understand English, you don't have to pound it into me."

He kept it up.

"Knock it off. You thump me one more time with that flashlight, I'll knock you down."

The cop said, "Oh, yeah? I'll take you in," and this and that.

So he thumped me one more time with that long flashlight. Retired Navy, big wheel. I just grabbed the flashlight and, "Kerwack," I hit him upside the head, and he hit the ground, I mean. Then I started kicking him 'cause I figured he might shoot me.

That other cop he had with him stuck a gun in my stomach and said, "Okay, that's enough."

He didn't take me to town. He didn't take me nowheres. Son-of-a-guns, they didn't have any business pulling a trick like that. But he got even. I'm sure he's the one who planted two liquor commission inspectors on us about a week later.

The inspectors came camping and claimed they were plywood workers. They kept telling Dennis, the storekeeper and bartender, they were plywood workers on vacation. They couldn't find anything wrong, so they set him up.

Every day they got to buddying up to him more and more and finally, after a week, talked him into a shuffleboard game.

155

Well, he won, and they said, "This is no fun. Let's do it for the drinks."

Well, Ol' Dennis beat them again and that's when they nailed him. They bought him a beer, and he kind of stepped back there in the kitchen part and was drinking it. They came right around and wrote him a ticket and Althea, too. She had seen him drinking it and should have stopped him. It took them eight or ten days to trap him, but they finally did it. I kept telling him those fellers are liquor inspectors.

"Aw, no, they're plywood workers," Dennis would chirp.

I came home that evening from logging in the woods and, boy, their faces were long.

Althea said, "Well, they caught Dennis."

I said, "Well, kid, you learn something from this?"

He said, "Yeah, I learnt that I won't be tending any more bar."

"I guess you won't be."

That's another outfit that ought to be turned over to local—county or city—control. The snooping federal men got to do setup deals like that and show something to keep their job.

It was a long time before we had a hearing. We had a lawyer—might as well had nothing.

He said, "Oh, don't say nothing, don't say nothing. They'll have more liquor inspectors up there than you have people."

I guess he was right. The Liquor Commission closed us down for ten days but hadn't set a date. I had a camp trailer then. I took all the beer except for a few cases and put it in the trailer.

They sure enough waited until elk season to close us down. They came and counted that damned beer that we had on hand in the walk-in cooler to make sure we wouldn't sell any during our shutdown—bunch of gestapos. Ol' Stutterin' Slim had 'em right. The restaurant was still open; we just couldn't sell any beer or wine.

156

I told the hunters what happened; and if they wanted a beer, just put your money in the can there in the trailer if they couldn't find Benny. Heck, the guys were glad to get it, and we made some money, too. That way the lack of income wasn't so bad during our ten-day shutdown. In fact, we made more money that way than if they were buying it inside. I know they paid more to get it. There was no way of making change out there. I didn't go near it. Didn't dare to. I just did a little more hunting than I might have otherwise.

# The Ice That Came from England

A guy came in to buy a bag of ice. Pete Stingley, the outdoorsman and trapper who worked part-time for us, sold the guy a bag of ice and said, "That'll be seventy-five cents, sir."

The customer howled, "By Golly! That's pretty high, ain't it? Seventy-five cents? Where are you getting this ice from?"

"Well, sir, England, my friend. Just got a shipment in this morning! Yep, yep, came all the way from England as a matter of fact."

# Bud Toy Remembers Ducketts

Every weekend toward evening everyone would start congregating on the dock. Every Saturday night there was a local group of musicians who would perform on the dock and all the campers and customers in the resort would dance 'til two in the morning. Lloyd had lights strung up down through the trees and to the dock.

There was a fiddler, Riley Finch, and his double cousin, Al Miller, who also played fiddle. Al's brother, Ed Miller, played guitar. The bass guitar player was named Charlie Parret. They all lived in Ash Valley and just played because they liked to get together.

I was the City Manager of Corvallis; had been for twenty years. I came down to Loon Lake on weekends. My two teenage sons were living in the dock house renting out Lloyd's boats, selling bait and tackle, and pumping gas.

They called me one time and said, "You got to get down here, Dad, it's just like in the movies!"

It must have been in the early seventies. One Saturday night, I was on the dock. Everybody was dancing and having a good time. I was dancing, too. Someone knocked somebody in the water. I thought I'd be a nice guy and lean over and give him a hand.

I got him up on the dock and I'll be darned if he didn't take a swing at me! I thought, 'What the heck?' and I popped him one. He fell right back into an aluminum row boat and, as if that weren't enough, the aluminum boat and him in it flipped over! It was better than the movies! And all through this the band never missed a lick.

# Roy Boys' Garbage Hauling

Roy Selander was married to a female judge presiding over the City of Canyonville. He got hurt on the job hauling garbage for some sanitation company and came to stay at Duckett's resort while he was recurperating. You couldn't help but kind of like the guy, but there were times when I could have killed him.

He was going to haul some garbage. He got the cans dumped into the trailer and had the kids from the campground helping him. He was just screaming at the kids—they weren't doing right, according to him. There wasn't anything wrong with the kids or how they were dumping the garbage, it was just Roy. I think he'd had one too many.

I told him to lay off the kids. He was just scaring them to death with all that cussin' and screaming. He made a run at me and that's when he landed in the garbage.

By God, I don't know how he got up on that pile, myself. I just got a hold of his arm and gave a little fling, and he was up in it. The kids sure got a bang out of that. I guess I did, too.

We've sure had some characters down in that place. Never a dull moment. Even taking out the garbage.

# Picking Huckleberry Brush

You know Althea and I were going to get rich picking huckleberry brush.

We had gone on the Umpqua in our boat and camped at Barrett's Landing. We'd picked brush and we'd been all over, up and down that river, picked at likely spots, and camped about a week. A lot of that brush had salt spray spots and they don't want that. And if it's under alder, it's got black on it, they don't want that either. So, we didn't get a whole lot; had to keep it wet under burlap bags.

Anyway, we were put-putting along with our seven-and-a-half horsepower outboard motor outside of Gardiner, no one there but us, just peaceful and quiet, when here comes a big high-powered boat and they wanted to swamp us, I mean drown us! They come in real close then turn the other way, the wake was pushing us. Pushed us right up into the mud flats. They were going at a terrible high speed. They weren't joking, they were mad. They made about three passes at us. If he would have made one more pass, I would have shot him with the .38 pistol. It took some doing with the boat rocking in that mud, but I got it out. It was down underneath all of our camping gear in the bow. They must have seen the pistol because they turned away from there that time in a quick hurry.

We finally got off the mud flats and motored down to Frank and Ethel Brookhart. It was about dark we docked at their shack.

I said, "You got a phone?"

He replied, "Oh, yeah."

I said, "Call the damned sheriff, get him down here!"

They were supposed to be brush pickers from Washington. That's what they were supposed to be. But they were butchering beef on the Hubbard Place, one of those islands down there. They were taking the beef (quartered up, probably) by boat over to the side of the river to where their rigs were parked and taking them out of there.

Cops got those rustlers that night.

Evidently, they thought we'd seen the son-of-a-bitches. We hadn't seen them, we hadn't been on that side of the river at all. We were out in the sand hills picking huckleberry brush.

# The Man That Crowed

Some of them guys you could knock crazy but you couldn't get them off their feet. Such a guy was this:

When Pierce died they had a young couple down on the dock working for them who locked Althea out of the house and store. She had gone into town to arrange for the funeral and other things and when she came back they were in the store and locked her out. Said they had a deal with Pierce. She had to get the police to get the couple out. They didn't have any paper or anything to show they'd had a deal with Pierce.

One time after that Althea and I were in the Foxhole Restaurant & Lounge and Althea says,

"Oh, there's that guy who locked me out. . . ."

I went over there and started pestering him, calling him all kinds of names—"chicken shit" and everything.

Finally he got through and he starts going and I just go and block the door.

I says, "I'll just go out with you." We get outside and I hit him a couple of lefts to the jaw and then a right in the belly and then another up side of the head with a good right.

Oh boy! That's when he went goofy. He started jumping up and down and making these funny sounds like the crowing of a rooster! He jumped clear up on the hood of a car—hopped on the front bumper and right on up. Ha! He crowed three or four times. I must have shook something loose up in there, must have rattled his cage.

Two or three people were out there, no comments, no one said a word.

Maybe he'll think twice before he locks someone out of their home next time.

# Rusty Nails

Old Boak was so tight he'd save those old nails that are almost rusted in two, the ones most people throw away. He'd have to hold them two different times with the vice grips to pound them. He'd get one grip on the lower part of the nail, pound it in, then change grips and holding the upper half pound the nail in the rest of the way.

He was thrifty and happy—whistled wherever he went. He must have been real satisfied making such good use of everything.

# Pappy DeWitt and the Chain

Pappy DeWitt had a chain in his hands. A young man in the resort asked him, "What are you going to do with that chain, old man?"

"Oh, I'm going to lock up a neighbor's gate with it."

"That don't do any good. We just came through Weyerhaeuser. We broke three chains just coming to here."

"Yeah, you look like the type."

"Oh, you're kind of a smart old son-of-a-bitch, aren't you?" guffawed the great, big kid.

With that Pappy came off of that barstool full tilt and caught that kid just perfect to the side of the jaw—hit him so hard he skidded clear across the booth seat till his head was in the fireplace.

Ray Crowder knew them. I got from behind the counter and Ray and I told the friend who was coming after Pappy, "Now, you just stay out of this."

Pappy said, "Turn him loose, too, I'll take care of him, too."

He had ahold of that chain and was going to really work him over.

Pappy later said, "I didn't mind him calling me a son-of-a-bitch, but I didn't think he needed to be calling me 'old.'"

Pappy had those big ol' long arms. He was used to splitting wood every day—he was cutting firewood then. I bet that guy thought a sledge hammer hit him. He was still kicking around in the fireplace when we told him and his friend to get out.

I bet the next time that kid will think quite a while before calling an older man a bunch of names.

"By God, that ol' fella had a whop to him," Ray Crowder said. Pappy always had a good sense of fairness, too.

Pappy DeWitt was retired from the International Paper sawmill in Gardiner as head sawyer. He also played minor league baseball as a catcher—another reason he had those big, long strong arms.

# Corvette Balanced on a Rock

It was summertime and a guy ran his Corvette off the road and cliff into Loon Lake. Well, it landed right on a boulder and the guy was still in it. Word got to us at the store, and we went to rescue him with a couple of blocks and some haywire, actually, logging cable. When we got there the guy was hollering his head off. He couldn't open his doors. The motorboats going by were making the Corvette rock. The way it was rocking around it was about ready to go into the deep. Ben and I were hooking up the straw line to pull him off of there. Up there on the road, a cop came by and was yelling at us to, "Get out of there! Leave him alone!"

So I just yelled back, "Oh, piss on ya, you're just one of those county mounties anyway, dollar-a-year job."

We just pulled him off that rock on to solid ground and left the cable on him. We pried the doors open and got him out of the Corvette.

The dollar-a-year cop didn't bother us any more. I think he was getting a lot of flack from the people up on top of the road, too. I think he seen he was outnumbered. These cops were reserves—men who had steady jobs but just worked weekends at the lake in uniform as county policemen. Some of them damned pretty good guys, though.

You can still see the scars on the big old growth tree where he hit before going over the cliff into the lake. The scars are all growed over. It's just this side of Beaman's dock if you ever get up this way to the lake.

      ☙         ☙         ☙

I don't remember what year that was, might have been the first year we got pavement. Got so they all went crazy then. Had a bunch from Florence coming up here that summer. Jim McCoy was one of them.

When he and the wife went to divorce, Jim said, "Okay, everything will be in half." He brought his chain saw in the house and cut the table in half; tried it on the bed but it didn't cut through those springs so good. . . .

Young Jim drowned up here in Loon Lake that same summer—some visiting hot rodders ran him off the road. A Corvette met him head on, and Jim, to avoid collision, ran off the road and into the lake.

Never did nothin' to that Corvette driver.

Then Chet and Marge ended up in the lake. They went off right down there close to where the Corvette went. They had a Volkswagen bus and Marge panicked and was going to open the doors and Chet said, "Oh, no! Don't open the doors! Don't open the doors! We're watertight, we're floating!" That Volkswagen bus *was* floating! A motorboat came along and pushed them to the shore.

# Fred Lang Killed

Ben and I went up there when Fred Lang was killed.

They were logging just a little bit past the Weyerhaeuser gate in them rock bluffs. The yarder fell over on him. The yarder and tower are all one unit mounted on rubber tires, and when it fell he was killed instantly.

What it looked liked happened is when that one guy line broke, Fred jumped out and started running. The tower is what hit him—drove him right down in the earth there. He'd been all right if he'd just stayed with the thing; the cab was never hurt.

Everybody was up there, a hell of a bunch. There was the state, the accident guys, Weyerhaeuser people, the loggers and their boss.

Fred left his widow and four young daughters on their ranch in Ash Valley. Mrs. Lang could have owned that layout; I tried to tell her so.

They were logging that yarder with only two guy lines on the tower. The electric motors that ran the winches to tighten up the other guy lines were still laying on the ground. I imagine the boss got a few citations from the state about the winches laying there, brand new, which he'd never put on.

We went to Ol' Fred's funeral; pouring down rain; one preacher bellered there for about a half an hour. Another one got up, he run out of wind, and then a third one started in. Leroy Stemmerman, the dairyman and logger, stopped him.

He said, "I think we've heard enough of this."

Ha! Not everyone was as religious as the Langs.

# "Oly, Oly, Oly"

Late one night a bunch of guys were naked and drunk, whooping and hollering all over the diving platform and dock.

All they were hollering was "Oly, Oly, Oly"—that was all. Whatever that means. Must have been advertising Oly beer.

I told Noel, "Grab a club." He picked up an old broken boat paddle and worked them pretty much out of there. Got them all except one guy up on the high dive platform. That platform was twenty feet tall. I climbed up there but he was kicking at me.

I climbed down and told Noel, "Get me a pole." I put my cap on the broken boat paddle and climbed back up, and stuck that up there. That cap did the trick. He saw that cap and made a kick at it and that was his mistake. I grabbed his leg and just hung on.

I flung him down, "Kerflap"—right smack flat of his back on the dock. I thought I'd killed him. Knocked all the wind out of him.

After a while he sat up and seemed to be all right, so I walked over to where his buddies were in the campground milling around a car and told them, "All right, go pick up your buddy over there and knock off all this noise at two in the morning. There's people around here trying to sleep."

No more "Oly, Oly, Oly."

# The Juke Box and the Shotgun

There was one logger that I used to hunt elk with that I never wanted to make mad. He was from the Willamette Valley and for the sake of the story, we'll call him "John."

Well, John was over there in the Valley, he'd been duck hunting and had stopped in at this tavern. There was a couple of guys in there bugging him about matching for the juke box (flipping a coin, whoever got tails had to pay for the music). To start with he said, naw, he didn't want to match. They kept buggin' and he says, all right. Well, they lost and then they didn't want to play the juke box.

He got up and says he was going outdoors and when he got back they'd better have the juke box a-playing!

He came back in there with his .12 gauge shotgun and says, "Okay, which one of you wants it first?"

One guy jumps up and he says, "I do."

So John, the duck hunter, blows his head off. The other guy didn't want seconds. He was just beggin'; I bet he played the juke box.

The cops got him and, oh yeah, he did time and worked on the Tillamook Burn as part of a work program. Old Charlie Crom, Sheriff of Coos County, got him paroled off to him. I always figured there was more to that than just that damned juke box.

John used to come up here hunting and fishing and the whole marianne. I was glad I didn't make him mad elk hunting with him.

Boy, I was glad to see that fella one time. He was about six foot three inches and husky. If he wasn't a logger, he sure could get around in the woods. We went up above on the ridge road and dropped down and into Salander Creek and all around.

We agreed if we didn't hear any shooting, we'd meet back

at the jeep. If someone did get an elk, we had agreed on a signal. The signal was to shoot one time, count to three, and then shoot two quick ones, Boom, boom, quick as you could— that was the meat call—and everyone would come help you with the elk. I hiked back up to the ridge, being no shooting or anything. Jesus, I thought the whole woods was afire. John had an old snag, a pitchy stump, afire. The CC's had fell that tree back in the 30s, it probably slid away down over the bluff, leaving just the stump right on the edge of the road. It was raining, half snow, almost dark, and, gosh darn, that felt good. We got a jug of whisky out from the jeep and talked and warmed ourselves. Oh man, that fire he built was a god-send. We stayed around that old stump afire until the rest of the crew showed up.

# Everett McClay

Everett McClay worked in logging camps all of his life. He had every penny he ever made, I imagine. He was milking cows, getting his Social Security and had sold part of his timber to E. K. Woods Timber and Logging Company. He had a little cash.

In the late 50s, early 60s, he hired me with my D-6 Cat to help him clear some land. Out in the middle of his fields, straight back from the corrals off the Loon Lake Road and around back toward Fredericksen's ranch, was a great big swale, kind of a huge, wide gulley. He had me fill that swale with ash, alders, maple, myrtle, willow, whatever. I just pushed them out of the ground, roots and all, pushed them into that low ditch and covered them with dirt. Plus someone had cut and left a lot of ash trees previously; they went in there, too. Boy, there would be some fine wood today—oh God, buried where the air can't get to them. And that ash, you could make just about anything you wanted out of it. Buried in the dirt the sap, just the outside, would be all that would be gone or rotten—the logs would be good. You'd get an inch or two into that sapwood of mud and moisture, but the sapwood's no good anyway.

Anyway, I covered 'em all with dirt; got a long ways back, just pushed dirt. I had to get a long ways back to get it from. I didn't get it from the creek or the hillside, which was too far away and covered with trees. I just lowered that field quite a bit. I don't know how many days I was just pushing dirt.

The old growths right there in that field where they got those cattle now; Everett chopped them—every one of them—down with an axe. Can you imagine? The myrtle and maples, too! He used a big, long, thin-bladed choppin' or a falling axe. To fall one of them with a cross-cut saw, you almost need another man—either that or drive a stake in the ground and use a piece of rubber inner tube to pull the saw back to the stake—so he just fell them himself; chopped them down. That was the way of the proud professional woodsmen of the olden days.

So those old growth firs, the clear stuff out of them he cut into wood for the wood stove; the tops and wherever it would get knotty, he'd just cut them into big long chunks and burn them.

Everett put his fence posts in the ground five foot deep! Every one of them on the place were put in five foot deep. They were just a full cedar log split in half.

One day I got stuck in a mud bog with the ol' Cat. There were no trees nearby, nothing to tie the winch line onto to pull myself out. I put some old chunks that were laying around there where I'd been clearing land—you know, poles and long chunks of wood—and stood them up against the backs and sides of one of his fence posts. Then I put a choker on the thing as low as I could and pulled myself out of there with the winch. There's not very many fence posts anywhere in the world that you could use to pull a Caterpillar out of the mud with. I bet those posts are still up there in the ground five foot deep.

Everett was old then, in his sixties, and he sometimes wore a little white beard. He'd have on one rubber boot, one leather boot, pants torn up the bottom, long johns shining through. He wore a clean pair of dashboards to town, though, and he bought one pair of pants a year—bib overalls. The reason why he had two different boots was that when one wore out instead of throwing away the whole pair, he'd wear the good one and some other type boot that was still good out of another pair. That's why he'd end up with one rubber and one leather.

He was quite a character. Neighboring farm kids said watching him build fence was better than going to the movies. He was built like a bear—big-chested and strong as an ox. He could pick up a 200, 250 pound anvil by the horn, set it up on his shoulder and walk off.

Old Tom was a great big ol' workhorse he had. If Everett couldn't pull on it, budge it and move it by hand, by God, Tom wasn't going to pull it either! Quite the pals. He wasn't going to overstrain his big, sleek, fat, elderly workhorse. Everett would pile his milk cans on a sled, and Tom would pull them to the road. He used the same home-made wooden sled—summer through the dust and winter through the mud.

He'd put another milk can on and test it out—see if he could still move it, and say out loud to himself, "Okay, Tom can take that."

One day he had Ol' Tom all harnessed up; he was going to go up on the hill and get a culvert. Pretty soon he came back and no culvert.

I said, "What happened?"

"Well," he says, "I got behind that and couldn't budge it; so, by golly, I'm not going to make Tom pull it."

"Well," I says, "Take the ol' jeep; it'll pull it."

"Oh, hell," he says, "That thing won't pull it."

"Oh, yes it will, go ahead and try it."

So he takes the jeep and comes back with the culvert. Then I couldn't get him off the jeep. He went around using it for everything.

There was a junk car at his driveway (where the gate is now) he'd sit in. One time I walked across the field; he didn't hear me, and I heard him talking—he'd answer, too.

"Well, Everett, there comes those loggers again (the crummy of my men were coming). And they're going to stop right there and open that gate. See that? They did, yes, sir. And they'd better close that gate. I've got my rifle right here. . . ."

He was real particular about that gate, he didn't want his

milk cows out on the road. He had plenty of milk, cream and butter, and one day he said, "Yet, (his word for "yep") my next milk check, I'm going to buy me a 'frigedairy.'"

He got one and built it into the log cabin so no one could steal it.

Some say he got sick in later years, but Everett McClay sick? Not that I had ever known. He was very robust. Any man that could chop away on those big trees all day long like a madman would have to have superb health. He never stopped—only to whet that axe a little bit with his whetstone.

Shoot, you had to watch him; you'd cover him up with the Cat. I got him all tangled up there one day—like to tore his clothes off. He was in there choppin' those limbs off, and I didn't see him. I finally seen him running. I had a limb stuck in his ol' underwear, and those long johns were about half torn off. He wouldn't have gone much further; no way he could get away—long handles had him caught. He was feisty. He had to get in there and chop limbs before we buried them, I guess, so they weren't sticking up.

"Yet," he says, "We ought to get a D-8 and just log that timber" (on his hillsides).

I should have took him up on that.

"Just you and me," he says, "By God, we can make 'er."

Everett told a lot of stories about Abraham Lincoln. One was that old Grandma Liz caught Abe out there in the tater patch with a Negress. She got him off of there with a hoe and ran him off.

"Yeah," he'd say, "Old Abe was nothin' but a Nigger lover."

When I was up there clearing, I took a newspaper up. We'd read the paper at the resort, and I'd take it up the next day.

One time he was reading, and he says, "My God! I see old Harry's up there in Portland!" (President Truman came through there on some conference or something.) "I sure would have liked to have known that; I'd went up and talked to old Harry. I don't give a damn about old Harry, but I'd sure like to know how the folks down home's doing."

And he went around saying, "If that flocking old Army cook gets elected as President, old IKenhauer, I'll sell every damned cow on the ranch. Why he's nothin' but an Army cook in the first place."

And when Ike got elected, he did; he got rid of every one of them. He sold all his cows. He didn't call him "Isenhauer," called him "IKenhauer."

Everett told his neighbors, Nels and Rick Fredericksen, that he drank an egg and hatched a lizard in his belly.

"Yet, I watched the doctors put it back together after they got it out. Nothin' but a lizard."

You see why I was hesitant about going into business with him on his timber.

Everett had four or five cherry trees, and they were his pride and joy. He'd shoot the livin' dickens out of those blue jays. What dog'd I have? He had run a coon out of one of the cherry trees and on up on the hill. Everett followed and shot the coon with his shotgun. He thought the world of that dog—that was one fine dog after that—helping him protect his cherries. Then he hung the damned coon on the fence to scare the others away, I guess.

The word was that years ago Everett had gone down to the doctor's office and had himself castrated. Some say he was broken-hearted by a girlfriend who jilted him, and he swore he'd never have another one. Others say he thought he was spending too much of his money on the ladies in the houses of ill repute. I should have looked him over when I rolled him through the bushes there with his clothes half tore off of him.

The old logger was never married. I think Tom went before Everett. Then they found Everett dead. It looked like his shotgun had gone off when he was trying to clean it.

I thought he was awful careful with that damned ol' gun—he'd shoot coons out of his cherry trees with it and took it with him everywhere. People said he took sick and ended his life.

He had willed his property to the Portland Zoo. The Zoo sold it to Champion International Timber Company, who logged it. Champion got bought out by the Hancock Insurance Company, who, while they owned it, had the Campbell Group Timber managers overseeing it. Hancock sold to C&D Lumber Company of Riddle, Oregon. Why it changed hands so many times is anyone's guess.

The pasture is leased by Bobby King Logging and Cattle Company so it's not quite the zoo, but it does have a good-looking herd of cattle on there. And the slopes are covered with beautiful fifteen-year old fir trees, twenty-five to thirty-five feet tall, just as thick as the hairs on God's head, and the slopes are about as steep as the back of His head.

Everett McClay worked that land and had a good life there. He was one fine neighbor.

*Everett McClay's Cabin*

# Killed by Bull

"Loon Lake Farmer Killed By Bull," read the Coos Bay *World* newspaper headlines. "July 14, 1936 A. E. Cardelle, age sixty-four, dairyman, was gored by prize and tame bull while family were away. He was badly trampled about 7:00 P.M."

Cora Mae, his daughter, tells the story: Uncle Rook called up and said, "Come on, we're going to pick grass seed up Coos River." That was one job I never did like so I took off in the brush.

My mother and my brother Ollie went, and before going Ollie had told Dad, "Don't let Eddie out of his pen."

Eddie was the prize Jersey bull. Another brother, Archie, had shown him in 4-H and he was just a big pet. He had won first prize at the County Fair and then at the State Fair. Next was the National competition, but Mother said we didn't have the money, and he wasn't going to go.

Some friends wanted me to go swimming with them down at the lake, so I came home to put on my bathing suit and Dad was sitting by himself reading the Sunday paper. I asked him if I could go, and he said something like, "Go ahead, Honey, you're only young once."

While I was gone Mr. Knolls came down and dropped his Jersey cow off to be bred. Dad turned the cow and Eddie loose to run with the rest of the herd up the canyon. Later on Dad brought them all in and had the cows in the barn, stanchioned, ready to be milked. He must have tried to "shoo" the bull into his pen, but you know how that would go, with a cow in heat and him being such a big pet and all. Something must have happened. Eddie was running loose and when we all got home from our various outings, there was Dad laying in the bull pen, dead. He had tried to get under the barn but did not make it. The little Ranger dog was with him, laying by his side. This faithful little companion was not hurt, but he just wanted to help out somehow and give him some protection. A great grief was felt forevermore, by all in the family, for our beloved father.

# "If She Keeps on Cooking Like This, I Think I Might Marry Her!"

You know, I never knew who turned this in, but I always figured it was Marvin Haskell, the rascal. He always knew when it was dinner time and would show up.

Althea would say, "Well, get back there and get washed up, we've got plenty to eat."

He'd get the cow manure washed off his hands. He'd always comment on how good the food was.

One time I said, "Yeah, if she keeps on cooking like this, I think I might marry her."

A while later here comes the Liquor Commission. Althea was tending the store, and I was out in the woods, logging. When I got back I heard all about it. I guess it really humiliated Altee (my nickname for Althea)—first they wanted to see our liquor license, then they wanted to see our marriage license.

Somebody called them. Marvin didn't call them, he just talked. He told it to somebody and somebody called the Liquor Commission. I guess them guys left satisfied, though, after seeing the marriage license.

Hell, I think I married her even before she did any cooking for me.

# Wreck in the Umpqua River

Noel Taft, a longshoreman, and I were going into town—going down river. Coming up from Reedsport and meeting us was a car coming like a bat out of hell. It was coming broadside. All of a sudden it must have gotten traction or something because it shot out into the river and lit on some rocks.

By the time we got there, a young man and woman were standing on top of the car! They even had their suitcases with them on the roof.

I ran back to Echo Resort and called the wrecker.

They were hollering they couldn't swim. Then someone in a pickup came along and threw them a rope and soon the passengers and luggage were pulled safely ashore.

They were a couple of college students travelling from Coos Bay to Eugene—broadside for part of the trip. It was a lucky thing that rock was there and they landed right where we could help them.

# The Shells That Misfired

I was in the back end getting beer into the walk-in cooler. I never even knew any motorcycle riders had come around. Our hired help, Pat, knew where I was. She came back to the cooler, opened up the door and says, "You'd better get out there, the damned motorcycle gang is fighting with Althea."

I had to come clean from the back to the front and along the way was a cubbyhole I kept rifles and shotguns and stuff. So as I went through, I grabbed a .12 gauge over-and-under shotgun. When I got out to the front, this one wild-looking motorcycle gang member had Althea, banging her up against the building. She had a water hose in her hand. I learned later they'd been fighting with some of the tourists. Althea was going to fix them like we fix a dog fight, spraying them with the water hose. I warned the man to turn her loose.

"Turn loose of her!"

And he just gave her a shove up against the building. That set me in a rage.

I went to shoot and the gun misfired. I pulled the trigger on the other barrel, and it misfired, too! You hear about Divine Intervention, well, that must have happened here because that over-and-under had never misfired before. I had shot it a lot.

Althea got a broken finger out of the deal and some bruising, and the thug got a busted head 'cause the shotgun barrel fit right around his head. The barrel didn't do so much damage as the stock did. The barrel knocked him down, and he cussed and rared and he called me a bunch of names.

He got back up and by that time I got hold of the stock. The shotgun flew all apart when I hit him, the barrel completely busted off of the stock. I put him down with the wooden stock, and he didn't get back up. I told the rest of them, "Pick up your trash here and get the hell out of here, 'cause this is not the only gun I own."

I think they were believers by then, anyway. Blood had just flown out of his head and was all over the cement and even the window was covered with it. They took that guy to the nut ward in Salem. His motorcycle and terrorizing days were over.

Months later he came with some older people, probably his Dad and Mom. I think they were figuring for a law suit. He had cleaned up a little, but I recognized him. He must have been up to Salem in the puzzle factory because he was being escorted around; he wasn't doing it on his own. They never came in the store, didn't even talk, just looked and walked around. They never came back.

I know a $750 shotgun went to hell. The barrel was bent so badly, never did get it repaired. People liked to look at it; kind of a conversation piece, I guess. John Layman got off with it; he was going to get it repaired. I think John died, I'm not sure.

One thing—that motorcycle gang of lazy floaters and loafers—they might not have known I pulled both triggers, but they knew how mad I was. They never came back.

# The Pinball Machine Artist

Pete Stingley, the trapper, ran the Rainbow Club for many years.

He once told a guy, "These pinball machines are for amusement only."

The customer was one of those jokers that had some kind of little hand drill he poked into those pinball machines and turned a handle attached to a wire and hit the jackpot. He had been down at the Waterfront and drilled a machine down there. They tipped Pete off that he was around drilling the machines.

So when he came down to the Rainbow and was getting change to play the machine, Pete told him, "Now we don't pay off here, son, this is for amusement only."

The man started playing the pinball machine.

Pete called home to his wife, Dorcus, "Bring down my shotgun."

So she brought down his shotgun, and the guy, he finally got 'er drilled and stuck a piano wire in there. It just tripped a lever or something inside there, and it started adding up the points—bells a-ringing!

The guy came over to the counter and wanted his pay.

That's when Pete said, "I told you to start with this was for amusement only."

The guy said, "Okay, I'll either get what's coming there or I'll tear this place apart!"

Pete just picked up that shotgun, and he said, "Yeah, okay, mister, you can just do that, and you'll make a fine-looking corpse. Yes, yes, I do believe you would make a fine-looking corpse. Now if you don't believe me, you just go ahead and try it because they'll just take you out of here feet first, mister, right on over to Mr. Unger's place. That's the funeral home just a block down the street. It'll be the last trip you make."

Then the guy said to Dale Wilson on the bar stool, "Good God, man, I think that guy's crazy."

Dale agreed, "Hope to shout, he's serious, I've seen some go out of here feet first."

Pete said, "That's right, mister, you'd better listen to what that man is saying because it's only been three days since I shot the last one. The last one was a big, fat Choctaw! Yep, yep, if you ain't out of here, you'll find out just how crazy I am."

That must have scared the guy because he forgot about tearing up the place or getting his money; he just hightailed it out of the Rainbow and was never seen again.

# Hundreds and Hundreds of Green Bottles
## Told by Ben Shadley

Old one-eyed Carl Collins lived in his trapper's shed on Lake Creek. He used to drink wine out of green bottles. His porch was right over the creek and when he had emptied one he would throw it in a big log jam that was in the creek.

One time a freshet came through there and washed the log jam out. I'll never forget the sight of hundreds and hundreds of green bottles floating down the middle of Loon Lake. They floated neck to base and base to neck like a green parade of smoothly gliding gems. They stayed packed together in a wide flotilla stretched out for a mile. Zoom over the gorge the strong flood current took them. I'm sure a lot of them made it the thirty miles to the ocean without breaking.

Beings how Carl Collins was a bachelor, if he'd put a note in every one, think of how many letters he might have received, back then before the days of phones. Some gal beachcombing might have found one of his bottles and written him a love letter back.

I'll never forget there was a fight there at Duckett's and the police were there trying to straighten it out.

Carl Collins came out on the porch of the store with a shotgun in his hands and told the cops, "You'd better get right back in your cars there before I shoot you. I'm dying anyway and I don't care if you shoot me!"

And they did. They just slithered in their cars and drove away.

It's sure not like it used to be. I remember the first day I came to Duckett's with a friend, Lloyd was putting in a dump station back of the resort. He asked if we'd both help him. I stayed on three or four years living and working with him.

When the cabin cesspools got too full, Lloyd would put dynamite in there and blow them a little deeper—worked really good!

One day I made three runs to Coos Bay in Lloyd's red pickup to bring back Blitz beer. I filled the pickup just as full as I could pack it in. It was the Fourth of July and we went through 350 cases of Blitz beer. I would carry it into the back door, Bick would stack them in the walk-in cooler, and they were sold by the bottle before they had a chance to get cold. We couldn't keep 'em moving fast enough. They wouldn't even have a chance to cool off; they took them out of the front doors of the walk-in that fast.

Most mornings somebody would knock at seven o'clock and come in and have a beer; they'd stay all day 'til late at night. The loggers would show up in the afternoons.

# The Dock

Ben: I remember one Saturday there was a dance at Duckett's. Seemed like all of Reedsport came up—must have been two or three hundred people out on the dock dancing. So many that you were getting your feet wet. The next morning I woke up with wet feet.

Lloyd: Hell, yes. That dock would go down. I was standing out there knee deep water with the fire hose and pump, blowing snow off, to keep it from going clear to the bottom. That was in the big, big snow, the winter of 1969.

# Blue Jays Clean Out Hornets

I used to shoot blue jays around here to keep them from eating up all the cherries and other fruit as it ripens in the trees.

We had a big hornets' nest. It was about one and a half feet across by two and a half feet long. They can build that large of a nest in one season. This one was hanging in a maple tree by the stump in the front yard.

One day there was half a dozen blue jays out there in the limbs of that little maple, just screaming and screaming. Boy, they ganged up on that nest. They were right by the hole in the bottom getting hornets as they were coming in and getting them as they were coming out. They were picking off hornets right and left. Must have been eating them; I never saw them spit any out. They cleaned that nest out. "Thoom, thoom, thoom," they got 'em all. I have the empty nest in my attic guest room. Guests often asked if there's hornets in that hive.

"No," I tell them. "Don't worry, they're all gone."

I never shot any more blue jays after that—figured they can eat all the cherries they want, long as they keep eating hornets, too.

# Nellie's Timber

Ol' Nellie Judy's husband, Luther, had been dead for years and years. She had some big old growth logs scattered all over the mountain, and she asked me to log them, and I did. These logs were left over from during the war when E. K. Woods Timber Company logged their adjacent land and hers also. They pretty well clear-cut it; but left the logs on her place. I don't know why they were fell and left. Maybe they decided they were over the line. Anyway, Nellie said they were hers and so I proceeded to make a road up to where they were. The logs had already been bucked; we just bucked the ends off of them, and they were good wood. This was in about 1955 or '56.

One day I went to the house. I had to get some water for the Cat. I knocked on the door and waited and waited and finally she come to the door. She had an old cupboard and here was Ol' Carl Collins' ol' shoes sticking out of there. I used to tease him about that—oh, yeah, Ol' Carl Collins knew all about that.

"Oh, yes! I know all about that."

But she'd been a widow many years and Carl had never been married.

One day Ol' Ed Seabloom showed up.

Ed says, "What are you doing logging my timber?"

Seabloom was the big manager for E. K. Woods. He was it as far as the woods end of it was concerned.

I said, "Nellie Judy is having me log this."

Ol' Seabloom claimed it was theirs. Nellie's son, Benson Judy, agreed with Seabloom that I must be on E. K. Woods' property.

He remonstrated, "Lloyd, you should have got ahold of me before starting."

Well, Seabloom said he'd let me finish up what I got and pay her. Anyway, I said to hell with it, and I never finished that logging job.

Now I think Ol' Nellie was right. The property changed hands in 1987, and the new owner, Audrey Bates, wanted to know where her lines were. Whacking around through the brush, I found corners up there marked off good. Another Seabloom bunch of balderdash; I don't think he knew where his property lines were. Those old growth scattered all over the mountain were Nellie Judy's after all.

An interesting thing with a dog happened while I was looking for these corners. Althea had passed away at the time and my future wife, Ellen Judy Fiocca, lived down the mountain from where I was, across the valley floor and up on the other side of the mountain in a little log cabin a mile away. Her dog, Lobi, must have heard Audrey and me talking or, on a breeze, picked up my scent. The dog knew I was there somehow and came across hill and dale to see me while I was looking for those corners—heard or smelled me for a mile away and found me up in the woods. Anyway, there she was with me.

That Cat road I made to get up to the logs fifty years before is the same road that Big Steve Brockman and his wife, Betty, use today to get up to their house. There was not a lot of timber there, so I just made a fast road up the mountain and made a flat landing there where their house stands today. To bring the logs down, I didn't bother winding around on my road, I just went straight down from the landing to the county road, about where the mailboxes are now. So, in other words, I wound around up slow and came down fast.

One day one of the field mechanics from Papé Cat came by; I don't remember what in Heaven's name he was looking for me for—I guess he was just in the area and wanted to say hello. He saw me come down that hill full tilt with a load of logs and said, "Jesus, Keeland, you're living a little reckless, ain't ya?"

I told him, "Hell, this weren't steep!"

I've logged steeper places, up in Willamina. They wouldn't even stay in the chokers. I'd cinch 'em up real tight and put a cable clamp in front of the bell to keep it from backing off. Then I'd back the Cat right over the logs, winch 'em up tight and that way we went along as one unit, they couldn't slide downhill faster than the Caterpillar was crawling.

A flat-lander would have a hard time imagining some of these things.

# Haircut Recommended

Jim McCull was driving and I was in the car with Kemo and one other guy. I don't remember what in the heck we were riding around with Jim for, or where we were going, but we were there in Reedsport and passed three hippies thumbing on the side of the road. All their stuff was piled there with them. Whoever was in the back says, "Hey, Jim, they flipped us a bird."

Jim says, "They did?"

So just up where another road joins in and there's kind of a wide spot, that's where Jim turned around. He wheeled in to that vacant lot where the library is now and flipped a cookie in there and man, had the dust just a-flying—right across from the police station.

We drove back to where they were and stopped. The window was down and that one run up to the side of the car and I says, "Where ya going?"

"Eugene," he replied.

I asked him, "Don't you think you ought to have a haircut before going to the big city?"

He says, "No one is going to cut my hair!"

And about that time I had him by the hair of the head. Jim, he was out of the car chasing one down in the ditch. Kemo and the other guy never did get out. Shoot, about that time there was all them pretty lights flashing behind us. Boy, I turned that S.O.B. loose that I had. Jim came running back and got in the car.

The cop says, "What's going on?"

"Sons of bitches trying to sell us some dope, by golly. Better shake 'em down."

We pulled away and shoot, went back up, way up the road that time to turn around—at Schofield Creek. As we came back and passed by them again, the cops had their crap scattered all over the shoulder of the road in front of the cop car. Ray Haas was one of the policemen. They all knew who we were. By the time I got back to the resort, Ernie, the Liquor Inspector, had already beat me there.

He was waiting for me and said, "Any more of that haircutting and I'll take your license."

I says, "That's a crock of baloney."

"What do you mean?" he asks.

"It's not in my name, it's in my wife's name—she ain't cutting no hair."

We left it that way. That way if we ever lost it permanent, we could get it in my name. It had been in her name twenty years before I ever came to Loon Lake. That's the reason we were able to have the oldest liquor license in the state when we sold in '75, it had been in her name since 1934.

I think whoever it was in the back seat just made it up about the hippies flipping us a bird because they just ran right up to us when we stopped. If they would have done that they wouldn't have come up. Been more people got on those sons of bitches the country wouldn't be in the shape it's in. That loafer didn't get his hair cut but I bet he remembers that to the day he dies—scroungy little potlicker.

# Henry Hudson Helps at the Boat Dock

Recently I was watching a husband and wife float their boat back onto its trailer at the boat ramp. The husband was driving the car and the wife, knee deep in water, was maneuvering the boat towards the trailer. Man, you see some awful goofups at the boat ramp.

Ol' Henry Hudson, Althea's brother, used to just torment those people trying to load their boats back on their trailers. Henry was a very exact, charming and dapper man who worked as an engineer on one of Hindsdale's tug boats. He was the mechanic in the engine room and his wife, Bertie, was the cook in the galley. The tugboat pulled the log rafts down the Umpqua River to the Hindsdale Mill in Reedsport.

When Hindsdale sold the tugboat, he sold the crew right along with it and so Henry and Bertie got to go to Hawaii with the boat. They were there when the Japs bombed it. Anyway, after they got back from Hawaii, he used to come up from Reedsport to help us about the last part of April. That's when there was an opening to the fishing season.

One time one guy was trying to park a trailer. He'd back it in, then Ol' Henry would have him run it ahead, "Nope, got to back it this way about a foot." Then, "Nap, go ahead, come back over a little more this way."

Althea and I were watching from up at the store. The guy finally got out of the rig and went back to where Henry was standing guiding him. Their arms started waving in the air and pretty soon Henry went down on the ground, his little white cap just a-flying.

Althea told him later, "Guess you tormented him enough, looked like he hit you!"

"Well," he said, "I was slipping anyway."

Didn't want to admit the man knocked him down.

Then he would tie their boats up—oh my goodness, ha! People would get mad. The way he had them tied, it looked like you had to take the boats through the metal rings to get them loose. They'd work and work trying to figure out his knot.

Henry was a good-looking, very tough man, and a good fighter. One man from Florence said he was the toughest guy in the country and thought he'd come down and try out Henry. The fight happened at some square dance. He might as well saved his gasoline and his reputation, he was no match for Henry.

*Henry and Bertie*

# Kemo's Billboard

Kemo and Sarah Couteure lived in a little cottage in Ash Valley nestled against a timbered hillside. Green pastures spread to the front and to the sides of the cottage, on which grazed the neighboring cattle. No other homes could be seen, but the myrtle groves along the creek which sheltered the cattle from the flies and hot summer sun and the winds and cold winter storms. Deer plied their way through the tall clover and bear could sometimes be seen foraging at the blackberry patches. Elk frolicked and played tag in the ponds in the fields or loped in big arcs around the grassy meadows. At night they bedded down in an old orchard. Fish teemed in the cold, wide creek meandering through the fields. Fresh water otters, muskrats and beavers made their homes along its banks.

Smoke curled up from the chimney of the cottage and the ring of an axe could be heard as Kemo split wood in the yard. Sarah was weeding by inching along in the garden, out of her wheelchair. Crippled by polio as a child, she never let her paralyzed legs get her down, but was a cheerful soul to all who knew her. Born in Oklahoma in a preacher's family, and half Indian, she loved working in her vegetable and flower garden. Kemo kept the little yard immaculate and they were happy in their home. Music from Sarah's accordion or organ could be heard wafting from the cottage, often accompanied by the lilt of Sarah and Kemo's voices singing the old songs.

Although content with their cottage and gardens in this idyllic scene, Kemo and Sarah wanted to have some television. They could get the voice, but they couldn't get the picture. Kemo pointed the antennae at the highest hill behind Everett McClay's place, Mt. Brown, and got the voice coming in good. But with the hillside and treetops at his back and being surrounded by more distant hillsides and treetops, he couldn't get very good reception.

Kemo had some of that aluminum that they use in walk-in coolers to reflect the heat back outside. It was a great, big six foot roll, real thin, and he had it stored in his garage. Remembering it, he had a brainstorm! He came and got me to help him. We took the aluminum and went up the county road, then walked in on an old Cat road. See, they logged that once. We stretched it out, put it around trees and brush and tried to keep a view of it like a great big billboard fifty feet long pointed toward the house. It shined up good. Back at the house he set his antennae aimed at it and got good TV reception!

Acting as a reflector for the waves in the air, it worked good until the Forest Service came along and put it out of business. It wasn't long before one of their employees came looking to see who put it up. They knocked on Kemo's door and told him they were going to take it down. Navy planes flying maneuvers out of Charleston had detected it. Seems it was fouling up the radar signals out of the Army radar station in Hauser, over the ridges from Mt. Brown. Did he know anything about it? Didn't know anything about it and that was the end of the good television reception in the Couteure household.

# Sarah Shoots at Lloyd

They were having a big party in Kemo's garage. I went up there. Oh heck, there was Curley and Mrs. Dodge, Ray and Mrs. Manekee, Shorty Idson, a whole bunch of them there, and Ol' Ray LaMar. We'd always heard that Ray and his brother George, when we weren't there, not to our face, would call me Ol' One Eye and Althea, Big Tits. So I walk in the garage and hadn't been there but just a minute or two when Ray says, "What'd ya do, sneak away from Ol' Big Tits?"

I says, "You know, I've been waiting to hear you say that."

So I went for him and I took a swing at him like I was going to hit him in the ribs and then I just lifted 'er up and caught him right square in the button. He went down and went down through Sarah's coffee table, broke it all to pieces. I told the Ol' Rip that I'd get her another coffee table or pay for it, which I did.

She left and went over to the house on her crutches. Outside the garage Rick Miller and a belligerent joker were in a disagreement. They weren't in any big scuffle, just arguing, and I thought, oh shoot, I'm going home, this is getting out of hand. I started out past them two guys and, "Pow!"

That's when Sarah shot. The bullet went right past my ear. You can tell when they're close. It didn't take me but about a second to drop to the ground fully stretched out.

Someone said, "Oh, my God, she's killed Lloyd!"

They seen me on the ground. I said, "Oh no, I'm all right, I'm not hit."

If you'd ever had one come close, you'd know it by the sound of it, it just cracks. She claims she shot in the air. She shot into the air all right. She was always shooting and so that was it. I came home. I think it was a .22 by the sounds of it, but they can kill you just as quick as a big one.

# Otters in the Beds

When Mr. and Mrs. Horn vacationed at Duckett's Resort, they stayed in the floathouse. The otters, Humpy and Dumpy, would climb up into the floating cabin and get on their bed. The Horns got a kick out of it. Mr. Horn would roll them up in the bedspread and take them both back outside at once and dump 'em in the lake. It got to be a game with them.

We let them into the store, but we didn't let them into our living quarters. With two of them we didn't dare; if they'd got up in the house, they'd have everything torn up, the way they played. That was big games to them, just rip and tear—mischievous little fellers.

Our first Humpy used to get up in the cheesecloth-like material under the mattress and burrowed in there and made like a hammock for himself. That's where he slept, hanging there under the bed.

Those otters are smart. The second Humpy and his brother, Dumpy, never went in our house or bed, but they picked up on beds from Mr. Horn—from going in his bed and getting dumped out.

Don Groat came down to the resort one time and, by God, he was mad! The otters had swam up the lake, up Tom Fool Creek, went up the upstairs of his house and got into one of his kids' beds. He couldn't get them out, so he got me and gave me quite a tongue-lashing. I just went up there and threw them out. Oh, they knew they were in trouble when they heard me coming up the stairs yelling at them.

Humpy would ride on the back of the seat when we went to town. He'd just stretch out and lay across there—clear across the damned thing. Everybody wanted to mess with him.

198

People would be fishing off the dock. They'd pull up their stringer and find a stringer full of heads. The otters had swam by underwater and eaten the bodies, then swam up the creek that ran through the campground past the store. The only reason they hadn't eaten the heads is that they knew the metal or poly rope stringer went through there. When the fishermen came in to complain that's where they'd be, back inside. Humpy and Dumpy would be sitting on the stools mounted at the counter as if nothing had happened.

"What are they blaming us for?" Then they'd get into something else.

Old Vern, the retired longshoreman, used to come all the way from North Bend every day just to bring something to those otters. He just loved to play with them. He'd bring a little sack of something, it might be a boiled egg, or, you couldn't tell what it might be. They knew him well, they liked all the customers, and were in and out of the store all day.

They slept in the dog's bed on the back porch with Bozo, the dalmatian, and a white cat. The white cat thought he was an otter. He would lay out on a boomstick in the water and when the otters were catching fish or swimming around there, he'd spot a bass close by and "boom," reach down and pull him right out of the water with a front paw.

The otters went off the diving boards; they could get right up the steps to the high dive, too, and go off that. They were really graceful diving, and they got along good with the people swimming, too.

That Vern would sit down there and laugh at them, he really thought they were amusing. Later, Ol' Vern got ran over and killed on the highway down there at North Bend.

# Bick & Stutterin' Slim

Vernon Bickford was a bachelor who lived on our place many years. "Bick," as we called him, worked for us part time sweeping and mopping, doing yard work, filling the beer coolers and pumping gas. He stuttered and could hardly get the words out sometimes. He lived in an old trailer we pulled up there for him for thirty years until his death.

One day a customer pulled up to get gas. It was Stutterin' Slim, a longshoreman from Coos Bay. He came up here a lot to fish but had never met Bick. He had a darned ol' Volkswagen bug and he stopped in front of the gas pump and raised the hood. He had the cap off the gas tank and that's about when Bick went out to help him. Bick lifted the nozzle off the pump and got over there by the rig and said, "Shall I f. . .f. . .f. . .f. . .fill 'er up?"

Stutterin' Slim said, "F--- you and go to hell."

He slammed the hood down and spun out of there.

The next time Slim came up to go fishing, I told him, "Hey, Slim, that guy wasn't making fun of you—he's messed up just like you maybe worse. Bick has the same speech impediment as you do; he meant no harm. Now why don't you get on an understanding level with him and make friends. He's a prince of a man and so are you."

# Brookharts

Frank Brookhart had a father named Walter Brookhart who had one eye. A bunch of toughs came up the river from Gardiner and somebody did something. . . .

Walter picked up a shovel and knocked this guy's ear off and then chased them up and down the dock, and out of Scottsburg. They got in their boat and went back down the river. That's the only way you could get there, in those days there was no road.

Walter was going way over to Smith River side one time to set up a new trap line. Them darned boys of his took his traps out and all his trapping gear and filled his sack with that many rocks. No wonder he was mean and ornery. He hiked from the mouth of Mill Creek, clear up over Well's Creek Guard Station, down towards Smith River and over towards Watson Lake—didn't have his food or nothing. Had a sack full of rocks. His boys, Frank and Dutch, played a practical joke on him. I bet he knocked *their* ears off when he got home.

It was a coincidence that Walter got his eye knocked out in a fight and so did his son, Frank. Frank and I got in a fight, and I hated that the rest of the days that Frank was alive. I knocked his eye out—blinded him. Didn't knock him out. Damn, he'd fight with anybody. We were good friends. Didn't make any difference.

He died of the DT's or out of his head anyways. He was under the bed screamin', thinking people was after him. He was down there on the Klamath River in Hoopaw, California, when he died.

He's buried right there by the gate at the Scottsburg Cemetery.

The day we put him in there, his brother, Ken Brookhart, walked over there and said, "Well, you ornery thus and such, what do you think of it down there?"

# Nels and the Bull

Nels Fredericksen, when he worked for me, almost got killed by his bull. The bull had a ring in his nose and then he drug a log chain. It was long enough so he could step on it by his back feet. That's the way all the old farmers used to do the bulls.

The bull hit him and knocked him down, and then he started ramming him. The only thing that saved his life was that he horned him under the fence. Nels was black and blue from one end to the other.

Ruth Fredericksen, Nels' wife, tells her version.

"That's right! What it was is that we had come home late from town and had to get the cows into the barn to milk. It was in the spring of the year, and the bull was with them. He had to be, you know. The bull was always put in a little pen by himself when we milked. Nels usually had a bar he put in the ring of his nose to handle him with; but being so late he said he'd just lead him with his chain. Well, the bull couldn't get in the barn with the cows, and he raised all kinds of Cain.

"The bull started running at Nels. Pretty soon the bull was running faster, and Nels was running faster, and the bull hit him in the middle of the back. He tore all the ribs off one side of Nels, squishing him against the ground. Right there was the fence, thank heavens, and he was able to get under it.

"Nels went to the doctor, and they wanted to put him in the hospital.

But Nels wouldn't go, claiming, 'That's where people go to die, you know it?'

So they taped him up and sent him home.

He got well and worked in the woods again, but he always had a great ridge down the center of his breast bone there from the ribs cracking."

# Stealing a Boat Dock

The dirty bastards tried to get me for stealing a boat dock. Wintertime around this lake with high water—the incoming creek, Lake Creek, up to ten feet and overflowing its banks, other times up to fifteen or twenty feet above summertime level; the outgoing gorge just a rushing torrent dropping a couple hundred feet to Mill Creek—there's often enough current everywhere in the lake to break docks from their moorings.

I towed logs in that we cut into firewood. I used to supply wood for the campground down there. The water would come up, and I'd see a log out there on the lake, go out in a motor boat and tow it in and float right up and tie it up in the middle of the campground. The water would go down and, hell, we'd start cutting wood.

Well, one time I had cut up an old log we had towed in there that was just an old log—something old Shorty Harrison had turned loose—I think, it had been in a bridge. Old Lady V. and Mrs. S. had seen us hauling that log in during high water. They claimed it was their boat dock and that I had stolen it. Their dock was down in the gorge. We took pictures of it after they called us thieves and caused one big ruckus.

The cause of their gripes was this. We'll start with Mrs. S. Her child set the house afire—an old Ash Valley farmhouse; they rented and burnt it to the ground. They had found the boy a few times before that playing with matches and trying to start a fire in the closet. Well, he finally got the job done, and the whole family had no place to go. We gave them Cabin 7—fixed it all up and gave it to them all winter—never charged them a dime. Mr. S. worked with Tony Martin— ran yarder, if I remember right.

The ladies of the valley made them a beautiful quilt; they put hours and hours right there in the store making it. I saw the quilt in the storage shed we had back there near their cabin with the dog sleeping on it. I jumped her ass about that.

I said, "Jesus Christ, if you didn't want that quilt, why didn't you give it back to them?"

That's one reason for them pulling that on me. The family went to Alaska and after that.

Old Lady V., she started the BS. I think she might have been pissed because I had worked over that gosh-darned goofy brother of hers. This brother was shoving and knocking an old man around. I told him to knock it off, leave him alone, he's old enough to be your granddad—what the hell you think you're doing?

Oh, he jerked off his glasses, slapped them on the counter there and challenged me, "Maybe YOU want some of it?"

"Yeah, I'll give you some of it."

That was her twin brother—maybe she had something to grind there.

So that was the status of the two ladies—just trouble-makers.

The next thing I know I got a warrant from the sheriff to either go to jail or put up some bond—they got me for larceny over a stolen boat dock.

I tried to show the Assistant District Attorney something different but that little bastard wouldn't go for it. We went down in the gorge, took pictures of their dock all broke up down there. Gordon Docket was the D.A.'s assistant; he handled their case.

Hell, I was in court four or five days—jury and everything. I had Dan Demmick for a lawyer. The newspaper article said it was just like a three-ring circus.

You know, they'd set those witnesses up there on the stand and, JESUS, old Demmick would tear them up. They were sorry they ever were up on that stand.

I never testified that first day. Mrs. V. and Mrs. S. presented their case. Ol' Lee Shipley didn't help things. He was the deputy sheriff. He came and went through the wood pile and found where that log had been a bridge. Got a chunk with some kind of notch or something—figured it must have been their boat dock.

Both ladies claimed they saw George Ogden with his red hat helping me in the boat get that dock towed home. They claimed you could tell it was him because he always wore a red hat. So they got George Ogden on the stand and asked him, "Mr. Ogden, do you wear a hat?"

"Yes."

They brought his hat out for review.

"Well, you don't have a red hat?"

"No," he answered, "Never had a red hat in my life."

He had one of them old yellow ones; you can buy yellow, red or black felt-type hats—you know, soft floppy things all the loggers wear. A little bit of muffled laughter was heard through the courtroom. He never did get it back. Last time I seen him he was still whining about that hat.

"Oh," I told him, "They keep that as evidence, I guess."

At one point Gordon Dockett said, "And it's a known fact this man rules that country over there with an iron fist." There was laughter throughout the courtroom and the old judge rapped his gavel for, "Order, order, order. No more of those laughing outbursts."

The saw shop guy got in on the act; the women got him to testify. When he came in there and said he owned the dock, I said, "Oh, hell, no, you never owned that dock. It belonged to Al Firshaw."

So they sent the sheriff after Al and subpoenaed him into court, and there they asked him if he owned the dock.

"Well, I built it," he said, "And I just left it there, so I guess I own it." This dock was parked at the BLM camp spot called Eastshore; the women and the saw shop guy used to ski off of it, that was all. They never took care of it; they let it break loose and go down in the gorge. Docks since then, that the BLM had built and put in there, have gone the same route.

Oh, those two women got mad as hell when they got on the stand and were cross-examined. That's when it was said it was a setup.

The jury voted unanimously with a not-guilty verdict. Every time I would see that son-of-a-bitch saw shop repairman that guy'd move out in high gear.

# Rose Bushes Out the Window

There used to be a big sprawling rose bush outside the window of the resort. The window opened on its hinges as does a door. Many a man has been knocked out of that window. A certain kid from across the lake, we won't name who, had his turn. The place was full.

Chet Craig says, "Hey look at that guy, he's pissing out the window!"

"You've got to be kidding."

"No, he really is." I never liked that young man anyway, and I walked over there and thought of shooting him. Instead I hit him right in the back of the neck and rolled him right out of that window. He landed right in the middle of those rose bushes with nothing but swimming trunks on and his hand on his ding dong.

# Stutterin' Slim

Stutterin' Slim was out fishing in a rowboat. The game warden was standing on the dock and wanted him to come in so he could see his fishing license.

Stutterin' Slim told him, "Go to hell, you're n..n..nothing but a Gestapo."

The game warden replies, "I'm not a Gestapo. What makes you say that?"

Slim says, "Well, you've got the b..b..b..b..boots!" He didn't come in, either. The game warden had real shiny black boots like some of them wore.

# Garbage Comes Back Home

Somebody was leaving garbage around the garbage cans down in the campground—just scattering it all over down there. People camping told me who it was. It was a group of "summer homers" coming across the lake every day. Those cans were for our campers, not for someone living across the lake.

One of the men dumping garbage from his summer home was a telephone company employee. When I confronted him on the subject, he whined, "We spend a lot of money in your place."

I said, "So what?"

He kept leaving his trash around our cans, and so I got their address off one of their checks.

I had to take Cougar Bill up to Portland. I bagged up all the telephone man and his wife's garbage, found out where they lived and went right up to their house. I knocked on their door first then just scattered their garbage all over their front lawn.

He comes out and says, "Hey, what are you doing?"

I said, "I'm seeing how you like garbage spread all over your place. . . ."

"You can't do this. I'll call the cops!" he shouted.

I said, "That would be a mistake. . . . You do that, and you'll be needing an ambulance to get you out of here."

I stepped up on the porch with him.

"You'd better not touch me. . .," he warned.

That was all it took.

I shoved the sucker around a little bit, slapped him I did and shook him up a little. Then I left.

After that our cans weren't full of his garbage nor was there any left around on the ground. I must have reformed him. He learned how to dispose of his own garbage.

# The Cop and the Skunk

Before his married life with Ruby, Wes Phillips got a skunk out there in Glide. He got one of the kits from a whole family of them. He named him "Stinky." Anytime Wes would get in the car or truck, Stinky was right along with him. He never did any stinking. He'd thump the floorboards a time or two, but he still wouldn't spray.

A cop stopped Wes one day when he had seen that skunk in the car. The cop got out and picked him up.

Wes told him, "Better watch out, HE IS NOT FIXED."

The young hotshot cop threw him up in the air and Stinky just sprayed all down the front of him.

He wanted to give Wes a ticket for transporting a wild animal and that older, other cop said, "No, you don't. You was warned."

Boy, he was mad.

The older one says, "You have to walk all the way back to Roseburg. You're not riding with me!"

He put him out walking—about nine miles to Winchester and another five miles to Roseburg.

I bet that veteran cop thought that was the best thing that ever happened to that recruit. He thought he was real hot stuff, the "Real LaCoy," as Wes would say. It was exactly what he needed. He was warned!

*Jack Phillips working at one of the sawmills in
Reedsport as a security guard.*

Wes Phillips' dad was named Jack. He loved to dance.

Butch Thompson of the Thompson Ford said they used
to have those dance marathons. When they opened the
McCullough North Bend Bridge, Jack danced thirty-six hours
without stopping. One night at the Eagles, Jack died dancing.
Just pumped those old gals around until he keeled over.

# Ollie and the Dinner Steaks

One time Althea had some beef steaks set out thawing for dinner. There was a half a dozen people in the store. One customer sitting at the counter said to me, "Some guy just walked through your place and took something off your kitchen table. It was that foreign-talking guy you had in here."

Well, Ollie had been on the bar side, then he'd been over there shooting the breeze, like he always did, with the people on the restaurant side, and from there he must have come back around the counter through the kitchen and out the back door.

I ran out the back door, is what I did to start with, and didn't see no Ollie.

'Bout time I got back, Althea had finished waiting on some people, and I asked her, "What'd you have laying there that he could have taken?"

"Oh," she replied, "Our dinner steaks."

Then I went out looking for Ollie. I hadn't seen him in the back yard so I went around in the front. I caught him out there in the front of the store. I asked him, "Where's our steaks? What'd you do with those steaks?"

"Ollie no take them steaks."

I said, "You confounded liar—you did take those steaks."

"Oh, Ollie no lie."

So I started wailing on him. I knocked the hell right out of him and he still wouldn't admit he'd took the steaks. About that time Helen, our helper, came out on the front steps of the store and said, "What are you beating Ollie up for? He's an old man."

I said, "He's not a hell of a lot older than I am, besides that, he stole my meat."

About that time Ken came up from the dock, also the tourist who had seen him go through the kitchen, came out, and the tourist says, "I ain't leaving this place 'til we find whatever he got."

So we started looking—Ken and the guy that seen him and myself. I think Ken found them—they were in a hollow hole in a myrtlewood tree back there—he'd stuck them in that rotten hole in that tree.

By God, we still had steak for dinner and Ollie had a sore head.

## Ernie Selle's Auto Wrecking Yard

All right, there was Barry and Bill McKinney and myself and Ollie, of course. Ernie Selle had a wrecking yard. We went there for something.

Ernie met us at the door and said,

"Okay, you go in, and you go in, and you're all right. . ., but you. . ." that was Ollie.

"You, we're going to weigh you in and weigh you out."

He put him on the scales, and he did—he weighed him in. He probably only weighed about 170 lbs. After we bought the part we were looking for, Ernie put him on the big standing scales again, looked at his weight, said, "Okay," and we left.

We got down to about Butch Thompson's Ford dealership. We got to teasing Ollie about it, and he says, "Ernie don't need tink he's smart. Ollie got this."

Ollie had a little, tiny end wrench.

So Bill McKinney knocked all the hell out of him, and we turned around and made him take that wrench back.

# Locals On the Dock

I remember Wes Phillips being down on the dock. He had a power saw, laid it down on the dock running, idling along, and then went off and left it. I was scared to death some kid would run into it or something.

# Sow Bear in the Tree

Ed Thomas and I used to go up there by Wes Phillips' on a drive. There used to be an old growth tree right in the middle of the road. You could go around it on either side.

A big ol' sow bear was running down the road ahead of us and run right up that tree making the bark fly. Got up there, hung right on the side of the tree and was looking back at us. Ed honked the horn and she wet all over the tree.

Ed was talking to her, "So, so, big gal. Don't be so scared, we're ain't going to hurt even the first little hair on your hide."

I tried to console her, "Hey, we don't mean to scare you! Quit acting so nervous."

We went away and left her alone.

# Duckett's Helps the Strikers

I remember when Crazy Otto and I fixed up the boys on the picket line at the U.S. Plywood mill below the highway bridge in Reedsport. Crazy Otto had the Chinese joint there in Reedsport. He brought the food and sandwiches and I told the beer truck driver, Nick, to stop by the picket line and drop off beer.

"I'll just take it off for breakage," he said his company allowed three to five cases for breakage.

I said, "Okay, and after that just put it on our invoice."

After that once a week Crazy Otto and I supplied the four or five picketers who were pulling their duty with sandwiches and beer. That strike lasted five or six months. Then the longshoremen went to sympathizing with the striking mill workers and that brought the management to their milk quick. The longshoremen said they weren't on-loading lumber on the ships while the mill workers were on strike at the mill. Now after this many years of hiring people, I might be more on the side of the management.

# Bill Andersen's Wooden Leg

Bill Andersen got in an argument at the Weyerhaeuser gate with his brother. The brother shot Bill's leg off; otherwise Ol' Bill would have probably killed him. There's no doubt about it if he hadn't have shot that leg off.

So Bill Andersen, Helen Abel's brother, ended up with a wooden leg. He would go to a bar and get half drunk. Some woman would come in and he'd take his knife and "punk". . . stick the knife in his wooden leg. One time in the Rainbow, he forgot which leg. He jabbed it in the wrong one. Whatever woman he was doing it for probably wasn't impressed, and had to stick around to doctor him up, besides.

# Pappy and the Skateboard Incident

Oh golly, right there in the bend of the road by the calf barn, a skateboard came rattling out on the road in front of Pappy DeWitt. On it was a girl, who lived up the hill from there. Pappy almost hit her and ran his pickup out into the ditch to avoid having an accident.

The father comes down the driveway, and Pappy says, "By golly, Sam, why don't you control these kids?"

The neighbor got mouthy with him and Pappy just dumped him. The neighbor told everybody he was hit with a jack handle—ha ha! He probably thought he was hit with a sledge hammer. It was just Pappy's fist.

The neighbor's venerable father was right there, too, and he started sounding off. Pappy was going to get him, too, but the old man left when Pappy went back to the pickup and got his little thumper from behind the pickup seat. His little thumper was a piece of lead wrapped in leather attached to a spring. The spring was wrapped in electrical tape and was used as a wobbly handle for the lead—just a small wholloper that he used in the picket lines. Pappy was always strong in the Woodworkers Union.

The venerable father was lucky Pappy didn't use the little thumper on him. He wouldn't have had to anyway; he could handle him without it.

The kids were a lot more careful riding onto the road after that.

# Haircut with the Pinking Shears

He comes in the store, dirty long-haired, regular mangy bastard. He ordered a beer and I said, "You don't get any beer in this place until you get a haircut."

And he says, "There ain't nobody big enough in here to cut my hair!"

And, "Oh, yeah?" and about that time he was captured. Elmer Baird and a couple of other loggers held that sucker down and we gave him a haircut.

"Snip, snip, snip, snip," I just grabbed the first ones I come to—Althea's pinking shears. He didn't want any beer after we got done with him. He left out.

Well, God, it must have been months; it was a long time. Man, he walked into the store there one day all cleaned up—like, I mean slacks, sports coat and a tie. He says,

"Remember me?"

"No, can't say as I do."

He says, "I'm the guy you give a haircut to with the pinking shears. That's the best thing that ever happened to me, I just had to come by and thank you."

He got his act all straightened up and had some kind of real good job.

# Wrecker Gets Elk

The old-timer, Clyde Butler, got a bull elk out of season in the middle of the night. He called Jeff Shinn's wrecker service out of Winchester Bay to come pull it out with his tow truck. I don't imagine Ol' Shinn even knew what he was getting.

Much to his surprise it wasn't a vehicle at all, but a bull elk! Jeff Shinn must have gotten it pulled out where Clyde could get ahold of it, but he was probably mad being called on to get an elk poached out of season.

# Monkeys, I Guess

Labor Day in Seaside used to be hard on the community. It was because of punk college kids tearing it up. They would get up on the roofs, tear the bricks out of the chimneys and throw them down on people.

One weekend a bunch of them came here. They were up on the roofs of the cabins, which is never good. On asphalt shingles those little shoes and boots can disturb things and cause leaks.

Vern Monroe, Frank and Tom Powell and a whole bunch of loggers saw them.

Vern says, "Lloyd, we're going to take them out of here." I got a double barrel shotgun and aimed it up there while Vern hollered at them, "You've got about one second to get down off there and hit the ground. And when you hit the ground, you'd better be running. If you don't we're going to knock your heads off and run them up and down the road like footballs."

They just jumped off and left. I guess that barrel of the shotgun was looking mighty big from up there.

I don't know yet how they got up there on that cabin. Monkeys, I guess. I think that's what they had planned on doing down here—taking the cinder blocks off the cabin chimney and throwing them down.

# The Campground

## As Remembered by Jim and Marianne Avery

It was late at night, and dark, about 2:30 A.M. when we drove into the Duckett's campground. We were in our big Ford pickup with a camper pulling a boat, and got about halfway down the campground driveway. We couldn't get any further than right there. From our vantage point we looked down into a car that was parked and blocking the roadway with a man and a woman inside. They weren't really doing the Samba, they weren't really doing the Basanova, but they were doing something pretty compromising. It wasn't too long before they put all their hats and shoes and clothes back on and drove out of there and we were able to park in our reserved camp spot by the lake.

Kind of a funny thing happened at that camp spot one time. It was the Fourth of July and we got to celebrating. Well, Marianne got a little tipsy. She decided that the tent was too hot and stuffy; we had four kids and a tom cat in there, so she went out and slept on the picnic table. She had gotten warm and taken all her clothes off, and in the morning there she was, in broad daylight, asleep on the picnic table without a stitch on. Later on we discovered that somebody had taken our beer and our watermelon. There was no beer, but our watermelon had been hollowed out and the inside eaten and put back together. They had cut it nicely in two, ate it and put it back. She was laying right there when all that was stolen and she never even woke up to catch them.

Boy, this place was really swinging then.

"Yeah, I caught them, though," says Lloyd. "We had a run of teenagers here for a while that was taking beer and taking coolers and all. I had an old meat gamble that was chopped out of a two by four. "I went after them and that one said, 'You'd better not strike us!' That's when I went to bustin' 'em in the ass and all over the place. That was an awful bunch from another locality. I guess they passed the word, 'Hey, that guy beats on ya! Stay away from there with your thievin'!'

"About that same time we had been missing beer and pop out of the storeroom. Ah, them little boogers, we'd kept it locked; we couldn't figure how they'd been getting in. There was a board missing on the side of the building. The drivers had piled the merchandise on the inside right up against that missing board. So all they had to do is reach in there and get it. And that's when they came alongside the building there with the goodies. I met them out front. On the way out the door I grabbed a bull whip that had been left there from the night before. Ed Miller had brought it in and everyone had been trying it out, snapping it all around the place—'Snap! Snap! Pop!' He hadn't taken it home for some reason and I just took it there and used it on those big scamps and Americanized them—you don't steal."

Margaret Finch, a long-time employee, friend, and Ash Valley resident, recalls, "I remember the first time I met Lloyd, he was working over some young men—right in front of the store—with a big, long, leather bull whip! I thought 'Oh my, what had those boys been doing here? It wouldn't happen again, whatever they'd done!'

"Both my husband and I got to love and respect Lloyd and felt honored to work for him. He was good-hearted, always fair and expected everybody to be fair with him. Don't cross him."

# Peeping Tom

While camped on a private piece of land, called "Miller's Cove," a gentleman used to frequent Duckett's Resort. We'll protect the guy and call him "Mr. D."

Mr. D. made a peephole in the partition between the men's and women's toilet. He was watching the women on their side. Noel Taff and I waited 'til he went in and Noel went right in the women's right behind him.

Pretty soon Mr. D. took a little wire and poked all that toilet paper out of the hole he had made.

Noel grabbed that wire and poked it right back at him and said, "Now what do you see, you galoot?"

All was silent for a little while. Then, all of a sudden, he came crashing out of that door. That's when I hit him over the head with his own guitar. He had left that guitar outside of the toilet—that got his attention.

Old Lady Smith knew he was peeping through that peephole and commented, "That was really entertaining." He might have been sticking something else through there to entertain her.

# Squashed Beaver

I can't remember who it was, but somebody told me that he came across a beaver squashed by his own tree. The tree wasn't barber chaired either, just fell on him and squashed him dead. That's pretty unusual.

# When I Broke the Army Sergeant's Leg

In 1964 we were 'way out there under Mount McKinley—miles from nowhere in Alaska. We came across two kids—young men, really—they went out on this frozen lake and picked up a caribou they'd shot. They had it in their pickup. They got back and just got their front wheels on the bank when the ice caved in on them in the rear. There wasn't anything left above water but their hood. We still could have gotten a cable on it easy.

There was three or four Army guys hunting also who were there in like a weapons carrier or command car or something all enclosed with a winch on it.

I asked them, "Come on, run that thing up here, and we'll run that winch out and we'll pull these kids out of here."

The sergeant says, "Oh, we can't do that without permission of our commanding officer."

"Well, where is he?"

"Back at Ft. Richardson."

I said, "Jesus Christ, that's 150 miles from here. I suppose you guys got to call the son-of-a-bitch before you can sneeze, huh? What kind of sportsmen are you? Out here at the taxpayers' expense."

They got in the rig and left. If they're going to run around up there in government rigs and hunt, they ought to at least be sportsmen about it.

We got the kids in the car. They were about froze to death; I mean froze. We put them back there between Althea and Faye and kind of covered them up. I hauled them down the road, oh shoot, I don't know how far. I don't remember if it was a place of business or someone's home or what; but the man who took the boys in said he'd put them up overnight and take his snow machine or some rig out there and haul their pickup out of the lake the next day.

When we got back into Delta Junction, we called the boys' parents and told them the situation, that they were in good hands.

Oh hell, it must have been a week or so after that I went in the Buffalo Lodge. That sergeant was sitting in there. He made some kind of comment like, "Oh, there's that gol-danged civilian who gave the Army hell." Then he says, "Don't you understand military regulations? Weren't you ever in the service?"

"Hell no," I says, "I was 4-F. Can't you tell looking? I got one eye."

I guess that got his nerve up because that's when he wanted to go outside. Well, we started outside, and he was real anxious to get out there and just before we got out the door, he tried to kick me in the balls. He missed and got my leg, it was all green and blue later. I just grabbed his foot and took off with it. He lit flat of his back right on that frozen ice in front of the door.

I says, "Oh, you like to kick, huh?"

Then I just jumped on that infernal leg of his—just jumped on it. I could hear bones just snapping and popping.

Then I said, "Now I'm going to kill you."

Then Smokey, the owner of the Buffalo Lodge, and about a half a dozen of 'em pushed me back inside. He had a buddy there. I guess it was his buddy. Another military guy.

I told that guy, "Hey, I was in the Marines. I walked over better guys than you just to kill a few Japs."

They loaded him up and took him back to the fort—big Army base, Fort Richardson.

We were up there about five weeks. We were moose and caribou hunting, and we visited with the stepdaughter, Faye, and her husband, Sam Hughes. We were also just looking the country over.

We saw a caribou migration and that was worth the whole trip. And they talk about the wolves getting the sick stragglers. Malarkey. That big wolf pulled that bull down—big healthy animal—right before our eyes. You could hear their hooves clicking—click, click, click, hear them for miles. That cold, still air, you could hear them especially out on that frozen lake. You could hear them 'way before you could see them—thousands of them, a mass of them just as far as you could see.

The day we were leaving there to come home, we stopped at the Buffalo Lodge to tell Smokey and his wife goodbye. The Army sergeant was sitting in there with a cast on his leg. (I forgot what that son-of-a-gun's name was. I used to know his name.)

Anyway I says, "Oh, there's Sgt. _____."

He started hollering, "Don't mess with me, man, don't mess with me! You've already cost me four weeks of extra duty. . . ."

"No," I said, "you simple-minded phoney, you brought it all on yourself."

Sam Hughes, the son-in-law, was with the Federal Aviation Agency. He kept the airstrip open for the military—kept the lights and snow plowed off and all that sort of thing.

Ol' Faye says, "Now if we go over there to the base, I can take one of you in, either you or Mom. But you can't buy anything."

"Oh, you can take your mother."

So I went up to the gate and had my card I got discharged from the Marine Corps with, and I flashed that card on the guy there at the gate. He looked at the captain's signature down on the bottom, and I guess he saw my picture and I guess he thought I was a captain because he came to attention and gave me a salute.

I had a couple of drinks in the NCO Club and looked all around. I met up with Faye and Althea looking at meat in the commissary.

"What are you doing here?"

"Never you mind, I'm in."

# Humpy Gets Lost

One time Humpy, the otter, was lost. Well, he wasn't lost, little stinker knew where he was. We were traveling and hunting in Alaska, near Paxon, when this herd of caribou came across the road in front of the car. They went out just kind of a little ways and stopped, and I thought, "Oh, boy, this is going to be easy." So I took a shot at this one's head and neck and they just looked at me. "What the heck's going on?" I thought, "Well, shoot, how'd I miss that?" So I took a rest across the station wagon and aimed right behind its shoulder and still missed it. That's when I figured something was wrong with the scope, I guess it got banged around on the trip coming north. I took a hatchet and started beating that thing off there so I could use the open sights and that's when the caribou left—"Whist." Althea wanted to stay in the car as it was cold outside. I told her to keep the window down a little bit and that way she could still run the motor and the heater when she got cold.

With the scope off, I took off after them; the otter and I went out there about a half mile and there they were, in kind of an amphitheater effect with us up above, looking down on them.

I laid down on my belly in the snow and zeroed in on one, and the damned otter was laying right up on my back. I got the one first shot, then I got the next one. I killed two right there. I could kill three; a resident could kill five on a tag. Humpy stayed with me until I was gutting them out and then he went to playing. When I got done he was no where around. I figured he went back to the car. I headed out that way and, nope, he hadn't been there. It gets dark about two o'clock that time of the year, and boy, I mean dark. I drove down the road about two or three miles to Summit Lake Lodge, it was out from nowhere, and asked the owner if he

228

could fly around and see if he could see him from the air. He was just changing from wheels to skis and he said that as quick as he finished he would fly around up there. I told him I'd go park back where I had walked in, so he knew where to fly around, and anyway he'd see the carcasses of the caribou in the snow.

I was waiting for the plane and I happened to look up on the bank and there that little S.O.B. was. I went up there and he knew he was in trouble, I was yelling at him. I discovered what he had been doing—sliding in the snow and tunneling in the drifts, hiding from me. I seen him do it, or if I hadn't seen him he'd been hid again, little bastard. It wouldn't have done the plane any good, and the owner had already gotten airborne by the time Humpy showed himself. I got out of the car and saw the plane in the air, the pilot made two or three circles and came back and landed right near us.

I said, "What do I owe you?"

"Oh, nothing," he said, "I wanted to try out my skis anyway."

It was getting almost dark. I wasn't going to get the caribou out in the dark there in bear country. When I went back I took the .348 with me—that'd change any bear's mind, quick.

Humpy never did that again. By God, he went with us. A guy on the base had a plastic toboggan he loaned us. Jesus Christ, if that wasn't a battle, getting those caribou out across the tundra. The brush grows up through it and there's holes everywhere you step in. We got both buck caribou out on the toboggan with Humpy running along in the snow nearby. Everyone was amazed at that otter minding ya, until he wanted to go skiing.

# Waterskiers Behave

Althea and I were camped over across the lake in Little Salander Creek, hunting. We had gotten a deer, skinned and gutted it and brought it over by boat to put in the walk-in cooler. Ol' Bert Shipey decided he'd go back across the lake with us to the camp. He must have been up in his eighties then. We were out there in our little ol' boat—little three-horsepower motor, "putt, putt, putt," and we were just moving along slowly. The only boats out there were a rowboat with a couple of ladies fishing and a cabin cruiser pulling two waterskiers. Before we knew it, the cabin cruiser went on one side of us and the skiers on the other. We ducked down as we saw the tow rope coming. We were practically laying down. Ol' Bert must not have had his head down far enough because it took his hat off.

That was before the BLM boat ramp was put in, and I knew they'd have to take their boat out of the lake at our ramp at the resort; so once back home and Althea and Bert safely ashore, I just waited for them—Noel Taft and I waited.

I waited about an hour, and the longer I waited the madder I got. Finally, here they came and one guy came buzzing in on the ski to the shallow water of the boat ramp, kicked it off and took off running up the shore—Noel got in one punch as he went by, but the guy was in high gear and Noel couldn't catch him. We weren't going to hurt the lady waterskier, just do some damage to the men.

The boat operator stayed in the boat. He wasn't going to get out. He must have known what was coming because he kind of hunkered down there with his head down on the steering wheel. He didn't want to get hit in his pretty face. That made it all the better. I jumped down in there with him and gave him a couple of fists in the kidneys—that straightened him up, then let him have it in the jaw. I then let him have another one, and he went right overboard backwards. I didn't care if he drowned. I bet he was surprised to see me coming down in the boat after him; he thought he was safe down there.

His wife was in the background hollering, "You barbarians, you're nothing but barbarians up here."

I informed her, "We are not barbarians here, lady, we just about got our heads taken off by your tow rope zinging over us at forty miles an hour. You had the whole lake to play in. Just one other woman and her mother were fishing and us."

The boat operator was hollering he was sorry, and I guess you know they didn't pull that stunt on anybody again that I know of.

# Putting in Water Line

Ol' Crazy Walt Hansen said, "Lloyd, remember when we put in a ditch for the water line down there at the resort with the walking plow?"

"Yeah, pulled it with the jeep."

"It worked pretty good," said Walt, "You were pulling me all over the place."

I imagine it was fun back there; that ol' thing would hang up when it dug too deep or roots came along. I had the line tied on the back bumper with a heavy block on it to keep the line down. We were putting in the mainline down through the park. We'd back up and dig it again.

# "Peace, Woman, Peace"

One time in the store, two women, Kitty Mouse (Muriel Johnson) and Chris Christianson, were in there. Kitty Mouse's beau, the old trapper named Pete Stingley, was at the front door about to come on in.

They were teasing Pete and locked him out. In the playing around, Kitty slapped at Pete and just sent his cowboy hat rolling.

A long-haired hippy type was sitting in the back of the store. He jumped up and ran right up to the two women.

With his hand up in the peace symbol, the two fingers shaped like a "V," he said, "Peace, woman, peace!"

They flogged him until he left the store with his arms about his head.

# National Line Record Bass

Fishermen got me up early one morning for a boat, like about four o'clock in the morning. So I just got a rod and went to fishing.

I caught a bass that Saturday morning that weighed over eleven pounds on a four pound line right off the dock. That was 'way over the state record for weight. They wouldn't let you use your scales, though ours were legal, tested by the state; they thought you'd cheat. Althea had to go to Roseburg the next Monday, so she took it over to a sporting goods store to get it weighed in. By then it had dried out some being in the walk-in cooler and only weighed ten pounds four ounces.

My line had to be sent to the National Spin Fishing Association to be tested. It overtested so they jumped it up to the next size up, the six-pound line. I still ended up with a national record of a ten pound four ounce large mouth bass caught on a six pound line. Years later some guy down in Alabama or somewheres caught a bigger one and broke my record. If my line wouldn't have overtested and we'd had the fish weighed the same day before it dried out, it still wouldn't have been beat as a world record.

After Althea and I got back to the resort from Roseburg, we were unloading the car. We brought that fish in, and I told the kid working for us, "Here, go take care of it."

I meant—take it into the walk-in. Pretty quick he came in with fillets—he'd took care of it. I was going to have it mounted.

# Weiner Flies Under the Elkton Bridge

Terry Gates, affectionately known as "Weiner," thought it was a beautiful day back in 1968. He didn't have to drive log truck that day so he thought he'd take his airplane for a spin. He fueled up at Beckridge Field in Roseburg and took off. Once in the air it was too good an opportunity to pass up; he'd been thinking about it for a long time so he sailed on over to Elkton.

There spanning the Umpqua River is a long-spanned bridge, which takes the traveler over Hinder Road (County Road Number 11). Weiner had always wanted to fly under it and had already stepped off the distance between the piers—120 feet. His wing span was forty-three feet.

The spring Chinook salmon were running and coming under the bridge. Ed Mitchell, his employer and four others were fishing off it enjoying their high vantage point over the river.

"It was a great day and a great flight under the bridge," Weiner recalls, "Until it cost me $163.00. I had to buy all those guys' fishing poles. All that fishing line and poles got tangled up in my propellers. I was doing 165 miles an hour. I would have done more than that except for my brand new engine I was breaking in. I was bringing her up when, 'Beeep, beeep, beeep!' the low air speed sounded. I couldn't get any more lift, so I had to drop back down and take a more level course to gain my altitude.

"Everybody in Elkton was mad at me. George Parrish was pounding shingles on his roof. When I went over, the shingles went flying everywhere. When I went back to the airport to get gas, everybody was waiting for me. They had received a lot of calls from cowtown, you know.

"The FAA fined me $650.00 and grounded me."

# Deer Runner Stopped

We had a half-Shepherd/Collie type and half-Lab. Rings was his name—he had a white ring around his neck. He'd go with me to the dump on our own property when I hauled garbage from the campground. He got in the habit of finding a deer to chase every time I was up there. I was having trouble breaking him.

These deer seemed to take the same escape route about ninety percent of the time. This one day Rings had 'em going. I figured, well, a deer is going to come through here and off that four foot bank again, and that's where I was waiting.

The deer went past—he leaped right off the bank. Very shortly here was the dog. He made his jump and I caught him right in mid air with that old rotten club. I thought I'd killed him. He laid there kicking and a-quivering. Finally he got up, staggered around, followed me back to the unloading, and to my knowledge he never ran a deer again. If he did, he done it out on the quiet all by himself; he never did any yipping. So that solved that. I thought I was going to have to shoot him to get him stopped.

He lived to die of cancer. Well, he didn't die—we had him put to sleep.

# Flood of '64

Ben Shadley's stepdad and mother, Bill and Bernice Hakki, live in a house at the edge of Reedsport which overlooks the Umpqua River. During the flood of 1964, they counted more than 400 cows, dead, that floated down the river. One cow was still barely alive—identified by the ear tag as coming from Roseburg. It was out in the ocean by Port Orford.

They didn't know how many trailers and houses floated by; thousands of sheep, dead. The beaches all over were covered with rattle snakes, washed out of their dens and holes.

Ben Shadley drove to see his mother and father during the first part of that flood. He and his wife and boys had come up from Medford. Highway 38 flooded, so they had to come through Mapleton and Florence, and his boys' hands touched the water as they hung them out the window of their Mercury Cyclone. One of the electric company men working on the power lines said, "Watch out for that second dip in the road, it's deep." It was, that's where the boys' hands were dragging in the water. Mom and Dad gave them royal hell for coming down to see them in weather like that.

During the same flood, which was at Christmas time, Althea and I worked all night putting things up on shelves because the lake was way up in the store.

Finally we went to bed in Cabin Number 3, which is farthest and most elevated from the lake.

Right before daylight I woke up and let my arm swing down off the side of the bed, and "Uh, oh!" my hand was touching water. The level of the lake had risen up and into the cabin in which we were sleeping.

When we went down to the store that day by rowboat, the water was four foot deep and floating aspirins in their little tin boxes off the shelf.

## Green Chain
### As Remembered by Benny Shadley

A guy working on the trim saw got his fingers cut off, like this, 'way back to the knuckle of the hand. I was working pulling lumber on the green chain when the glove, fingers and all, came down to me on a piece of lumber.

I hit the kill switch. They took him into the hospital and sewed his fingers back on. The funny thing was we just had a few days to go before we won a prize for so many days without an accident.

Then there was the preacher who started working there who was a diabetic. He tore a hangnail loose on his thumb and went to the hospital to get that fixed. That was another time when we had just one more day to go without accidents to get the award. They gave away all kinds of things—Zippo lighters and everything else.

One of the other guys pulling green chain said if he ever saw that preacher in the streets, he'd bomb him a good one.

# "What Happened to the Boat?"

Ben Shadley and his father-in-law at the time, Zeke Springer, were going deer hunting over to Chiloquin. Zeke was a big ol' tall, skinny, long-necked guy who worked for the county road department. He and Ben were looking forward to a good deer hunt around the Klamath Indian Reservation of Chiloquin. This good hunting territory is in the beautiful pine country of Central Oregon.

As they traveled along, ahead of them ran a pickup with a cabover camper pulling a big, fancy boat.

All of a sudden that pickup ahead of them veered off the road. Ben didn't know if a rear tire blew out or an axle broke or what caused the truck to veer, but as the truck went crashing off the roadway, the camper shell was thrown off in one direction. The ball hitch where the boat was attached broke and the boat and trailer took off through the brush in the other direction.

The guy went running to see if the boat was hurt, yelling,

"What happened to the boat? What happened to the boat?"

His wife and children had been asleep in the camper, which was all crushed up after flying off the pickup. The camper had hit the side of the road and the wife had a broken shoulder and four or five broken ribs. He never went running to see how they were; he was just concerned about the boat.

Ben flagged down a car and sent word for an ambulance. They waited and waited and waited; no ambulance ever showed up. So they packed the wife and kids in the back of the station wagon to take them to the hospital.

The husband wanted to come, too, but Zeke said, "Oh, no, you're staying right here, you blank-blank potlicker, with your boat."

Left him out there in the freezing nighttime with his big, fancy boat he was so concerned about. Why, it seemed he cared more for that than he did his family.

# Lloyd Keeps the Peace

Don Fitzlaff: "I was drinking at Duckett's. Somebody was mouthing off on the stool.

"Ol' Lloyd says, 'Shut up!'

"He kept mouthing off.

"Lloyd walks down there and says, 'I told you to shut up!' and then backhands him right off the stool."

Lloyd thought a minute and then says, "He must have been talking dirty or something. You know, with all the things that went on down there, you never did hear them talking the 'F' word or anything like that. I used to tell them, " 'Now do you talk that way in front of your mother?'

" 'They'd say, 'No,'

" 'Well, then that takes care of that.' "

Don Fitzlaff: "One time I had a guy on either side of me. They got lippy. They were going to stomp me into the ground.

"Lloyd comes over and says, 'Now, you two, none of this nigger stuff. Let's make it legal, shall we?'

"Then he knocked both of their heads together and down they went."

Lloyd: "If I remember right, that was just a couple of kids. 'Course, Fitzlaff was just a kid himself about then, wasn't he?"

Benny: "It was probably that it was his head was one of them that got knocked. That's the reason he remembered."

# French Canadian Guide

Moose hunting in Alberta, Canada (Peace River country), was a great and special event; I guess I went five times taking employees, relatives or just my wife with me. You had to hire a Canadian guide or hunt with a resident. But if you hunted with a resident, when you took the meat back to the States, you had to take a bunch of papers to a guide and he signed them, then you could go to the Royal Canadian Mounted Police or Canadian Fish and Wildlife, and they would make out permits to get the meat and the trophies out of the country.

One time I hunted with a resident named Mervin, and he had a friend who signed my papers for me only charging me the price guiding me for one day—$100—instead of guiding for a whole hunt like they normally do.

So anyway, we usually hired a guide. They were all Frenchmen. And here we are with our guide; one night the ol' Frenchman says, "Well, I guess tonight I'm going to change socks."

He took one off, shaped like a foot, really dirty, and put it on the other foot. Thought he was being funny. He was dirty. He'd peel potatoes leaving peelings on the floor. There was six of us living in his bee truck—what he hauled bees in. It was eight feet wide. You know it had to be illegal to go down the road with like that, it was too wide. It was sixteen feet long. He had built it. He hauled the bees clear from California in it. This big ol' box he had built was on a Dodge truck, single axle. It had a side door in it and a ladder to get in there.

One night I heard him pissing in his potato peelings. Never did wash any dishes. We just wiped plates off with paper towels. He had a metal fifty-five gallon drum full of water in there to dip and drink out of and wash with, what little we did wash. Boy, that was crude. It's a wonder we didn't catch some diseases or get sick or get the dysentery or something. Damned wonder.

He had a damned wood stove in that bee truck; that's what he used to cook on. It'd get too hot, then it'd get too cold—miserable, miserable.

Vern Johnson, the long-term BLM man from Coos Bay, and Richardson, another Swede from out in Central Oregon (I thought he worked for the highway department, I'm not sure) were with us. Althea and I, Vern and Richardson were old, old buddies.

The French guide had to hire a guy to help him. Early one morning we'd all been outside. We all had to use the brush (outdoors) for our toiletries; we overheard the hired man ask the guide, "Well, shall we get the Americans their moose today?"

"No, to hell with them," was the answer.

That's when I decided to hunt on my own. He'd leave me in different places and then he'd go off on that snowmobile. I'd seen some good trails and hunting areas we just passed up.

That day, as usual, I stood behind him on the snowmobile as we went two or three miles from camp. We were in the third cut line from camp. Oil exploration makes a cut line, cleared of brush and timber about every square mile just so they can get a Cat down it, oh, about fifty feet wide or so. The timber they just push out in a pile, no place to harvest it; most of it's just cottonwood, little ol' scrubby spruce, poplar. He let me off, told me to go out in a swamp. I went out about a 100 yards; I knew what it was, a swamp, and first thing I knew I was sinking. He'd told me he was going over about five, six miles to an old sawmill to look for moose. Coming in for lunch I saw the track where moose had been crossing, going right over the cut line—looked like a herd of cattle had gone through. I wasn't supposed to be there, so I got in a bunch of logs and brush and sat down and waited.

Pretty soon here came three—"zip"—they trotted on by. Then I heard the brush crackling and a cow and two yearlings. Next was bulls, I got two—a cow and a young bull. They must have heard my shots. He came back, the Frenchman did, Johnnie Dufrennes (Gaston Devalle was his helper) and gave me all kinds of hell for being there.

"What are you doing here? What are you doing here? I left you over by that swamp."

Yeah, I thought to myself, nothing in that swamp. A moose would sink; he has better sense than to be out in a swamp like that.

Then he said, "You shot it from where?"

I told him, "That pile of logs."

I got the bull right behind the ear and the cow a little further back. The bull just went down, dropped; the cow, I don't know why she didn't just drop, but she went twenty-five yards—bled, the snow was just covered with blood. Had two nice dead moose.

Johnny Dufrennes said, "That was a fluke."

He hadn't seen the other one yet—the cow that had run off.

I said, "Well, there's another fluke right over there!"

"Aw," he jabbered off a bunch of baloney in French to Gaston and said, "We got to get a trail chopped into there—get those moose out of there."

So Gaston returned with an old chain saw that was dull and an axe that didn't amount to much, and we got a trail into there.

Gaston brought the Ski-do in to where the cow was. By then Johnson and Richardson showed up. We picked the Ski-do up by hand and turned it around, pulled the cow out and hooked it behind the bigger snowmobile and away they went. The guide and two hunters and a moose behind. They must have been going about thirty-five, forty miles an hour. That guide was just a little bit mad still—had to do a little work.

243

I don't know if they hit a stump or log or what buried under the snow going up that cut line, but at one point the moose almost came over on top of them.

These two moose ended the hunt. I think we went out hunting the next morning if I remember right. Then Johnson and them said, "Aw, the hell with it."

Johnson and Richardson were perturbed about the thing we were living in. I shared my meat with Johnson and Richardson when we got back home. They wouldn't take any up there, figured I should take the animals whole across the border.

The cost of the guide was $107 a day per hunter. That's probably why Johnnie Dufrennes didn't want to hurry and get us anything. I think the guides had to get five days worth of pay as a minimum. That guide told a lot of simple and corny jokes.

Later they and their wives stopped in to see us a couple of times on their trips down to Reno.

We exchanged Christmas cards with both Johnnie Dufrennes and Gaston Devalle until they both deceased, long gone over the Great Divide.

# Manley Watson's Garage Door

One night Manley Watson, owner of Watson Logging Company, came home after having some strong drinks. His wife, Adeline, was asleep so he thought he wouldn't wake her up.

A few hours later, in the early morning, the milkman, Larry Hill, was delivering milk to their house when his foot missed the clutch and the milk truck went through their garage door. The milk truck was one of those stand up clutch jobs. Larry Hill knocked on the door and hollered what had happened, "I just went through the garage door!"

Adeline said out loud, "Oh dear, Manley just came home," and went back to sleep, thinking the loud crash was her husband hitting something with the car.

Manley didn't say anything the next day. He just repaired the garage door.

# Sheep Dip Bath

Allan Boyce, the Curry County Sheriff, didn't take any flack from the mangy hippie types wandering through his county—he cut their hair and sent them through a bath of sheep dip.

The long-hairs didn't stop in his town of Gold Beach. They detoured or just went on through.

# Caught In an Avalanche of Mud

We were clam digging in Clam Gulch, Alaska, where our daughter and son-in-law lived. We had dug our limits and went back to the Blazer. I spotted a waterfall a couple of hundred yards away and I said, "That's a good place to clean up my boots, shovel and stuff before we get in this vehicle."

Later Althea said she was coming along but I did not hear her. There were jet planes flying around there low, making a lot of noise. The little dog and I got to the waterfall and I got one boot washed off and I changed sides, was washing the other one and I heard the rumble and roar and I thought, "Another jet." The dog knew different—she left.

About the next instant I was showered with sand and rocks and I was still washing on a boot and leaning on the shovel and the sand and rocks must have hit the shovel just right and knocked me back against the wall of the bluff, which was real lucky! The stuff kept showering down, the trees and stumps and roots—well, hell, boulders, everything imaginable—regular avalanche of mud. My cap was gone, my glasses gone; never did see the shovel again; I was holding my hands over my head to protect my head—it still has gashes. Beat my fingernails off, they still ain't right, come out split when they grew back.

Well, when it ended up, all the rumble and roaring, I was in a hole about the size of a refrigerator and twelve to fifteen feet deep. After I got the sand and mud out of my eye, I was glad to see the sunlight up there and climbed out, straight up.

The falls was about forty feet high. There was debris and mud a couple of thousand feet running straight out into the clam flats and the bay. We had a hell of a time getting through it, driving way down next to the water with the Blazer.

Faye says, "Oh, my God, there's blood coming out through all that mud on his head and hands. We need to get him home and wash him off—see if he needs to go to the hospital." By golly, I had that mud and sand in my ears—I was just covered with it. When we got to the house, I took my clothes off and laid them in the yard and just hosed them.

I'm sure glad I didn't hear Althea or waited for her. She might not have been as lucky. Both of our guardian angels were along on that trip!

# Bent Over the Ice Machine

Two brothers got in a fight over Beverly, a one-eyed gal. She was really dolled up and had on green chartreuse glittery pants. The brothers and the gal had taken the Reedsport taxi the twenty-five miles from town to Duckett's Resort. Reedsport only has one taxi, so it was unusual to see it pull up and a really dressed-up gal step out, along with these two brothers. One brother was a commercial fisherman and the other was a bush pilot from Alaska, goshdarned goofy son-of-a-gun. They were Piercie Dickensen's kids—kids, shoot, they were grown men.

They came in and wanted to rent a cabin. We didn't have none. Duane, our worker, said that the taxi was still waiting for them and pretty soon they got in it and went up the valley to Sarah and Kemo's. Then they came back in the taxi from Sarah and Kemo's. Althea and I were just getting set down to have our lunch. I heard a big rumble and a big roar and a crash, and Althea says, "Oh, my gosh, they're fighting!"

I run out there and the one had his brother down and was stomping him in the head. I mean really stomping him— had blood running out of his ears.

I grabbed that son-of-a-bitch by the arm and spun him around. I jerked his arm up behind him and got him doubled up across the ice machine in a double whammy. He was flat on his back across there and I was about ready to break his neck when Duane held my arm back and he got away.

Duane said, "You're going to kill him!"

Boy, I would have, too, I was mad. He came after me again and I got ahold of him and just slammed him up against the goshdarned wall there right between the door and the machine. He just slumped right down to the floor.

I said, "You son-of-a-bitch, you set right there until the ambulance gets here. You get up, I'll kill ya."

The ambulance came and took his brother away. The cops came and took him back to town. It was kind of funny, they told him to get up.

"Oh, no," he says, "I'm not getting up until he says so." I guess I put the fear of Christ in him. But the cops finally got him out of there. Duane, who was working the counter, could have stopped that fight before it even got started. He wasn't doing a thing—just standing there a-looking.

Ah, them son-of-a-guns just think they can tear people's property up, do what they want to do and you're supposed to like it. So maybe that brother will think twice next time before tearing things up and stomping someone.

## Any Loons?

People would come in the store and ask the same questions, such as, "Any loons? Where's the loons?"

"Well, some of them are sitting there in the back bar and some of them are over there in the campground."

Another one was how deep the lake was.

"You can stand up and drink," Don Schultz told them.

# Suicide Cuts

Roy Sealander (a good-looking, square-cut, middle-aged man) used to come fishing at the lake. He'd leave his home in Canyonville and wife, who was a city judge, and come up just about every weekend during the summer. He worked for the Canyonville garbage collector and drove the truck. I think he got hurt on that job, got his knee smashed up. When he came fishing he drove a pink Lincoln and I mean pink. Then he bought a Dodge pickup and pulled a travel trailer behind and we were stuck with him. Just a regular nuisance. He wasn't so bad until he'd get his snoot full of that vodka, then he was impossible. We had him all summer. That's when he decided he was going to cut wood and sell it to the campers.

This guy, I forget the guy's name he had staying with him there, one of his drunken buddies, came down there to the store and he says, "Better come up there," he says, "I don't know nothing about falling trees, but I don't think Roy's doing it right." He was cutting alders. So I come up and I see what he was doing, he was making a saw cut in the front, and then he was going around back to the other side and cutting there and all around and the damned thing could just fall wherever it wanted to fall. So I picked up the saw and went over there to fall one of the bigger ones. I made a face in it, shut the saw off and was going to tell them to get out of the way, and I didn't have to tell 'em. Ol' Sealander was hollering to his friend, "Jesus Christ, let's get out of here, he's put one of them suicide cuts in it." With a face, yeah. They were leaving out of the country when I fell the tree. And I kept a-falling them. Got enough down to keep them working for a few days so he wouldn't kill himself. Boy, he's lucky he didn't do that to one of them bigger ones.

It would have barber-chaired on him. The little ones had barber-chaired but they weren't split up very high.

He stayed with us for ten or fifteen years, and always liked to fish. Out of the lake he caught bass, cocanee, rainbow trout, cut throat, blue gill, and cat fish. He fished off the dock and fought with the game wardens. He'd tie a rock on the end of a line and put it in the water and let the rock sit on the bottom, then he'd get another pole out and fish with that one. A game warden would come along and think he was fishing with two poles. He'd look things over and say something like, "Well, what you think we're doing here?" Then the warden would pull up that first line and there would be that rock tied on the end of it and he wasn't happy with it, you could tell by his expression. Then Roy Boy would laugh and cuss him out. Then the warden would really look over Sealander's other one good, see what he could find there.

One time Sealander was fishing on the creek bank. He was right there alongside the Loon Lake Road with that open bottle. The Sheriff, Bob Migas, stopped to tell him and his buddy there they'd have to move. Ol' Sealander threw him in the creek. That was a mistake. Migas took him down and put him in jail, the buddy, too. They had to face the judge; Sealander had to face the judge when he got home, too.

# Fight Over a Pool Game

The pool table—I wouldn't have one when I owned Duckett's Resort—starts lots of fights.

One time at the Rainbow Tavern, my brother, Leonard, and I were having a drink. His wife and mine were out shopping; it was Christmas Eve.

I went to the "head" in the back. On the way back out, Harold "Dutch" Johnson was playing pool with another guy.

I said to Harold, "Better be careful—that guy's going to take your money."

Something to that effect. I didn't know the guy at all. They had four or five dollars there, they must have been betting.

I went over and sat at the bar. After a while, "Whop!" Somebody hit me up back of the head. I turned around. It was the guy Harold had been playing pool with.

I said, "Well, you son-of-a-bitch, if that's as hard as you can hit, you're in trouble."

I had seen a star or two and that's about it. I got ahold of him and off toward the restaurant we went. I got him bent back across the lunch counter, I was knocking him the whole way, and that was as far as he could go—working him over.

About that time a brother and an uncle and a couple of cross-eyed cousins got in the fight. Leonard was pounding on some of them, "Dutch" was taking them on, too. That was one big fight. A couple of them were unconscious on the floor when the bartender and other customers got it broken up.

About that time Althea and Audrey came in.

Althea says, "What's going on here?"

They were mopping up blood all over the floor.

252

Mickey, the bartender, said, "Some guy hit Lloyd and made him mad."

The uncle ran the Eagles—all the Oakies went back there to their little hidey hole.

Leonard and Denny Jackson and Cliff Ammons and half a dozen guys that got in the tail end of it there said, "Well, if those guys want to fight, we've got even numbers here, let's just see how they can fight."

The Eagles said, "Oh no, we'll call the cops!"

We said, "No, you already called the cops—we haven't done nothing yet." Boy, they were nervous and gave us free drinks.

That might have been the reason that guy hit me. He'd lost the pool game to Dutch Johnson. That's why I never let a pool table in the place when I owned it—just too many poor losers.

## "What Good Are The Cops?"

Reading an article about cops not wanting store owners to have guns, Lloyd asked, "What good are the cops? Those riots in Los Angeles proved that."

"Yeah," said Benny, "Like the time in Reedsport when the hippies and the loggers were getting into it in the Waterfront Tavern. The cops were too scared to even come in. They just stood outside and waited for them to come out, then arrested them. Out of thirty-six pool sticks, only two weren't broken, and the pool tables were all covered in blood. That was one time when even the fishermen stepped in to help the loggers, and half of them have long hair. But even they didn't like the hippies."

# Deer Caught in the Fence

Damned choker setter was riding with me one day in the log truck. We hit a deer. The deer ran and got its head caught in a hog wire fence. (Hog wire is heavy woven-wire fence with squares about six inches big at the top going down to smaller at the bottom.) The choker setter ran over and was going to get him out of that fence. He was going to cut his throat. That damned guy didn't have any pants left when the deer got done with him—the hooves, you know, they really cut.

I jumped out of the log truck and got the cheater bar you tighten the chains with and ran up there and whopped that deer on the back of the head. And there it was. I had to cut the deer out of the fence by cutting that hog wire and take that guy back to town. Took the deer right then, too. The choker setter forgot that even though the deer had his head caught in the fence, he still had feet left. That guy got a hold of something he couldn't get loose of.

# Cement Contractor Boxes Long Hairs

Charlie Holmes: "I know a fella that would stop by the side of the road and kick the B'Jesus out of them. He was a cement contractor and I used to work with him. First time I saw him do this, I got to work a different way rather than ride any more with him.

"But he sure had a good boxing style that was impressive. He knocked one unconscious and then the next and there was two of them and only one of him!

"People don't realize how strongly a cement contractor feels about this state being infiltrated with hippies. This guy was about as square as they come."

# Flood at Duckett's Resort
## As Told by Benny Shadley

We had a flood down there. My cabin was Number Four, second farthest one from the lake, that's why I say "down there" to where the lake was. Ours and Number Three, furthest from the lake, were the only ones that didn't have water in them. Old Bucket Mouth and I were running off a batch of whiskey in a pressure cooker. You're supposed to use regular corn, all we had was cornmeal.

Down closer to the lake, the Mexican tree planters were leaving their cabin. A boat had been tied up there to their cabin for their convenience to get out if they had to with the water getting high and all. Well, they got in that boat and they couldn't paddle, they couldn't row nor nothing else. They were in the trees over there where the current had pushed them, caught up in the bushes. Don Cookston and Duke went out in another boat and retrieved them. About every boat in the place was flooded. The bar was floating around. Lloyd and Althea were in the house.

Just a picture of wintertime in Oregon's beautiful vacationland.

# Shetland Pony Sold as Elk Meat

My cousin Sylvia's husband, Ralph Leadford, sold an elk for $200 to a man. It turned out to be a Shetland pony he bought and butchered. He got the pony from someone who wanted to get rid of him down here on the Umpqua River.

The receivers of the meat were older people; I doubt they ever knew the difference; maybe they never had eaten elk meat before.

# Hippies Thumbing on the Road

The log truck driver, Terry Gates, has been known to run right at them—the hippies would dive for the brush, but he'd get their luggage.

Another gravel truck driver's been known to straddle the rubber dividers and open his trailer belly dump at them when he went by. Of course, he wouldn't dare do this with a full load of gravel—that's all he hauled with his dump truck and trailer. If the truck and trailer were empty, just the sound of the air-operated dump gates—a "Whoosh!"—was enough to scare them. Also any leftover gravel that sticks in the bottom would be knocked loose and hit the pavement.

As someone riding with him attested, "Just like a row of pebbles flying out like this. . ." his arms flinging out to the side.

# Shit Happens

A hippie with a tee shirt which read across the back "Shit Happens," was in the Loon Lake Lodge.

I said, "Oh, my God, it did. Here's a big pile of it right here!" pointing at the guy.

# Bert Shipey

Bert Shipey didn't like everybody. He liked me.

When he was down at the hospital, he wouldn't let the doctors do anything. They wanted to do something and he wouldn't let them. They had to come get me—way out in the woods—to go to Lower Umpqua Hospital.

"What's going on, Bert?" I asked him.

"Egh!" he growled, "What do you think of this?"

"I think you'd better let them help you here, not be quite so ornery!"

It wasn't long after that I think Bertie must have been dying or close to it. Something finally busted inside of him. We were right there going up Schofield Hill, taking him to the hospital when he says, "I never seen such beautiful lights."

Christmas Eve it was, too. We had another guy riding into town with us and he says, "Holy Christ, let me out!"

Bert wanted to know if we'd seen them, which we hadn't. He'd seen them up in the sky. Said he'd never seen them before. With Bert saying that I would believe him.

Bert's parents owned 160 acres in the middle of Portland. Bert and his brother, when real young men, went down around Kirby in the Rogue River area and shot Chinamen and took their gold.

Then he was the handyman in a Coos Bay house of ill repute for many years. He did all the repairs to the building.

He could do anything—build a radio, electrical tester, an electrical converter—AC to twelve volts. He made a lathe and made lamp bases, candle holders, bowls; he did all the repairs of all kinds for many years here at the resort to the buildings and boats. He made cabinets and chest of drawers, end tables; all the hinges were home-made, too.

He never married, never talked much, just kind of grunted. After shooting Chinamen, isn't it something someone like this could be catching a glimpse of Heaven by seeing those beautiful lights up in the sky? We buried him in the Scottsburg Cemetery.

When they buried Clarence Wheeler in the Scottsburg Cemetery they put him right next to Harold Faircloth. Alive, these two men fought every time they saw each other. Buried side by side the ground is probably rumbling under there with those two fighting each other.

Maybe they saw blue lights, too, and got over their differences.

# Radio Repaired

I had a top-of-the-line radio in the resort. It was a home-base, permanent-type Citizen's Band radio that set right in the house. We had it mainly for fire protection; we could talk to all the lookouts. It went kaput.

I let a damned ol' insurance agent have it. He said he had a hobby of fixing those things in his spare time and, like a damned fool, I let him take it. He said he'd have it back in a week.

Probably ten days later we had to go to Coos Bay for our supplies so I started inquiring about it. I called his area supervisor, also in Coos Bay I think, and found out he had been transferred to Coeur d'Alene, Idaho. He must have known he was going to be transferred and reasoned that if he took the radio we'd never see him again, and he'd never see us. He probably never had any hobby of fixing them either; oh, hell no, he just figured he'd glom on to something.

That radio was our communication—a lot of people knew we had it. There were no phones in the valley until much later, in 1977. People would relay messages to us and make reservations. I'd talk to Bud Parker, up the valley, he had one, and Grandma Parker had one. So I bought a radio telephone probably the same day that I called the insurance company in Coos Bay. We couldn't go without it, that was the peak of our season, up 'til Labor Day.

After Labor Day it just so happened I was going moose hunting up in Canada and Coeur d'Alene, Idaho, was right on the way. The Coos Bay guy gave me his address—ha, ha, shoot, he told me right where he lived.

Yes, Coeur d'Alene was right on the route. That same morning a moose was in downtown Coeur d'Alene; they were all talking about it, but we didn't see it, we just missed it.

I found the insurance agent's house. I knocked on the door—boy, was he surprised to see me. First thing I did was punch him in the nose. Then we went to talking about the radio. He didn't talk much, the sorry excuse for an agent. He'd never fixed it. Old grandpa intervened there pretty quickly; grandpa wasn't too old, either!

Grandpa said, "What's going on here?"

I told him, "You got a thief here. He's got a radio that belongs to me." He told the dolt standing there holding his nose, "You got the man's radio, you'd better go get it."

Then he inquired of me, "You come clear from the Oregon Coast to get this radio?"

I said, "Yeah, I'd chase a thief to the end of the world! He's lucky I don't shoot him."

(He never knew his house was right on my way to Alberta, Canada.) Sometimes I took some of the men that worked for me moose hunting in the fall—kind of a bonus for working. Such was the case this time. I had three real characters. Riley Finch, Kenny Spencer and Clarence Wheeler were out of the car and waiting for me when I came walking back with the radio.

They said, "Let's get out of here—they'll have you in jail."

"They won't have *me* in jail, that insurance agent just ran into the door as it opened. *Door* hit him in the face."

The old grandpa didn't look too honest himself so maybe it taught him a lesson, too. The grandson, after that correction of his sticky-fingered ways, might have jumped sideways everytime he saw a radio. I bet he doesn't proclaim to be a radio repairman anymore either.

You know, I learned something there I didn't know. And that is that this particular insurance company paroles men out of prison and makes insurance men out of them; that's where you get all them crooked, thieving potlickers.

261

We had insurance, and a lot of it, with this big national company. We had an encounter with the agent that replaced the one that transferred to Coeur d'Alene. He was a kind of playboy type. He spent a lot of time at the boat dock and just playing around. He confided in Helen, who worked for us, that he was on parole and had to be careful with his drinking. After hearing that I quit those guys and got a different company. Who knows what *this* guy was going to pull?

One thing without the CB radio, the resort had better communication with the new radio telephone we had bought. It hooked right up to an operator in Coos Bay.

We had what they call an "answering service"—she would plug us right into the telephone company. They reached us through her, too. We could talk all over the country, all over the world if we wanted to.

*Ken, me, Clarence and Riley on our way*
*to the moose hunt.*

# Bucking Timber on Crutches

Mutt Williams, relative of "Rattlesnake" Williams of Reedsport, was on crutches and used to go out and buck timber. Crutches didn't slow Mutt down. A logging accident had left him permanently on crutches. I have seen him out there a-buckin' up out of Carlton, Yamhill, Gaston, up in that country. He had his old crosscut saw and got around in the woods just fine working like anybody else. Nowadays the state wouldn't let you with all their rules and regulations. He'd be called handicapped. He ran Cat a lot; had a place up there to lay his crutches.

And run hounds—he could get over a barbed wire fence while you were still wondering how to go about it. He pole-vaulted right over them with his crutches. Like many loggers, when he wasn't working in the woods, he was hunting or fishing in them.

# The Trap Line

I had a tent pitched out in the woods. I had canned food in there, a little air-tight heater, some sleeping bags, and a gas lantern. I left it there from elk season in the fall to when trapping season came along in the dead of the winter. Sometimes I'd spend a night there, depends what, if I had a lot of skinning to do, I'd just stay right there all night and do it—that way I wouldn't have to pack out the carcasses.

I had a ridge I trapped out—went almost to the headwaters of the Millicoma. One day I came back up the ridge to my camp. I didn't see the jeep; but I saw this guy—looked like he had the damned gas lantern—then I heard them talking. So I speeded up—they were leaving just about the time I got there. I got the license number off of their jeep as it pulled away. I would have shot the weasely jokers, but I had a rain jacket on, all zippered up, and shirt under there and the pistol in a sholster (shoulder holster), so by the time I got to it they were out of sight.

I kept watching jeeps for a license number. A month or two later, I came in and that jeep was parked out in front of the resort. I asked who owned it and here it was our, by golly, propane guy. Bud Parker told me ahead of time he thought that's who it was. I don't know how he knew—I guess the propane guy had come by and seen Bud and talked about where he had been or something.

I went in the tavern there and asked, "Who owns that jeep?"

"Oh, that's mine."

I said, "Oh, great, when are you going to bring back my camping gear you stole?"

"Camping gear? We never stole no camping gear."

"Well," I ventured, "If you didn't, you loaned your jeep to somebody else."

"It wasn't my jeep."

"Oh, yes, it was. I wrote down your license number on a Copenhagen can with a .22 bullet."

"Huh, hey, honest, Squint, honest!"

I says, "You're a pot-licking liar and you know my name. You call me 'Squint' again, I'll knock you flat of your ass."

"Oh, honest, no, I never, Squint."

"Okay," boom, I just skidded him down under them stools. I picked him up by the shirt and whacked him a time or two. They must have bought that six pack to go or something; that's when his ol' gal started hitting me on the head with the beer bottles. I think someone pushed her out of the tavern part of the store and got her out of there. I think Larry, my nephew, was there and was pulling me off of him.

Those were good sleeping bags, too, and the scoundrel took my Beanie Weenies, too (little canned wienies)—all the goodies. Wish I'd got there a little quicker when he was taking all that stuff from the camp or he'd had a little more than a sore jaw—a little hot lead in the ass.

He didn't deliver propane to us after that; somebody else did from the same company.

That was a dandy trap line. I stocked the camp during elk season. Then as soon as trapping season came along, I'd go across the lake in a boat. I'd go up the main ridge between Little and Big Salander Creeks. I'd go up to the old CC road and there, after about a quarter mile, was the camp and tent.

I'd set all my traps out on the ridges. I'd go down one ridge to the bluffs and walk back. Then I'd walk to the old CC road—had traps set out all along there, check them and come back. Then on another ridge I got almost to the "old cedar cabin," as everyone called it—that's where I could almost put my feet in the headwaters of the west fork of the Millicoma River. I'd hike in there and out. That was the trouble with it up there—had to walk back each time, so I generally spent the night in the tent. The last set of traps I'd check were along a ridge from which I'd drop down on to a Cat road now known as the "1000 Road," and I'd walk home from there.

I caught bobcat in them damned marten sets, and you couldn't even give them sons-of-bitches away. Just shoot them and get them away from your traps.

Marten were going for twenty-five dollars. I was trapping them for the Museum of Natural History. They wanted the skulls for the brain surgeons to study. They did this under Dr. Murray Johnson of the Puget Sound College. He had written me a letter—must have gotten my trapper's license number or something, like the buyers who are always sending you a lot of stuff. So I sent the skulls up to that college in Tacoma, Washington.

I had to measure each one in certain ways—from the tip of the tail to the tip of the nose, the length of the tail, the length of the body, and the elevation of where I got each one. Also you didn't dare have damaged any of the membranes of the brain in the skull.

You didn't have to shoot them. Marten were always dead in the trap—must have heart attacks or work themselves to death. You could tell they fought the trap quite a bit.

Old Carl Collins said that in all his years of trapping he'd never seen a marten alive in a trap. So the next time I went out, it just so happened there was a marten looking at me, just calm as can be. So I just untied the trap from the tree and put marten and trap both in my packsack. I got down to the resort and told Carl, "Here's your marten!"

"Gosh darn you, Keeland," he growled, "If I said there were no elephants out there, you'd find one and bring it back. Now get on out of here!"

With all the brain surgery going on nowadays, maybe my trapping did some good; me and the little marten might have helped out somewhere along the line.

# Keeping Bob Off the Power Pole

One time right before the Fourth of July weekend, the Douglas Electric Cooperative truck shows up.

Their long, tall, skinny worker named Bob starts putting on the spurs to go up the pole and switch off the electric to the resort! He claimed he had orders to terminate the electric because we hadn't paid the bill. That was all nonsense because I had the cancelled check from Douglas Electric from the last month's bill.

I told Bob, "You go up that pole and I'll get the .348 and knock you out of there!"

I called and talked to a woman at Douglas Electric and told her I want to talk to Harold Bracken.

"Why, that's the manager!" she exclaimed.

I says, "Well, who the hell you think I want to talk to?"

The boss of the Douglas Electric apologized. The bill had gotten mixed up and our payment accredited to somebody else. I knew him just as well as anybody; he used to come over here fishing and stayed in Cabin 6. He even tried to get me to go on the Board of Commissioners of the Co-op.

I wouldn't have hit Bob up there, just fired a shot below into the pole—the sound and the percussion of it would have brought him out of there.

# Lady Bird's Program

When Lyndon Baines Johnson was President, his wife, Lady Bird Johnson wanted to beautify our highways. She thought things would look better without any signs, advertising or billboards, and had them torn down all across the nation.

Oregon State Highway 38 became classified as a Scenic Highway and all private signs had to come down, including ours. We got a letter from the State Highway Department giving us no alternative—we either tore them down or they were going to tear them down and bill us. These signs were beautifully and professionally made, in good repair and a help to us. They let travelers know what kind of business we had off the highway. One read, "Duckett's Beautiful LOON LAKE RESORT & PICNIC GROUNDS. FISHERMANS—VACATIONERS—PARADISE. BOATS, MOTORS. 15 MILES—LEFT AT MILL CREEK BRIDGE." The other two were about the same. After people made that left they had to go nine windy miles up Mill Creek on County Road 3 to reach the lake, then three miles to the resort.

I wrote back to the highway department that these signs let travelers know our business was off the main highway and I refused to remove them. More letters were exchanged, including registered letters at the end. They won out and I tore them down.

The first one was up on a curve at Weatherly Creek. That was a beautiful location for people to see as they slowed down. It was a tin sign eight feet tall by sixteen feet long, framed with wood, with a great big jumping bass on it. That one came down. We always paid Mr. Weatherly something every year to have it there.

Then we had one right inside the Loon Lake Road. That one was a great big one, but they could see it from the highway, so we had to take it down, too.

We had another one across from Boye's Canyon in that field—we paid Mr. Boye by the year to have it there—had to take that one down.

When we sold the resort to Dave and B. J. McGruder, the second short term buyers, they changed the name to Fish Haven. We could have stopped them but we wanted to be cooperative. If those three big signs had stayed up, Dave and B. J. probably wouldn't have changed the name, not wanting to spend the money for the name being repainted on all three. The Fish Haven sign is still on the store twenty years later, but many people yet call it Duckett's.

Back to Lady Bird's day, after we got them torn down—see, you had to have a license on them—I started writing the son-of-a-bitches in Salem. I wanted a refund. They still had a few years to go and still would have been there if they hadn't have forced me to tear 'em down. By God, they finally sent us a refund. I bet a lot of people didn't get theirs, probably didn't even think of it. They were about as mad as I was and didn't want anything to do with the state. That was just the starting of all the control we've got nowadays. That must be when the Burma Shave signs had to go then, too.

We had some little bitty guys out on the Loon Lake County Road, too. Each one had a catchy phrase. I don't remember what they were, but under them was the miles you were from Duckett's. One of 'em used to say, "Duckett's," so many miles. And there was one closer, at Camp Creek, which read, "5 Miles to Duckett's." And there was one right over there by the first cabin—"Duckett's, At Last!" We lost most of these signs when the county widened the road. They got pushed over and bulldozed. We didn't bitch about *them*, the county was helping us, getting a good hard road in to us.

270

Since that time, in the late 1960's, the government has put up a lot of signs along the "scenic" State Highways 101 and 38 and the Loon Lake County Road #3. The Bureau of Land Management has built a big and a little campground at the lake, and put up signs to advertise and direct travelers to these campgrounds. This is something that anyone in private enterprise still cannot do to this day—advertise on the highway.

My wife made signs for Loon Lake Lodge and Fish Haven Resort which were put up on Elliott State Forest land but were torn down either by the State Highway Department or BLM. BLM guys took down our Coca Cola sign, which also said Duckett's—4 miles. We had put that one up at the Cougar Pass logging road, which doesn't belong to BLM, but Elliott State Forest or International Paper, one of the two. The kids that were working there at BLM told me they tore our sign down. They told me where they threw it. That one knew me; he was from Carlton, his folks owned a big dairy right out of town. This removing of our sign was probably ordered by that old Russian son-of-a-bitch, Valda Marulof, that was managing the whole works down there in Coos Bay.

Recently, my wife Ellen counted forty signs, put up by county, state and federal agencies. Within thirty miles of home, she started writing them down, starting two miles south of Winchester Bay and ending at our home here behind Fish Haven Resort. None of these signs have as much originality, color, good lettering or general snap as the old private ones. Not much purpose either, only that the government is competing with private campgrounds and announcing some private land they've confiscated and now spend money on. None of these government signs say anything that anyone wants to hear, either, except maybe the Elliott State Forest sign. This model forest is logged on a sustained yield basis, bringing in an annual revenue for the state, forever. This means about ten million dollars a year, a hundred percent of which goes to the public schools. So, not including traffic signs, just traveling in one direction, here's what's on 101, 38 and County Road 3 in a forty-five minute drive from home:

1. Douglas County
2. Umpqua Soil and Water District
3. Scenic Byway
4. This lake provides. . .
5. Umpqua Light House/Oregon State Parks
6. Viewpoint
7. Dune Country—Camping, RTV, rentals
8. Salmon Harbor Recreation Area
9. Oregon Coast Bike Route
10. Sportsmen's Cannery
11. Salmon Harbor Recreation Area
12. Discovery Drive Bike Route
13. Scenic Bikeway
14. Camping   1/4 mile
15. Camping

In city limits of Winchester Bay and Reedsport, signs on places of business, then back to:
16. Oregon Dunes National Recreation Area
17. Umpqua Discovery Center,
    Dean Creek Elk Viewing Area use Highway 38
18. Entering Dean Creek Area
19. Approaching Elk Viewing
20. Elk Viewing next four miles
21. Adopt a highway Verla Black
22. Elk View Point 1/4 mile
23. Dean Creek, Elk Viewing Area
24. No hunting/trespassing
25. Elk Viewing Area
26. No Parking

272

27. No Parking
28. No Parking
29. No Parking
30. Elk Viewing
31. Oregon State Parks 1/4 mile ahead
32. Historical Marker
33. Umpqua Wayside
34. Umpqua Wayside
35. Umpqua Wayside
36. Loon Lake Resort Area 1/4 mile
37. Loon Lake
38. Loon Lake Recreation Area
    BLM   Day Use/Campground 7 miles
39. Elliott State Forest
40. Loon Lake Recreation Site
41. Adopted Highway next 5 miles-Grange
42. Smokey the Bear
43. East Shore campground-BLM


Salbasgeon Inn (the old Echo Resort), Loon Lake Lodge and Fish Haven Resort do have signs on their own premises, but no where else. There's about forty environmental, socialistic, offensive-looking government signs one way, and the same amount going back. So eighty little green signs have replaced ten or fifteen bigger colorful ones. These private signs, made by local businessmen and women, were unique, informative and tailor-made to the needs of the business, real works of art. We can applaud them who are still running their establishments without the benefit of roadside advertising.

After Althea and I were running the resort, I engaged Tom Stevenson to help me clear out the brush and repair our sign at Weatherly Creek. It was leaning 'way back from being totally overgrown and the wooden posts had rotted at the ground. We removed the brush and berries and put new underpinnings under it. Originally Bert Shipey had made the sign, painted it and put it up, but the paint had flaked off and it was looking pretty scabby.

We hired a sign maker to repaint it. He was just passing through, doing some work over in Roseburg. He painted it off of ladders right where it stood.

Note the bullet holes in the picture of the fish. Our sign just couldn't be resisted by all, screwballs and everybody. The potshotter had a fairly tight pattern to the left which he corrected with his next rounds and brought up higher and to the right to hit the bass. The elongation of the holes shows he was probably shooting at an angle on the same side of the road as the sign. Probably didn't want to shoot across the road and get in trouble with the police. He would have wished "trouble with the police" if I'd have caught him.

The ol' advertisement brought business. A lot of people commented on it, they had seen our sign.

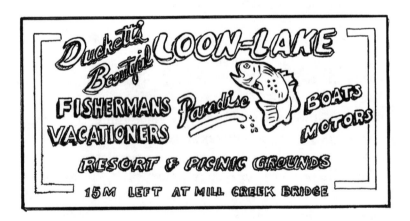

# Flue Fire

Vernon Bickford lived in his trailer which was located on a wooded side hill overlooking our house. One time he ran down into our living room and said, "Ah, Ah, Ah, Ah, Ah. . . ."

Pointing up and pointing up. Then he run back out and Althea was outside trying to understand him but couldn't make out a word. He just kept pointing and saying, "F. . . f. . .f. . .f. . . ."

When he would get excited, he couldn't say a word. This time he couldn't even talk. Finally, Althea said, "Well Bick, for Pete's sake, just spit it out."

"F. . .f. . .f. . .flue fire!"

Black smoke and flames were pouring out of the brick chimney on top of our house.

Somebody was visiting. I think it was Harold and Donna Cushing. I'd cut the ends off the creosoted pilings where I was building the shop. Whoever it was visiting brought one of them down here and threw it in the fire, then closed up the doors of the insert. That sent the flames shooting four or five feet out of the chimney and cinders a-flying. I guess we put some wet sacks in the stove and shut 'er up to contain it. Good thing we had Bick around to help watch the place.

# Anti-Loggers

Clare Allan's father shot his employee for stealing cream off the milk. It wouldn't have been so bad but the man was given all the milk he and his family needed. No court case was ever held. The employee was probably selling the cream. In those days people's main income was from selling cream and milk. This shows that Clare came from stock of people that didn't put up with thieves.

Clare Allan and his logging crew arrived at his logging show out of Eugene early one morning. They drove up in the crummy and could see by the tracks in the dew someone had been up there before them. They got up to the gate and there was a car parked there all locked up blocking the road. They pulled the car out of the way with the pickup and unlocked the gate. As they were opening it, a voice yelled down at them from an old grouse ladder (a tree with many, many limbs in it clear to the ground) which was right beside the gate, "You are not cutting any more trees in here!"

Clare couldn't believe his ears, "What?"

"Yeah, you are not cutting any more trees in here. You're all done."

"What?"

"Yeah, that's right," the voice intoned, "You're not taking any more trees, we're taking you to court."

Clare looked up and there was a guy—beard down to here, hair everywhere, and Clare sends a guy to bring the Cat. And then he gets out his chain saw and fires it up. He gets a face cut in the tree, little ol' bushy tree the guy was up in, foot maybe two and a half foot through. Then he starts on the back of her, starts backing it up, the guy is still not coming down. Finally, he has the tree just leaning, like this, when the guy jumps down. As the man is running away, Clare runs after him and grabs him by the back of the hair and spins him around. Then he smacks him around a few times.

Clare says, "Now, you're getting off easy because the bulldozer is on its way. You're lucky I don't bury both you and the car, nobody would know the difference."

"Oh, yes they would," the guy says, "There's two more!"

Clare and his crew look around and sure enough, there's two more up in trees. Clare grabs his saw and runs over to the next one's tree. He didn't have to fall either one; when they saw what happened to their buddy, they came down out of their trees.

Clare figured they'd have to be in court, but nothing was ever said of it.

### Words on a Bumper Sticker
"Hug a logger, you'll never go back to trees."

# Marvin Haskell

On a hot summer's day, with the dock loaded with people, Ol' Marvin Haskell would come for a swim.

He'd go in clothes and all. He'd just go off the dock there and jump in—he could swim like a fish. That was his form of taking a bath. I don't recall him bringing any soap. He was about as dirty when he got out as when he got in, caked on him anyway. The bar oil and power saw gas, sour milk and cow manure never left his clothes entirely.

He enjoyed coming in the store. He'd even come in after his swim—it didn't make him any difference; you'd have to mop up behind him. He never bought anything, maybe a pack of cigarettes and a glass of milk, but others would buy him cookies and things. He was a well liked by everybody and everyone liked hearing his stories told in an Irish brogue and most amazing style.

*Marvin Haskell in 1977*

# Battery Blows Up

I loaned Mr. H. the brush hog, that goes behind the tractor, and, shoot, he took it over to his house and broke it all to hell. Well, when I sent someone, I forgot who it was, over to the house to inquire about it, Mr. H. says, "No, you ain't getting that, I've got a $170 bill against it."

I think all he did was broke some bearings. All he had to do was put in some new bearings. They came back and told me what he said, so I got on the phone and said, "What's the $170 stuff? It was in good shape when you got it, so I'm coming after it."

He says, "If you come, bring the sheriff."

I says, "I don't need a sheriff."

So Bill Connelly, a neighbor and refrigerator repairman, was here; Queery Gary, the gay new resort owner; and Ken Spencer, my trapping partner and helper who lived with us; and I says to them, "Let's go and load that brush hog up."

It took four men to lift it. We go over there and Mr. H. had it hooked up on the back of the tractor.

He says, "Oh, okay, I'll go start the tractor."

Ken and I went around the shed to help him get the tractor started. It had a dead battery. Mr. H. had brought a good battery around to jump start it with. So when he started to jump it, the battery blew up with a "Bang!" Sounded like a gun going off.

Hit him right in the damned face. Boy, we grabbed him and got him to a water faucet and got the battery acid all washed off. Ken and I were dealing with him; but Queery Gary and Connelly were around the other side of the shed and couldn't see what was going on. So when that battery blew up, Queery Gary thought it was a gunshot and asked Bill, "What's that?"

But Bill Connelly told him, "Oh, my God, Ol' Keeland's killed him!"

They didn't wait to find out. They got in Connelly's car and hottailed it out of there. Just spun on out up the loose gravel on that steep, steep driveway.

Mr. H. and I were in a pretty hot argument, I admit. He went back in the house and Ken and I had to load that brush hog on the trailer by ourselves.

# Don't Drive That Pickup!"

Right after my knee replacement, our slightly intoxicated neighbor, Jerry Fredericksen, came visiting us in our new house. I wasn't there, but my wife was. He had walked from his ranch, or the resort, or somewhere, but he was afoot.

After chatting for a while with Althea, he asked if he could use our pickup. Jerry did not have any driver's license. If they caught him driving, drunk, they'd have everything we own.

Althea told him, "Don't take that pickup," but he took it anyway.

He drove it down the driveway to the resort and parked there. When I got the word from Althea he had taken the pickup against her will, I drove down to the resort.

I went in there and said, "What the heck you doing with the pickup? Althea told you to leave it alone!"

I was telling him about it, and he attacked me. That was a mistake he made. Freddie Humphry seen that. He said, "Oh, I know he made a mistake."

He came a-chargin' right at me—gol dang, I guess he was going to flatten me, that's just what he was thinking. He was swinging like a wild man and "smack!" I punched him right through the swinging doors. Right behind the bar is where he went.

Then I took him home after they cleaned his darned head up.

That broke him of the habit of not doing what he's told, around this place anyway. I don't know how Nels did with him up there.

# Pete Stingley Runs the Rainbow

Pete used to go to the bank and take out thirty thousand dollars on a Friday just to cash paychecks. They'd be four deep waiting at the bar to cash their checks—longshoremen and the loggers.

Same thing at Duckett's Resort. We kept about ten or twelve thousand dollars on Fridays, or more than that, to cash loggers' checks. The economy has changed desperately. Now you're lucky to take a $300 check up to the Lodge and have it cashed.

The loggers not only cashed them there but spent them. Vivian Ott, who cooked at the Rainbow for years, remembers Friday nights when the loggers would come in. There was an alley outside and there'd be three fights going on at once. She had a hard time cooking for watching the fights. They'd swing a few blows, then put their arms around each other and be pals and go back in and be the best of friends again. This comradery and boxing went on all night long.

# "It Warrants a Fire"

In the Yukon Territory, a little short retired Army guy and his large wife ran a lodge with a gas pump and grocery store. Althea, George and Jody and I stopped there to fill up the motor home. I think they had some cabins out behind there, the way it looked.

A young man pumped the gas. He came in the store where we all were to tell the wife how much we owed.

That's when the little Army guy come in from doing something and said, "Well. . .I think it warrants a fire!"

His huge wife just came unglued.

"You leave that alone! Just leave the stove alone! I told you not to mess with that stove! We don't need no fire!"

Ol' George sure got a kick out of that—"Well. . .I think it warrants a fire."

I guess it didn't warrant a fire. Crazy ol' woman.

# World Record Grayling

Our daughter and her husband and two boys, Sam and Larry, had lived in Alaska twenty-five years. We were up visiting with our other daughter and her husband, George. George caught a great, big grayling—twenty-seven inches. We ate it. Come to find out, the world's record was twenty-one inches. You would have thought that Sam and Larry, who lived up there all their lives and were real fishing advocates, would have known that. Instead, they just ran around and acted like a bunch of wild Indians.

# The Canadian Wildlife Official

Coming back from Alaska in 1964, we stopped at Hundred Mile House, a town in British Columbia. We had parked the car and when we came back, the car was surrounded by a whole bunch of kids looking at Humpy, our otter, inside. They were tapping on the windows and making him stand up. A large older man was with them and he said, "Is that your car?"

"Yes, that's my car."

"I'm going to have to take that animal."

I thought he was just joking. I didn't believe him.

"Oh, yeah?"

That's when he brought out his badge from the Canadian Fish & Wildlife Department.

I told him, "Wait a minute, I have a permit to have him in the State of Oregon from the Fish & Wildlife. He's had his shots—rabies and everything. We are just traveling through your country. We went through Customs going into Canada, went through Customs going into Alaska, and coming back came through the same B.S."

"Well, that may be all very well, but I can guarantee you that I'm still going to have to take this animal."

"Well, I can guarantee you that you can take him after the fight."

That's when all the kids started clapping.

There was a woman there, too, telling the wildlife official he was crazy.

I told Althea to get in and lock the doors. She got in and one, two, three, four locked all the doors.

He said, "That animal's got to be taken and turned back in the wild."

I told him, "I don't think you have enough help around here for you to take him."

I think he could tell I meant business then and that I was that mad. He said no more and I just went over to the driver's door, Althea unlocked it for me; I got in and we drove off. I was half expecting to be followed by the Canadian Royal Mounted Police, but we made it to the border and through U.S. Customs—not a question was asked. Well, they did ask to see his papers; they always did that. We made it back to home and to Humpy's own little playground—Loon Lake.

# Don't Trifle with Sgt. Preston and the Canadian Royal Mounted Police

Boy, you talk about police brutality! These bleeding hearts down here haven't seen nothing compared to the Canadian Royal Mounted Police! Our policemen ought to take a lesson.

It was in Alberta, Canada, that Clarence Wheeler and I were staying in a bunkhouse out on a ranch. I don't know where in hell Ol' Red Nelson, the Canadian guide, was that night, he wasn't there. Ol' Clarence got pneumonia, couldn't breathe.

He says, "Oh, you got to get me to a doctor."

So I went to Falher, the closest town, drove around and around, the place was dead except for this hotel. I went in there and found out that to get a doctor you have to go to a hospital.

I was just leaving that place and two of those big Royal Mounted Policemen just about bowled me over coming in and I thought, What the hell!. . .They walked over to where three or four men were sitting and told one of them, "Okay, get up, you're coming with us!"

That sucker didn't budge. But when they got done jerking that guy up out of there and slapping him around, he led right along.

I have no idea what the guy had done or what they wanted him for; but boy, they knew who they were after.

# Jehovah's Witnesses

I darned near got slapped and darned near got a divorce, too! When I had the resort, they'd come to the door—you know, they wouldn't come in the store or nothin', they'd come to the living quarters and beat on that gosh darned door. . . . You'd never know who it was, but. . .

This one day Althea and a lady who worked for us went to Coos Bay—supply gettin'. Ol' Ken, guy worked for me, said, "Oh, there goes those Jehovah Witnesses up on the front porch."

I says, "Who are they?"

He says, "Three women."

"I'll run them off forever." I went and opened the door, unzipped and I says, "Which one's first?"

They says, "Oh, no, no, we never came here for that!"

"Well, why not, you might as well." They got back in their car and left. God, when Althea got back from town, Ken told her.

She said, "You didn't do that! To them women?"

"Well, why not?" I don't care if religion gets mixed up in it as long as the joke is good. It's a wonder they didn't hit me over the head with their purses and Bibles.

# Big Bad Indian of the Yukon

Our daughter and son-in-law and family lived up in Ft. Yukon. There they owned and operated the utilities of the town—a diesel generator for electricity, a frozen food locker, the water works, a barge and construction company. Being above the Arctic Circle, it's either one or the other—you come by boat or you come by air. We called from Fairbanks, "Is there anything we can bring?"

"Oh, yes, you can bring a load of whiskey, wine and vodka."

They met us there at the airport with the pickup. We were unloading the pickup at the office.

"Ah, boy. . .how 'bout a drink of that?"

A big 'ol Indian was wanting the hootch we'd brought in. He kept buggin' and finally came across with, "I'm the toughest son-of-a-bitch this side of the Yukon."

I told him, "You *were* the toughest son-of-a-bitch. I'm here now."

He shuffled away. Figured he wasn't going to get no wine. That's what he was wanting to start with.

When the liquor store did open, it was open for just one hour. They would be lined up for three or four hours before, sitting outside for that long, on a big ol' tree that floated in there from somewhere. They were comical to watch. It wouldn't be long before there'd be fist fights; those Athabascan Indians weren't striking much or many blows, just swinging as they staggered backwards. It was a regular three-ring circus to watch them.

# Protesters in Eugene

When Althea was in the Sacred Heart Hospital, we were down by the University of Oregon. They had it blocked off, a certain street there, so the damned Vietnam protesting could go on. Babe Pardee was with me.

The students put their hands on the station wagon and started rocking it. They had already turned over a little Volvo in front of us. They had gotten lost in the town of Eugene, too, and gotten on to that blocked-off street. The students rocked and rocked until the little Volvo rolled over on its side. There was a man and a woman in there.

The students were really starting to rock us good.

I had the .22 Ruger under the seat. I just stuck that under the fellow's chin who was by the door rocking the station wagon.

I said, "Hey, you don't want to turn this one over. . . ."

He calls to his friends, "Hey, he's got a rod!"

We got the hell out of there 'cause here came the damned cops.

Dirty scoundrels—didn't want to go to war but raise hell with everybody.

You'd think they'd go to school to study instead of to turn cars over.

# Practical Jokes

Elaine Fullhart, Ash Valley's mail carrier at one time, liked to bake. She would bring big plates of divinity or fudge or cookies to the Post Office.

One April Fool's Day she made cookies and put cotton that had been soaked in red pepper in them. The policeman, Walt Miller, ate one and got that hot cotton stuck away back in his mouth where there was a tooth with a hole in it. It about drove him wild stuck in that tooth back there. He was jumping around before he got it out.

She used to put strips of flannel in her husband's pancakes.

Bob Fullhart, her son and owner of Fullhart Insurance Company said, "She pulled that on Dad a number of times."

# Mrs. Haskell Speaks

One time the store was just packed as it always was. Margie Haskell comes in there. Bud Parker sitting having a cup of coffee says, "Margie, I wish you and Marve would get things settled between you. We're logging and I can't get him to come out before ten o'clock in the morning."

Margie replies, "Well, I won't come back until he promises me he won't have any more affairs with any of those cows."

All kinds of people were in there. The place just roared!

# Free Trip to Hawaii

In the years 1973 and 1974, Althea and I won the award for the most Blitz beer sold out of one establishment in the state. This didn't include a big chain like Safeway stores, but just stores and businesses, bars, lounges—any one account.

The Blitz Company paid for a week in Hawaii. That got us over there, and we spent a month. I got to see Maui, where I had trained with the Fourth Marine Division before being shipped overseas in World War II.

We would have won it the next year if we wouldn't have sold the resort about the middle of summer. The new owners didn't sell much beer, food or anything else. Those potlickers didn't know how to treat their customers and let it go to pieces real quick.

We also had the oldest liquor license in the State of Oregon when we sold in 1975. Our liquor license had been issued in 1934 right after liquor came back into the state and remained under the same name until we sold. Then the ownership of the oldest liquor license went to Bill and Millie Arrante who owned the hotel in Kerby, Oregon.

# U.S.S. *ARIZONA* Memorial

You can see part of the Battleship *Arizona* sticking up there out of the water. They've got a platform built all around that thing, and a big billboard there telling the names of all the sailors and the marines that were on it. Part of it is chained off—a smokestack or gun turret or something sticks up there out of the water. You pay for a tour, which includes a boat to take you out there. The whole thing's a government park.

I was there with my wife, Althea. Japanese tourists were out there pointing and laughing and jabbering in their lingo. They seemed to think it was pretty funny.

I told them, "Knock that laughing off or you'll be down there on the bottom, too. Got anything to say, say it so the rest of us can know what you're saying."

"Amen," said another American tourist and a few people clapped their hands in agreement. The Japanese quieted right down.

That's when those young government park rangers came swarming around—they thought we were going to really get things stirred up out there.

I said to one, "You got a problem?"

"Oh no, but I just hope everything is all right over here."
"Damned right it is. Everyone is showing a little more respect now for what they're looking at."

# Cane Whops the Coyote in Hawaii

Althea and I were on our free trip to Hawaii in 1976. One night in a Holiday Inn motel in Maui we were asleep in our beds. I heard our door unlock from the outside. There was a chain barring the door from the inside, too. We had locked that. "Click, click, click." It was the click of that door that woke me up. I had my aluminum cane laying right there by the bed. That hand came in. He was in there reaching, trying to get that inside chain undone. I just eased out of bed and picked up the cane. Pretty quick that hand came in again and fiddled around with the chain. I just, "Kawhap!" came down with all my might on the hand. A great big "Ow!" was all that came out. By the time I got the chain undone, he had gotten away down the hallway.

The next morning I told the motel clerks what happened.

I told them, "You've got a burglar around here. He'll be easy found. All you got to do is look for someone with a messed up hand or wrist."

They said, "Oh boy, we'll be right over there and change the lock on the door. We've had this trouble before and other complaints. We think we know which of our former employees is a thief; he's buddy-buddies with another one. He uses his master key to get into the rooms at night."

I said, "This aluminum cane I use is also what I use to knock them coyotes out with when they're in the trap. So I got another coyote, but I didn't get him stopped. I almost knocked the chain off the wall, too."

The woman manager comes to the desk and says, "God, oh thanks, I think I know who's doing it." They all agreed they'd keep an eye out for the sore-handed guy.

The next morning about five o'clock, just at daybreak, all hell broke loose. I heard all kinds of commotion going on and half a dozen  police cars. They  brought  him out of the hotel room he stayed in. Was he Hawaiian? Oh hell, no. He was a long hair. By the way, he had his hand all taped up, too, when they led him out of there all cuffed up. He was howling the handcuff was hurting that hand I'll tell ya. He was begging for them to release that.

I should have let him get his gol-dern head stuck in there. Then I'd a-had him. Boy, the handle end of that ol' cane is hard.

It's really an aluminum crutch the V.A. gave me after my first knee joint replacement. I broke off the little horseshoe shape you're supposed to put your forearm in—too hard on the arm. It's shaped like a tall "T." When I really want to hit something with it, I grab the walking end of it, and it'll deliver a powerful blow. Used right side up it's a pretty good machete getting through the blackberries. It really chops them back, chop, chop; you'd be surprised.

Boy, you couldn't believe the stuff coming out of the room where he stayed—cowboy boots by the pairs, luggage, briefcases, radios, cameras, golf clubs, "gee-tars," boxes of stuff; seemed they were a half an hour taking everything out of there. They put it in the vans and paddy wagons. They even had to put it in the trunks and back seats of the police cars.

We sure had a lot of excitement on our free trip to Hawaii, especially the big "ee-ow!" in the middle of the night!

# No Suffering with Aluminum Cane

You wouldn't want to tell the environmentalists how I go about killing those coyotes—oh God, they'd think that's awful.

How do you do it?

Oh, heck, you just hit them on their nose and boy, they're down. They can't take that. They are down for the count—knocked out. It doesn't take much of a blow—just a little ol' stick will do it. I carry that aluminum cane on my trap line just for that reason.

Then you just put your foot and step right behind their front shoulder. Just put the pressure and kind of push ahead, I do put some weight on it and my foot crushes their heart. Kills them instantly, no suffering.

Some old-timer wised me up to that. It might have been Kayo Mullins, the ol' government trapper, I used to go with him.

The coyote never knew what hit him, you don't have blood on the pelt you got to wash out, and there's no hole in the pelt.

# Coyotes

You'd better believe coyotes are smart. I've had 'em turn my trap over on its back and then shit right on top of it. When I saw that I went down to Winchester Bay and got several carcasses of bottom fish—tails, heads and rib cage, enough to make a stink, what's left over after they make a fillet. Then I went up on a hill and made a whole pile of it pretty close to the same area where she'd done a number on my trap—then I found about three trails and put a trap in each one. That stinky fish would lure her in. I hoped a deer or elk wouldn't come along and spring them, they just shake 'em off and keep on a-going, but they do leave your trap sprung.

I caught the coyote by the last foot she had. Front foot—she'd been digging my trap out by that one foot. This little female was just running on stubs that had healed over. I imagine I was picking up some of Pete Stingley's mess. S.O.B. wouldn't go out there and check his traps eight, ten days at a time, long enough for a coyote's foot to go numb and fall off. I had my sister-in-law with me at the time and I told her to go back to the rig because I didn't want her to see me kill the coyote. I almost turned that coyote loose. Anyone who could survive that good I had to have some respect for.

# Mr. Ralston

Mr. Ralston of the famous Ralston Purina Chows was one of my good customers and enjoyed fly fishing for large mouth bass. Every summer he came from the San Diego area to spend a week fishing at the resort. He used a fly rod and homemade lures he made from plain old bottle corks, they worked like a popper plug.

The first visit he wanted a boat and looked the boats all over and, "Eh, I'll take that one right there, that'll do it." It was a long wooden boat.

I said, "We can put a motor on that if you wish."

He said, "Oh, no, no. No thanks. I have my own motor."

So they get all their fishing gear out of the car and the Black man chauffeur, he packed the cooler and all that. They put Mrs. Ralston in the bow of the boat and he got in the stern and Ol' William, the chauffeur and outboard motor, he got in the middle and picked up the idiot sticks and away they went.

When they came back in from fishing, I went out and got the boat and tied it up to the dock so they could all get out. They all got out and he told William to take the cooler and go over and air condition the car. The car was a Cadillac limousine with glass between them and William that could roll up and down. Then out of his old fishing vest he pulled a flask of rum and he gave me a speel about having a nice place and good fishing and they would be back and we'll just have a drink to that. So him and I just had a little drink out of his rum bottle. And he wanted to know if we served good food in that restaurant. I told him, "Yeah, we have a wonderful cook. She'll put you out a good sandwich; or whatever she cooks is good."

Then the next thing he said is, "Will they let William come in?"

I said, "Anyone can come in so long as they behave themselves."

In other words, I doubt if they would have come in and had lunch if they couldn't have taken William. They were looking after him; hell, he had rowed all over that damned lake and on their return trips Mr. Ralston always wanted that boat; William liked that boat.

It was about the second visit I think when the otters were over by the fireplace wrestling around. Mr. Ralston came in the store and saw them and called out,

"Hey William, come look at the otters!"

I said, "That's just great you want to share things with William."

Mr. Ralston, who was way up in years, said, "William has gone with us everywhere. He has gotten to see the world and work at the same time. He gets paid to travel around the globe." I think William was just part of the family, really.

William said, "He ever give me a vacation, I'm going to bring my wife up here!" He must not have ever gave him a vacation, because he never came up, or who knows, maybe the old man died.

Some years later, it was a coincidence that Althea and I were picnicking under one of these shelters on a beach in Maui when a tour bus came up full of Purina people. They were on a tour around the island, they'd been up Mount Holliocula. This one guy came over and we started talking. He said he was with the Ralston Purina Company.

"Well hell, I know your boss, Mr. Ralston."

Then he looks at me like I'm an idiot. We got to talking about his fishing and homemade plugs and all. I mentioned William and, "Well, hell, you know that old man!" he said.

"Well, yeah, I told you I did, him and William and Mama."

# Glen Smith, Fits

Glen Smith hauled garbage for Dave and B. J. when they owned the resort. He had fits.

One time he had that Chevrolet pickup all piled high full of garbage. He got in, fired it up, and had a fit. Had it in gear, even. Then all at once she went wide open. His foot had the accelerator pushed all the way down. That big ol' myrtle tree was right there and that's what he hit. He had 'er floorboarded in low gear and the back wheels were going around. He just sat there and dug holes in the ground.

I was working outside in the front yard and I heard the motor roaring and then a crash. Then I heard Ol' B. J. down there a-screaming and a-hollering. That's when I started down there.

Pretty soon I heard, "Pow!" One back tire blew out and I thought, "Jesus Christ, Ol' B. J. has killed someone." Then after a while, "Pow!" The other back tire blew out. When I got there the rims were still spinning around and around. Dave and B. J. were standing there doing nothing. We pulled him out of the pickup and the engine died.

He finally came out of his unconsciousness, fits or grand mal seizures from drinking. That pickup must have had positive traction because both of those hind wheels just dug holes. Both back tires blew out and there set the garbage man.

# "Peanuts" the Powder Monkey

Paul Coates: "I was working in the woods over at Sweet Home and remember a guy who could blast a quarter mile of road at a time. When he'd touch her off, the whole ground would just raise up about six inches in a little mound and then settle down. There wasn't any rocks flying, not the first rock. They were blasting in solid rock. I don't know how he did it; he knew just how to drill the whole road and set those charges. And he was just teetotally, absolutely drunk the whole time! He'd have been in his thermos and been into his whiskey flask, too, he carried in his shirt pocket. We called him 'Peanuts' and his wife's name was Hellen.

"When you weren't supposed to get any rocks in the creek, he'd just move the whole dirt over up hill a little. It'd be all loosened up and the grader would just come through and take it down that one inch minus stuff he had all blown up there. In other words, the grader would smooth out the finely crazed and cracked up surface rock, which was more like gravel at this point.

"Peanuts could just barely hang on to his drilling air hammer handle. This is like a big heavy jack hammer, which is mounted on the back of a Caterpillar. They take off the winch and put this boom and air drill apparatus for drilling the holes the dynamite goes in.

"Peanuts had them all beat by a mile; sure was a capable powder monkey, been doing it so long he could do it in his sleep.

"Many more swigs out of his flask, and he would be asleep."

# The Old West Trading Post

The Old West Trading Post and Museum on Interstate Ten between Deming and Lordsburg, New Mexico, was run by Indians. In 1976 on the highway coming towards it, we were listening on the CB radio and heard some of the awfullest damned filth you ever wanted to hear. It went on and on until finally a woman came on the air and said, "What filth! What filth! That mike ought to be washed out with soap!"

That really set them off with a string of it. Then a man came on the CB and told them, "I know who you are," and described the car that these three young foul-mouthed men were traveling in. After another string of profanities aimed at the truckdriver, as he turned out to be, the truckdriver told them, "If you'll stop up the road, we'll settle this matter!"

It wasn't very long before we saw a semitruck, bobtail (without a trailer), parked alongside the road with a late 60s Ford parked beside him and two guys laid out on the ground—actually one was just helping the other guy up; looked like they were both pretty beat up. The third guy didn't get any, he was still in the car. He was probably the one who was doing all the bad talking. The truckdriver was just getting in his cab.

Later up the road we met that truckdriver and his wife, the woman who had told them they needed their mike washed out with soap. We had more or less followed them after they pulled out, and when they pulled into the Old West Trading Post and Museum, we pulled right in, too, just to meet them.

"I thought I'd have to help you," I said.

"Oh, I've got something to take care of guys like that!" he replied. Some kind of sap or a small club I hunched.

This truckdriver and his wife were taking their semi back to Los Angeles to pick up another trailer—something happened to theirs, not making any money traveling bobtail like that, no load.

We bought something there, and it was nice to see a little Americanizing going on. It's too bad a little more isn't going on nowadays. Those young men probably got the picture of what truckdrivers do and don't want to hear over the air.


## Customer Gets the Red Carpet Treatment

Rob Fairchild was eight-balled out of every bar in Oregon, including Duckett's. This was the result of just being a dinkhead, a regular orangutang, fighting and going nuts when drinking.

He came inside and I said, "What are you doing in here; you know you're not supposed to be in here."

Rob Fairchild got mad and says, "Why you oversized old hunk of baloney,. . .big crock of horse hockey. . ." and he comes after me right down the back of the counter!

I just gave him everything I had (I knew I'd better do this just right) and aimed a blow at him and landed him right up on the counter. Then I just got him in the gut and over the counter.

His friend, Ray McCulley, who had come in with him said, "What's the meaning of all this?"

"Well, he's not supposed to be in here. I hate to tell you, but that applies to you, too."

# Santa Ana, California, Customer

"If you weren't here, I'd go to the Santa Ana race track," said one of our old customers when we were visiting him and his wife at their home in Santa Ana, California.

I said, "Don't let that stop you." We were in our motorhome and stopped to see them. She was a nice person. She and Althea were great friends. He always insisted if we ever got down his way to stop in. I told him it wouldn't bother us if he went to the race track.

"Well, I can't leave you in my home. . . ."

"We could go, too," said Althea, "that would be fun."

Then he didn't want to go, the insulting ol' son-of-a-bitch.

We had our motorhome parked in their driveway. We looked all over for a trailer park to park the motorhome but couldn't find one so stayed there.

The second night we were there he said, "I've got some company coming."

I said, "Well, hell, we're out of here. We're on our way," (around an obnoxious host like that). Capt. Jack and I were already staying outside.

That was one reason the Santa Ana customer was acting that way; we had Capt. Jack with us. The Santa Ana customer was kind of gullible and during the summers when they camped at the resort, Capt. Jack pulled all kinds of jokes and tricks on him.

Another reason he was being so obnoxious is that I had asked him if he still had that crank telephone he had gotten from up in our attic the summer before. He had wanted a piece of myrtlewood I had dried in the attic, and I told him he could have it; Mr. Bickford would get it for him as we were going fishing in Wickiup.

We went fishing and Bick took him up in the attic. He got the myrtlewood, and he spotted those two old crank telephones. He told Mr. Bickford Althea had given that one to his wife—the lying bastard—and he got off with the good one. Althea hadn't given it away.

I didn't press the matter in his home there but when he came back for a vacation at the resort I said, "Well! The thief from California's back."

Then I asked him if his "supposed to be" company ever arrived. Then I began to really harass him, telling him what a cull bastard he was, thief, besides. Things got hot and he pushed me to get past and that's when I nailed him. Then Ol' Dave and all of them jumped in and he got away.

# Man in Sleeping Bag Ran Over

Early one morning, shortly after I sold the resort, one of my old customers, Bud Toy, come up to the house and he says, "I think you'd better get down there."

Those new owners didn't want a thing to do with an accident that had happened. I got down there. Here was a man in a sleeping bag back under a car.

I says, "Holy Criminy, we'd better call the sheriff. That guy's dead."

It looked like they'd been partying. Not only looked like it, but the rest of the campers said there'd been partying going on most of the night. There had been a dance all night in the store, too. After the man retired in his sleeping bag behind the car, the lady decided to move the car, I guess; way it looked. Looked like she'd run over him two or three times. She had got the car astraddle up on one of the cement fireplaces. It looked like she tried to go forward and her back wheels would catch ahold of the fireplace and when she backed up her front wheels would catch it. She was still asleep in the car when the sheriff got there. She claimed she didn't even know he was there.

Well, I brought down a handyman jack and we jacked the car up, drug him up from underneath so the coroner, who'd come with the sheriff, could pronounce him dead.

They took her back to town and questioned her. That's about it.

Gary and Ed, the new owners, were hiding. Probably wondered what they'd gotten themselves into up here at Loon Lake.

# Old Growth Bark

On the trap line Ken Spencer and I used to park at an old landing that was like a cul-de-sac, a dead end, and walk out the Cat roads from there and set traps. There was some old growth bark on the landing, must have been eight or ten inches thick. Boy that's the best wood you can get.Back in the old days that was the only thing that got hot enough to melt babbitt—old growth fir bark. We did that right out in the woods, melted the babbitt in heavy metal kettles and ladled it out putting new "D"'s on the ends of rigging straps, nubs on chokers; you could figure a day for repairing stuff.

Ken and I decided we'd take the trailer up there one day, leave it at the landing. When we got done with the trap lines we'd saw the bark into wood and bring it home. So that's what we did. We used the Bronco to look at our traps in other places. Then we returned to the landing, sawed up our bark and came out of there with it. A guy in a Bureau of Land Management pickup was waiting for us when we come back out to the junction with the logging road. We stopped.

He says, "I heard you sawing wood. Where is your permit?"

I had a .22 Ruger between the two front seats. I told Ken, "Ken, hand me my permit."

He handed me the Ruger, still in the holster. I held it in the air, where he could see it and said, "Here's my permit, to cut something like this."

He says, "Yeah, yeah, yeah, well I guess that ain't considered wood, that bark. It doesn't amount to much, go ahead and take all you want."

We drove away, no need standing there arguing with him. I told Ken, "Well, we ain't heard the end of this. We will probably be getting a little notice we attempted his life or something." We had that trailer full of nice big thick stuff, man. They must have set that out with the shovel or something when they were logging on the landing, some logger was going to take that home, but never did. It had been sitting there a year. Heck with the BLM guy and his, "Where's your permit?"

No doubt we need some control or people would go and fall timber for firewood right across the road like a certain neighbor of ours, Mr. Q. We'd have a lot of Mr. Q's. But the government makes the loggers burn up their landings full of wood just so the people can't get them.

# "You-all" Boys

Warren Turner had met these fellers in the tavern and they heard he was looking for some timber fallers. So he talked to them and they told a pretty good story. They were "you-all" boys, from the South, and said they were timber fallers. They had cut timber. So he hired them to clear a right of way; he told them where it was and all about it. He said he'd meet them there in the morning, and if he wasn't there, they were to go ahead, line it out and get started. He might be a little bit late, maybe a couple of hours.

Well, he got there a little bit late and no one was around—goodness! He saw a big ol' tree—looked like a rabid beaver had attacked it—no undercut, no face, no nothing, just cut all around. They'd started from each side and they'd gnawed around and it had just tipped over.

There wasn't any hide nor hair laying around on the ground, just a big note on the stump which read, "Guess we all ain't the timber fallers we thought we were. Thank you very much." At least the we-in's went home in one piece, after trying their hand at falling timber.

# Grader Gets Salmon

Ed Miller, resident of Ash Valley, operated a big road grader for Darrel Fromm and Bob Burton Construction outfit. One time they were making a road far up the Smith River. They had to ford the river to get to the other side where the construction site was. There was no bridge, but it was summertime and the Caterpillar went through, then he on his grader came next.

He had never gotten a salmon in his life, but they were running then and he saw a great big one as he drove across. He just let the grader blade down and caught it; pinned a nice big salmon right there. That's one that went home without punching the tag.

# The Dented Can Inspector

"Well, it says here we've got to keep this for our records," I told my wife as I was reading the mail one day. I was reading a notice from the damned Jerry Brown outfit, the gas company where a card unlocks the tanks so you can pump your own gas. This notice told all about the safety regulations and the two percent discount and the point we are, in fact, a farm.

"They could send a man out to make sure you had it."

She said, "I'm sure they're going to send a man out to see if you had that notice."

I continued, "Hey, any time the government sends a man out to check for dented cans, you don't know what they're going to send one for."

She asked, "The man came out to check for dented cans?"

"Yeah, in the store. We were covering for Gary and Ed while they went somewhere. An inspector showed up, got out of his car, put on his full-length white apron and came in the resort. I'd had dealings with that joker in the past. The guy came in and was checking everything. . .a regular idiot. He was looking for dented cans. He spotted the bleach up on the shelf and said, " 'You've got to get this down on a lower shelf!'

"I asked him, 'Yeah, how come?'

"'Well!' he said, 'In case it should spring a leak, it wouldn't dribble down on the things below!'

"Then Bozo came to say hello to him and he said, 'Oh, my God, you've got to get this dog out of here!'

"I said, 'Okay, that's enough, that dog isn't half as dirty as you are, you ignorant, mangy hippie. Now get out of here!'

"He said, 'What?'

"I told him, 'You heard me. Just leave before I throw you out!'

"He had put on a white apron before he came in the store to cover up some of his filth—long-haired, cruddy-looking guy. He left and Gary and Ed never mentioned anything about hearing from the government. I guess the guy never said anything. That was that ol' hippie bastard that used to come looking through the shelves for dented cans. I got even with the ol' worthless non-producer while Althea and I were watching the store."

While one wing of the government has you pour bleach in a perfectly good spring to ruin your drinking water, another wing of the government is worried about it leaking out on a shelf. Those inspectors are everywhere—there's more non-producers than there are people working to pay their way. One thing about it though, at least that one never came back.

## The Woman's Libist

Dave and B. J. McGruder, after buying Duckett's Resort, were sitting in a bar over in Empire. The woman sitting next to them was carrying on about the evils of men—damned men this and damned men that.

A man was sitting there reading the newspaper and drinking a beer. Pretty soon he got up to leave and walked over and didn't say a word, "Wham," knocked that woman right off the seat. Then he walked out, never saying anything. That shut that up momentarily.

All the time Dave and B. J. thought they were together. Dave and B. J. left so we'll never find out if being backhanded off the barstool shut that lady up or not.

# *Present*

*Here I am with Ellen at the Fish Haven Dock, March of 2000.*

# Dead Night Crawlers

Tuesday morning, January 6, 1990, we looked out the back door of the house and found hundreds and hundreds of night crawlers ruptured and dead by the back steps. The ground was just covered with them. It was just pitiful. This was a fisherman's dream if only these worms had been alive. We couldn't imagine what caused so many hundreds of them to come up to the top of the hard ground there and die.

This is the stormy winter time of year. Two nights before a tree went down and the power went off at nine-thirty and stayed off. Did they get electrocuted? One night before we were hit with 120 M.P.H. gusts of winds and rain. Did they drown? Were they too near the septic tank? Too near the greywater outlet?

"I bet I started the washer real late at night, and the bleach water came out right when the night crawlers were crawling around," Ellie said.

That's a good way to kill things—with bleach. That's probably about what happened.

# "It's Flooded, Not Shorted"

The 1968 Ford pickup was sputtering and lurching as my wife and I drove it down the driveway.

I said, "Flooded out."

She said, "How could it be flooded out in such a short time?"

"It's flooded, not shorted."

# Cow Swallows the Shirt

A big maple tree had fallen down in Tom Carley's pasture near the bank of the Umpqua River. He was down sawing it into firewood with his power saw. Though it was wintertime, he got warm working, took off his flannel shirt and threw it on a bush. He hadn't noticed, but one of his cows was grazing nearby and came over and found the flannel shirt hanging on the bush and proceeded to chew on it and swallow it.

He looked over and saw the cow standing there still chewing on it, and it was going down! Just one sleeve was left hanging out of her mouth.

This cow's name was Britches. He walked up to her, talking slow and steady all the time to keep her from running off, and got up to her, got ahold of the sleeve and tugged and pulled and finally got the whole shirt back. It was slimy and green. He washed it off in the river and much to his surprise, it was still in good shape, nothing wrong with it!

He wore it many more times—the flannel shirt the cow had swallowed.

# Donkey Eats Grease Rag

Tony, the donkey, was standing on the cement slab in front of our shop while I was inside doing some mechanical work to my pickup. I came out to scratch him and was talking to him when, for some reason, he got ahold of the grease rag sticking out of my hip pocket. It was really greasy, too. I tried to get it away from him, but no way you're going to get it loose once he's got his jaws locked on to it. He hung right on to it. Me, too. I hung right onto my end of it. He pulled and I pulled. Then he jerked his head back and got it away from me and trotted off and swallowed that grease rag!

He must have digested it; full of grease, WD-40 and everything—amazing it didn't kill him.

# Citizen's Arrest

Crazy Tom Woodard's brother, Jim Woodard, had a convertible painted with every color you could think of—bright fluorescent blue, red, pink, green, black. He just took a bunch of spray cans and doctored the convertible up with all different colors—just spots and streaks and whatever.

One day, while Jim and all of us were in the store, a state police cop car went by—just roared by about forty miles an hour—around the little horseshoe bend and up the valley. Bales is who it was; two cops in the same car.

Someone says, "Boy, those cops are really a-traveling!"

Jim says, "Yes, they're going too fast. I'm going to make a citizen's arrest!"

He got in his painted-up convertible and took out after them, a-honking. He went up the road blaring his horn—must have been gone about fifteen minutes.

After a while here comes the cop car back. Jim was right behind him, still honking. When the cops pulled over in front of Cabin Seven, Jim pulled over too, still on his tail.

The cop stepped out and said, "What do you want?"

Jim said, "I'm making a citizen's arrest!"

The cop said, "Well, let's see your driver's license," and after that, "Now, let's have a look at your car."

When he got done that son-of-a-gun had a ticket—must have been a mile long—muffler, defective light; oh, heck, I don't know what all. He got a citizen's arrest all right—all kinds of things to fix on his convertible.

# Jim, Gerald and Bud Parker

Jim Parker beat a Jersey bull calf to death with a hammer. Hell, that's the way they used to do them in those days, though, knock them in the head. Everyone had Jersey dairy cows that calved every spring. The heifers could be sold or replenish the herd as milk cows but the bull calves weren't good for anything, so as soon as they were born, they were knocked in the head and thrown out there on the manure pile. You can still buy them for twenty dollars, eighty years later in 1999 today, from the dairies, so you can see they still aren't worth much—they never get much meat on them and there's not much market for a dairy steer.

Jim had two sons. Bud was the younger son, and Gerald was the older one. Gerald had infantile paralysis as a baby, one year old. It affected his left leg, so it never grew as much, and it was shorter than the right leg. He was killed in a farming accident.

Bud tells how: "One fall he had taken the silage cutter over to the Harrison Ranch where they were cutting corn into silage. He was just helping out and he always ran the silage cutter, which was powered by a stationary gasoline engine. The engine had a big, big flywheel, and after he had run a load of corn through, he went back to slow the engine down; to idle it down. He was on planks, and it was wet and raining like it generally is when you're putting up corn. He slipped and fell into the big flywheel. The spoke of the flywheel hit him right across the forehead and killed him. He was twenty-six years old. That left only me to run the dairy and ranch with my folks."

# Menace to the Public

I went with a borrowed car trailer and my neighbor, Ron Weikum, on an August day in 1994 to Bouy's Canyon off the Umpqua River. There I had been given an old International four-wheel-drive truck. After a forty-minute drive we arrived at the site of my free gift. We couldn't see it for the berries but soon a block purchase and electric winch running off the battery of my old pickup got it out of the vines and up on the trailer.

We put a block in front of the wheels.

"Got it blocked!" Pulled the trailer away and "Crash, Boom!" blocked on wrong side of the wheels. The International truck had run forward on the trailer 'til the front wheels fell down and the International grill hit the pickup. We jacked it up with the handyman jack. Then we put planks under the tires and rolled it back slowly with a come-a-long onto the trailer, but too far—it rolled part way off the rear end.

So we backed the trailer up to about seven feet away from a power pole. We lifted a cedar fence post so one butt end was against the power pole and the other butt end was against the International, horizontal to the ground. Then we backed the whole works up and the International was jill-poked forwards on the trailer but this time with a chain on it so it couldn't run off the front. It stayed centered—just poked it so far. Finally tied her down front and back by cinching come-a-longs down tight and we were on our way!

Traveling contentedly down busy old Highway 38 that old trailer would whip; we could only go so fast. Then all of a sudden, "Scrrraaaapppe!" Ramp fell down. We pulled over to the gravel on the side of the highway. As we were attaching the loading ramp back on, Ron noticed the tail light bar was still laying in the pickup. We'd forgotten to nail it down in the back to serve as taillights on the wooden trailer bed.

"By God, how did we forget that? Get it nailed down before they stop us for no lights," Ron exclaimed.

I replied, "By God, Ron, we'd better stay in Loon Lake, we're a menace to the public!"

## Bit By His Own Dog

One cold, dark night on the Umpqua River, Tom Carley wanted to play with his two Airedale dogs. He was going to scare them by coming outside growling and snarling. He came out imitating a wild animal, and one Airedale bit him on the buttocks.

So much for the playing around; Tom came back inside and didn't do any more bear imitations for a while.

# Trick Driving

On election day, November 9, 1993, Benny and I went to Coos Bay to bring back supplies for building the new barn. We came back after dark with our old pickup, a 1968 Ford Ranger. We were loaded with groceries—cases of canned milk, pineapple, and other canned goods on sale, feed and hardware. We were pulling Scott Studeman's car trailer really weighed down with a load of steel rebar, angle iron, reinforcement wire for concrete, and lumber—the pickup and trailer were loaded to the gills and would sway if we got up too much speed.

It was dark, so we had our headlights on and were coming out of Reedsport towards home, following the Umpqua River. It was on the west side of Dean's Creek where there's kind of a big double curve in the road. All of a sudden we saw two sets of headlights abreast coming towards us instead of one! A pickup with a four-wheeler in the back was passing a big truck. Whether it was a chip truck or not, I didn't know, but it was an eighteen-wheeler. The passing vehicle looked like a BLM pickup—it was that same color of light green and with the four-wheeler in back, I'm pretty sure it was one of those guys who run around in one of them things trying to spot the bugs and owls. Dirty son-of-a-bitches—wonder where he thought he was. It was pitch black and there was not enough time to pull off to the side of the road so I drove right between them. Benny and I went right down the center of the highway with the semi on one side and the pickup on the other!

Benny said, "Oh, my God."

And when they went clattering past he rolled down his window and hollered at the passing pickup, "You no good dare devil!"

"You talk about some trick driving," I told my wife. "That's where the race car driving comes in handy from my days of racing. You don't lose your cool. I heard a lot of squealin' and a-rattling and a-banging, and I know the semi-truck hit that guard rail. He braked hard. I did too, hard enough that it shifted the whole load of lumber and rebar ahead about a foot. Ben and I and the pickup and trailer went right between them bastards, straddling the yellow line.

"The pickup driver knew enough to pull to the left and the semi pulled to the right. The guy driving the pickup just couldn't slow down in time to get back where he was supposed to be behind that huge truck. I had such a load behind me on that trailer I could hardly have slowed down if I wanted to."

He was damned lucky he didn't stop and park. We'd have went back and whipped up on him—that'd get his attention. Next time I went by I seen the guard rail bent 'way over and black tire marks all over.

# Voters Agree

The polling place in Ash Valley is the schoolhouse cafeteria. After the polls shut down at eight o'clock P.M. November 9, 1993, the election board counted up the votes.

Mrs. Coates, Keeland, Fredericksen, and Stingley noticed that out of thirty-three voters who voted that day, all thirty-three voted "No" on Measure 1, with nobody in favor of it. This set a record—all Ash Valley residents agreed upon something! Measure 1 was the five percent sales tax. The sales tax has been voted out ten different times over the years by Oregon voters, according to the Douglas County Elections Department. Sounds like nobody wants it, not even Ash Valley.

# Whistle Britches in Size Forty-Four

Charlie Holmes, a five foot three inch tall timber faller, went in a saw shop in literally rags—his pants were torn to shreds. They didn't have the loggers' double fronted denim pants in size twenty-eight inches. Forty-four inches is all they had.

Well, that didn't bother him. Charlie was just pleased as punch they had anything.

"Just fine! Just what I want!"

Charlie wore them, BIG as they were, quite a while, until he got his money's worth.

His partner laughed, "Yes, he can take off running and twenty minutes later his pants catch up to him."

Charlie says, "If these pants get caught up in equipment, saw or something, I could cut them off of myself."

That's one reason loggers don't mind loose pants. But not that loose, Charlie.

# Loading the Cow

Dean and Sonja Wooley were the owners of the Morgan horse and cattle ranch located at Dean's Creek junction with the Umpqua River. On this ranch was almost always a large elk herd, which everybody enjoyed seeing as they grazed along with Wooley's Morgan horses and cattle. Wooley's raised, bred and sold champion Morgan horses with Mrs. Wooley giving horseback riding lessons. She also invented, patented and sold a unique rubber boot for protection of hooves—horses, donkeys, etc. in wet ground.

In 1987, the BLM, who already own fifty-two percent of the state, condemned the ranch, forced Wooley's to sell and made an official BLM elk reserve out of the fields—the buildings are still deserted twelve years later. Why, the elk were more interesting to see when they intermingled with the cattle and horses! Now there is no more cattle, Morgan horses, the only true American breed of horse, nor workers in the fields, lights on at the ranch, hay in the barns, nor riding lessons nor good neighbors on the tax roles. Now it is a sterile, fallow ranch which tax dollars have to support. Back when there was people on it there was a lot of cattle transactions, neighborliness and fun. Here's an example:

Tom Carley had wintered his cow on Dean and Sonja's pasture. He came with his horse trailer to pick it up. It was springtime and the green grass was really growing.

You know how that effects the cows and loosens them up; just a green runny slop hits the ground and splatters in all directions.

Dean and Tom got the horse trailer hooked up, then they put the cow in the back door of it, and got her loaded up without too much difficulty. Tom was closing up the back gate to the trailer and noticed the cow's tail was out but thought, "Oh, well, horses all go down the road like that, if I put it in, it would swing right out again." About then Dean reminded him that up high there were little wing nuts to keep the door locked during the trip; better get them. So Tom was adjusting the little wing nuts above his head—got the left one and was working on the right one, when "blurp!"—the cow let out a green sloppy emission right in his face. She must have farted or coughed or something because it came out like an explosion—about the consistency of pancake batter. It was everywhere, on the brim of his hat, in his mouth, it filled his pocket full—his glasses were in his pocket—Dean was down on one knee he was laughing so hard. He roared and laughed so much, he was almost vomiting. Next he was hanging on to a fence post to keep standing up.

"Well, Tom," he finally gasps, "I'll have to wash you down with the hose, but first let me go get my wife to take a look at you!"

Tom patiently waited until the wife came out to see him. He got a good chuckle out of it, too; especially watching his good friend Dean Wooley hanging onto the fence post while belly-laughing so wildly and thoroughly at the sight. The manure was hosed off with all three of them still joking and ribbing each other. Then Tom got in the pickup and left for home with his cow in tow.

# "Going Around The World On A Tractor"

It had been raining here all spring—really pouring.

I went to town on April 26, 1993, and while at Bob Speck's Reedsport Transmission, saw a sign on the back of a small camp trailer, "Slow Moving Vehicle." The camp trailer was pulled by a 3100 Ford tractor—the same size as ours!

The thirty-five year old New Zealand man and his wife were getting an oil change there at Gil Hensen's Texaco station next door—oil change, grease job, going all over it.

A sign, "Going Around The World On A Tractor" was hung on the trailer.

The man in his raingear told me, "My windscreen is getting loose."

I didn't know what he was talking about until he showed me the windshield he had lashed up in the front of the tractor. It wasn't something he had rigged up professionally before he left. No, it looked like something that had happened along the way. He'd gotten a car windshield out of a wrecking yard and attached it with baling wire and boards. Same with his fenders.

The man and the wife had plastic bags over the back wheels of the tractor to keep water from being thrown back over them. In the back of the front wheels of the tractor, it looked like old plywood hanging there to keep road water from being thrown at them. Quite a remarkable sight and challenge.

They had come up the coast. It had been a downpour of water for weeks. Hensen was getting them ready for the next leg of the trip.

# Putting Up Campaign Signs

Getting ready for the general elections in the fall of 1996, I put up a lot of plywood campaign signs for our candidate who was running for county commissioner. I was down on the highway putting up one of these great big unusual-looking signs that my wife had made. She had jig-sawed out part of the plywood to make an "R" that looked like him posing. His name was Rafferty.

These signs called for a lot of posts to be pounded in, shoring up and bracing and nailing. This one was going up in the same spot we had put one up in the spring during the primary election. Why you have to put them up in the spring for the primaries, take them down during summer and put them up again in the fall during the general election, I don't know—one pain in the neck.

In the spring when we were pounding the dynamite bar in the ground to make holes for the posts, a big gust of wind came along and picked the four foot by eight foot sheet of plywood with our friend's campaign slogan on it and everything and sailed it across Highway 101, bouncing as it went. Thank goodness no traffic was going by right then or it might have ended his campaign right then. That might have been the end of our candidate but instead he won the primaries and went on to the general election.

I asked permission from the guy in the store, as I had before months earlier, and he said, "Okay, that's fine again, put it up."

The berries had grown up quite a bit since spring and I was clear out through them again putting the sign where it could be seen from the highway good, when a man across the highway started honking his horn and waving his hands above his head. I didn't pay any attention to him, just kept on with what I was doing. So he drove over. I was being nice to the guy at first.

He says, "You're trespassing."

Then he saw whose sign it was.

I said, "No, I got permission from the guy in the store."

He says, "Well, I'm the owner of this property, and I tore down a sign of yours last spring!"

That's when I said, "Who in the hell are you anyway; what's your name?"

He said, "Strever."

"John?"

He said, "Yes, I'm John Strever."

That's when I threw the sledge hammer and sign in the back of the car and said, "You (with an oath) dirty thus and such. I've owed you a licking for a long time."

He took off and got in his pickup and was cranking on the engine. I got him right through the open window. I hit him with all I could and connected right in the front of the ear—a little too high on the jaw, really. He went right over sideways on the seat. He stayed on the seat—either playing possum or stunned and out of it. I jerked the door open and said, "I ought to drag your ass out of there and give you a gosh darned good overhauling!"

I don't think he even heard it.

John Strever was the insurance agent for Althea and me for many years when we owned the resort. We had all our liability, cars, fire, and performance bonds, for when I was logging, with him.

One day, Althea and I had somebody rear-end us down at a stop light on 101 in Coos Bay. It hit so hard while we were parked at a stop light that it knocked me, all 230 lbs. of me, completely into the back seat and drove us into the parked car in front of us—a four-car pile-up. That old codger hit us, we hit the Mercedes and the Mercedes hit some kind of old clunker, ran him over the sidewalk and into a building.

I filled out an insurance form, gave the people the number and all that. The people in the car in front of us, once they found out we owned a resort, were suing for a million dollars. They got back with us that our insurance company had never heard of us—for years! This agent of ours had never sent in the paperwork, money or anything! That was John Strever.

A federal judge ruled in his favor—judge was asleep all during the trial—they had to shake him to make a decision.

He said, "I can't help but rule in favor of the insurance company; when a man gets a policy, he should check to make sure he's really got it."

The federal judge, in the federal building in Portland, let that crooked guy go free.

I went into the store and told the kid, "Hey, I'm probably going to get you in trouble because I hit that guy out there."

"Who is that guy, anyway?"

"John Strever."

The kid said, "OOOoooo."

When I came out of the store, Strever's tires were smoking that gravel, and he spun out of there. He had gravel thrown 100 feet back.

I thought to myself, "Oh, oh, I bet he's going to the sheriff!"

I still had to get chicken feed and Bossy feed so I went over to the Parent Feed Store from there. At Parent Feed I was still worked up and mad, and Old Grandpa Porky was trying to split some wood. Grandma LaJoy was laughing at me, "My, I've never seen you so worked up before."

They hid the campaign signs I was supposed to put up—hid them in the hay stack so maybe someone else could put them up the next day.

Then I said, "Here, let me have that splitting maul, I need to work some of this off!"

I split a few rounds of wood, then went to the Tide's Inn to pick up Ben. They said he'd been in and out in the morning but haven't seen him. Lake Price said to me, "Sit down, I'll buy you all the beer you can drink; there's not a man in town that wouldn't have liked to do that to that S.O.B."

I had a 7-Up and came on home. When I got home my wife told me she had put a large sign up there two weeks ago and spent an hour and a half bracing it up for the wind. That old agent must have removed that one, too, and demolished it. He put up the opponent's sign instead; the opponent was a practically ninety-five percent Socialist. If I would have known he'd done that, I would have been even madder.

# The Climbing Outfit

In 1992 a young twenty-three-year-old fella who had been raised in Ash Valley came to the door and asked to borrow my climbing outfit. He needed the whole works— spurs and belt and rope—to take down a cedar tree for Kirk Downing, lawyer-turned-rancher, up the valley. I had two climbing outfits—one old one and one that I had climbed with for years in the woods from a young man on. It was a good one and quite a prized possession. I didn't want to see the young man get hurt, so I loaned him my good one; I might add knowing full well that this particular young man was not too reliable. It's nice to give people the benefit of the doubt; they may have reformed over the years.

The young man never did take the tree down, no climbing outfit returned; never saw him either. Two years lapsed when finally I noticed a bunch of people over at the trailer, now rented, where this young man had been raised. I cruised by and noticed the young people had taken the motor out of the absent renter's VW van and had it laying on the ground.

I thought, I bet those crummy-looking sons-of-bitches were hauling that motor out of here in their Dodge Power Wagon.

I asked at the Lodge if this guy was there, and they said, "Yes, he's been in and out."

This was Saturday night, on August 6, 1994. The next day, Sunday, I went by to see if he were there at the old trailer, but nope, no Power Wagon, no car. So I went to the Lodge, saw a little blue car there, went in and sat down at the counter. I got a cup of tea and asked Angie, the waitress, "Whose little car is that out there?"

She replies, "Oh, that's so and so (my thief), he's out on the sun deck."

I said, "Oh, good, I want to see him. Couldn't catch him at a better place."

I passed Pappy DeWitt sitting on the bench by the magazines and plate glass windows as I went out on the sun deck.

Out there the young man was eating hamburgers with his friends. He saw me, turned around, stuck out his hand to shake hands, like that, and I said, "Oh, wait here, here! I've been waiting to catch up with you for two years. This isn't on friendly terms."

"Yeah," the boy remonstrated, "Why, what, what?"

"It's about my climbing outfit you borrowed!" I reminded him.

"I don't know a thing about your blanking climbing outfit!"

"Well, you're a worthless liar as well as a worthless thief, then!"

That's when the young man hopped up and I whopped him on the neck with my cane. This is the same aluminum cane I used to kill coyotes with on the trap line—not a good-looking cane, just real functional. The kid grabbed ahold of the cane with both hands and just hung there in the air like a monkey on a trapeze bar. I was holding him up. The little scamp was hollering at the top of his lungs, "Help, help! Somebody get Jim (the Lodge owner), get Charlie (manager). Somebody, help! Oh, just anybody, help!"

I told him, "You know, you sound just like a rat does in a trap—just screams his head off—just like the rat that you are."

Out comes the waitress, Carol, saying, "Oh, Mr. Lloyd, please, the place is full of people. . . ."

"I know, I know, I just want to let them know what a yellow cull he is."

Then to the monkey suspended off my cane I said, "All right, you little punk. Turn loose. I promise ya I won't hit ya."

He turned loose and went to getting out of there, around the backside of the table. He left the sun deck, came inside, looking for sympathy—he went to Pappy and everybody. Pappy just sat there and looked at him.

I went to drinking my tea. The thief was hiding behind Marquetta (wife of the manager), and I told him, "You just remember what I told you about coming back into this valley. If you ever do come back, you had better, by God, have a climbing outfit in your hand or you ain't walking back out of here."

"Oooooo, what are you going to do, shoot me?" the kid challenges.

"No, I don't need a gun for the likes of you."

"Well, I got a gun."

"Yeah, what kind of a gun do you have?"

I was hoping he would say a .44 Magnum (what shot up Randy Weikum's car).

Randy Weikum was sixteen years old and got his car front end over the bank and blocking two-third's of the Soup Creek Road, which leads out of the valley. He walked home. Ben and I went up and pulled it back on the road. Randy was taken to the hospital with a broken jaw and by the time he and his father came the next morning to get it, both father and son's fully complete tool boxes were stolen and the windows broken and the car shot full of holes with a .44 Magnum.

This same culprit and his crummy-looking friends in his little blue car passed Randy and his father coming down Soup Creek Road, turned around and passed them again coming back up as they were on their way to rescue the car.

334

The boys must have done their deed, hid the tool boxes and then got back out of the valley where they'd be safe figuring to retrieve the hidden tool boxes later.

The Weikums turned this into the police department, who did come out and determine it was a .44 Magnum; but what do you get with the police? Running up and down the road looking to see if you have a seat belt on or some other nonsense.

He didn't want to tell what kind of gun he had, just, "If you ever hit me again, I'm going to tear you to pieces."

"You little punk," I rejoined, "You ain't going to tear nothing to pieces. Get out from behind Marquetta and I can kill you right where you're standing."

Marquetta kind of shoved him out.

"Yeah," he says, "I'm coming back in this valley."

"If you ever come back in this valley again, you'd better have a set of climbing spurs on your shoulder."

Pappy, aged eighty-five, said, "Why didn't you really lay it to him?"

I replied, "I could have ripped the cane out of his hands, as I was really holding him up; but he was hollering so much. I figured I'd just let him humiliate himself."

The motor disappeared, so did his friends, but he's never been back; doesn't have a lot of reason to now.

# Wisdom of the Chickens

You know we don't have television, but our chickens provide us with a lot of entertainment. They're smart, just like any other animal. Here's some examples:

When Paul Coates logged here on our property, you couldn't always see him but you could hear him. He would arrive early to meet the log truck, fire up the loader, and load the trucks out with a load of logs. That was before daylight and so the chickens stayed on the roost. Later in the day, the chickens still didn't pay any attention to the loading of the log truck with big ol' grapple tongs or the sound of the yarder bringing in more logs. All that far away noise didn't interest them because the loader didn't move to expose grubs and goodies in the soil and the truck didn't uncover new dirt, either. Just packed it in.

Now as soon as Paul would start up the Caterpillar, that was a different story. Even if it was parked 'way up on a log road, here would come a-running some hens and maybe a rooster. No matter what time of day, whenever he'd fire the Cat up, they would follow getting worms and bugs.

When he had to grub out a root wad, they'd go down in that hole and really have a hay day—get all kinds of worms. He had to be a little careful; he was always afraid he would back over one. One little red hen in particular was always with the Caterpillar when it was running. He watched out for her as she stuck right with him no matter if he was going forwards or backwards.

"Those chickens are smart," Paul would say. "They can tell the difference in the equipment starting up—whether it's a log truck, yarder or loader. These are all big diesel motors but don't move dirt so you don't see the chickens. But start up the rubber-tired dought or Caterpillar, which are more big diesel motors, and with this sound you have chickens

336

with you hunting and pecking all over the place. They have pretty good ears to tell the difference in these motors."

Lloyd had another example: "Boy, you can't tell me those chickens are dumb. As soon as they hear my riding mower fire up, here they come! I park it in the woodshed and use it to pull a little wood trailer from the shed to the house, where I stack wood on the porch. When I start it up and position the trailer in a convenient place against the stack to load firewood and turn it off, that takes a minute and by then I've got a flock of chickens by the wood pile waiting. They like those bugs you uncover as you get wood off the pile. Boom, they got it. Then they follow the trailer over to the porch—as more bugs fall out."

＠　　＠　　＠

There's another couple of sounds they know. I have a porch right off the kitchen. There I knock against the railing or post, at regular intervals, the remains of two different containers. Both containers are about the same size, and both carry a hollow ring for quite a distance. The heavy plastic dish "bongs!" and throws table and cooking scraps out in a heap. Chickens come running as fast as their legs can carry them. The stainless steel pot "bongs!" and coffee grounds fling out and the chickens don't even look up. They know what's coming from the difference in those "bong" sounds.

Before we did under all the roosters, we probably had 300 chicks born every summer. The hens had nests everywhere, and every week or two, off the side hills would come another mother hen with a dozen or so chicks behind her. She might start off with a dozen and end up with three; the survival rate wasn't good. The tiny little black and yellow fluffy chicks would fall into holes they couldn't climb out of, try to nestle under a hen or rooster's legs and get pecked, and generally not be able to stick with mother on her wide roamings around the yards and back to the nighttime nest under ferns—just pooped out. We certainly didn't need more chickens, but we hated to see the little guys die of exhaustion, so we started to put hen and chicks in the coops and lock them up three weeks or so until they were bigger and more able to fend for themselves.

Those little chicks have a built-in instinctual smartness. To catch the whole group, we'd net mother with a smelt net and she'd let out a loud "squawk!" like she was being killed. At that sound the chicks would run in all directions and hide. Really go down and not move. They'd get down and stay down! not peep, not move a muscle or stand up, just freeze and just hide in the grass or flowers for up to an hour. If you could see a little yellow or black chick, you could pick him up; but the only way to get the ones you couldn't see was to keep coming back and grab them when they started to cheep for their mother. At that point they would run, too, and we would catch those chicks and re-unite them with their mother in the coop.

If not cooped up, a hen travels all day long hunting and pecking over the yard, an area of three acres. A mother hen at large with her chicks talks to them all the time. She calls to them, a low "cluck, cluck. . .cluck, cluck. . ." kind of low and under her breath telling them to follow her. Her children become occupied with things they find, get distracted and straggle along. Another more distinct "Cluck, cluck! Cluck, cluck!" means "Here's something good to eat," like a worm, bug, etc. With that call, they come running front and center to see what she has uncovered. A rooster will pull up a big worm out of the lawn and call his hens with the same clucking, then stand back and looks around to see there's no rooster coming with the lot. He's proud of his hens, likes to find tidbits for them, and calls them with his particular "cluck cluck..cluck cluck."

॰ ॰ ॰

A rooster crows, you know, at the break of daylight, and also during the day, and he'll also crow at night if you turn on a light in the house. When he sees that, he must think it's getting close to daylight. At one point we had thirteen roosters. I tried not to turn on a light too much at night to wake up the renters in the yard.

Little Red and Hitler were two roosters that were an equal match and sparred all the time. The Rhode Island Little Red was about half the size of the Big Barred Rock Dominique Hitler, named so because he did the goose step walking. One time they had spurred and ruffled and pecked at each other as usual, then Hitler ran all the way around the house and came back to where Little Red was waiting for him. Little Red put out his foot and whapped him—literally kicked him in the rear end—as he ran around the corner of the house looking for his enemy.

One day we got back in the evening from haying to find one sole little black chick alone in the chicken yard—we never did know what became of its mother. We tried

to pawn it off under another couple of hens with chicks by putting it under them at nighttime but couldn't get any mother to take the chick, so we raised her in the house. She became known as "Chick Chick," and became attached to us in a day. She never tired of being held with a hand held over her like a mother's protective wing. It sounds funny, but they need this as much as they need food and water. We had raised quite a few goslings and chicks from the incubator in the house, but a single one is always lonesome, more than if there's two or three or more where they can nestle into each other for love. You can't replace that mother's wing.

That little chick would sleep for a while but was definitely lonesome and would "cheep" quite a bit. Around 6:00 in the evenings, she could smell the food cooking and heard our feet and voices as dinner was being prepared. Then she would really "Cheep!" for attention, and the only way to quiet her was to hold her during dinner. I got tired of eating with one hand, and pretty soon we spent a month with that chick standing at the edge of our plates pecking here and there. It took one hand to fend her off the plate, guests turned up their noses at this but we got a bang out of her. Left to her own choice, Chick Chick had just as good taste in food as a gourmet person—bread and potatoes, unless they had gravy on them, she never touched. Rich food was it—cottage cheese, cheese, meat, butter, and toward the top of her list was fish, and the very top of the list was shellfish and crab. The chick went crazy for crab. And here we all think they prefer grain—it's just the cheapest thing to feed them.

Then if she didn't get put back in her box soon enough in the evening she'd get overly tired and carry on with that ear-deafening Cheep! Cheeaapp! until I went in and soothed her with the towel over her, a hand and a lullaby putting her to sleep. You see, under normal conditions, a chick nestles up under its mother a hundred times a day and receives security, protection and love. So this little chick caused quite a ruckus for lack of it. I took her to work with me in the pickup burnpiling at the ranch. I sing a lot of the time and that kept the little bird comforted. We took her to town with us and the shop owners liked to hold her, too, in her dish towel. She rode in my lap or nestled up against Lloyd's neck and under his collar. She'd sing a little song when warm and happy that sounds like "ppptttwww, ppptttwww, ppptttwww." The main time we were unoccupied enough to hold her was when we both went to town together.

She got big enough to get out of her towel and follow us outside. When weeding the gardens, I would point out worms to her. She ate one sow bug I pointed out to her (the gray bugs that roll up like a pill when you touch them) but would never touch another one. Sow bugs look good; but they must not taste that way—sour maybe.

One time the minister, Howard Spear, came by and was amazed to see Chick Chick perched on the back of the riding mower seat while Lloyd and I were underneath the mower deck replacing some belts. She looked just as happy as could be, which she was, same as any time we stayed in one place doing something. Wherever we went she was running right with us, fluttering her wings to keep her balance as she ran. Chick Chick must have had strong legs after going back and forth from the house to the shop many times a day.

She got past sleeping nestled under the towels and went to roosting overnight on the edge of her cardboard box. She'd greet us in the morning with a happy "Tttrrreeepppt, ppttreeeept" sound, like a chick does when he's real full and sitting in your warm hand and getting sleepy.

Another thing they do (and so do goslings and geese when they're contented) is to open their mouths and close them with their head tilted back, kind of like they're yawning. Well, all this happy life indoors and being a baby had to come to an end. One night we broke her to roost outside.

It took about five nights of singing hymns while keeping a hand over Chick Chick's head and body atop the saddle out on the porch before she would roost out there on her own. Then that chicken fought doors to get back into the house—for months. Five years later she still sneaks in the house any chance she can to check out the grease in the frying pan or the butter left out, etc. That is the last chicken we will ever raise in the house, if we can help it.

When Chick Chick had her babies, she kept them, or they kept to her, until they were full-sized chickens. By the time all the other young poultry were one-third full grown, they leave their mother's side; roost amidst various other aged chickens in various places; and hunt and peck around the yard on their own. Chick Chick's kept under her wing 'til full grown, the size of her; and when at night you'd shine a flashlight in the feed shed, side by side on perch could be seen Chick Chick and her four full-grown babies nestled together looking at you.

When Lloyd drives up to the house, she still greets the car. There is usually some tidbit from town he can throw out to her.

So much for Chick Chick.

Now these chickens are creatures of habit and instinct and like to roost overnight in trees, though we have a henhouse, a feed shed and a smokehouse with high perches for them to roost in. There's four semi-dwarf apple trees in the back yard and, at one time, about twenty chickens roosted in the limbs. One night we heard a big "Squawk! Squawk!" Something got one out of the apple tree. We ran out with the flashlight and the gun, but the raccoon had gotten away with the hen. We could see his tracks in the mud the next morning. The next night nobody roosted in that tree, quite a few had deserted the other trees, too. We got a ladder and removed the remaining hens from their perches in those trees and placed them in the smokehouse. The next night we had to remove about six, the night after, two and by the fourth maybe one—that's how fast they learn to relocate. We've trained them off the antlers on the front porch and the rafters in the shop by swatting them with a broom; it takes about one to five applications of that to train them to sleep a different place. An owl got a hen one night off her roost in the elderberry tree by our bedroom window. Just some loud "Squawk!"'s and then the sound of wings flapping away. Same thing—those chickens aren't dumb—or in varying degrees anyway, just like people—a lot of the tree was deserted by the next night.

Hawks just love little baby chicks and will swoop down, grab them and fly off. Our back renter saw quite a sight in the driveway in front of his trailer. A hawk swooped down on a mother hen and her ten chicks. She let out a "squawk!"

and all the chicks ran under the trailer house. Then she swirled to brace herself for the attack. She was fluffed up, wings spread out, feet apart and facing and watching the descending hawk. She was ready to fight! But the hawk just swooped her, not wanting a hen but a baby chick. He couldn't get a chick because they'd all ran for cover. They'd understood that tone of their mother's squawk.

Here at Loon Lake in the coastal mountain range, we have two types of elderberries—the red ones and the dark blue-purplish ones. Early spring, about May, the red elderberries ripen and are the first fruit of the year. The dark blue ones are sour but edible and make good pancake syrup when they ripen in the fall. They grow on a tall spindly tree in bunches like grapes.

Pigeons like to eat them and then disappear until next year about the same time. These red ones are edible according to some ladies who report they have made a lot of good jelly out of them, I don't know. Lloyd says they're poisonous, so we don't eat them. The chickens love them and that's what this is about.

The huge red elderberry tree off the corner of our back porch had ripened, the fruit eaten by chickens and pigeons and many months had passed and the fall was upon us.

While walking back home from the lodge, I came to a black elderberry tree growing by the side of the road. I picked up some sprigs of the edible berries which had blown off a tree and were laying on the road. I added them, the next day, to some apples I was canning and threw the one remaining sprig out mixed up with the "chicken garbage," table and kitchen scraps. I didn't think much of it. I knew they'd eat them there down on the ground, but the next thing I heard was a lot of commotion of flapping wings and squawking as the hens were climbing and fluttering from limb to limb in that huge red elderberry tree.

They'd get one place, look all around, then get to another place; looked like they were searching for something. They were flying up there looking for more. Hens make a certain sound when they think they've found something good and they were clucking like that, attracting more hens.

Our property only has the red elderberry trees. Though they hadn't had any for three or four months, they must have recognized the taste and as far as I can remember this was the first time our chickens have ever had the purple elderberries. The taste must be similar and that's why they got up in our trees looking for more even though there was four months' span between ripening of the red fruit and the purple.

Another case of when they have their wings, and when they have their freedom, their retention power is quite evident.

          ☙      ☙      ☙

Here's another case of their savvy: Our farmhouse renters, who lived half a mile away, ordered two dozen baby chicks through the mail. The chicks were a month old when the renters moved away leaving them in a chicken coop with an outside run. Another month went by and once a week or so I would replenish their water and feed. Raccoons started getting them, just like clockwork, about two a night. Under the chicken house and in their yard was a few heads and feet the coons had left. I kept telling Lloyd we've got to get up there and bring those chickens home. Finally there was only two left—about half-grown chickens. We grabbed them by the legs one night off the roost, put them in feedsacks and brought them home and put them to roost with ours. Would you believe those chickens must have known they were saved because for weeks afterwards they would run right up to our feet—they'd see us and run right over. You'd open the back door off the kitchen and they'd be looking at you right off

the doorstep. They liked the house, too. After seeing that many of their buddies killed, I imagine they figured they were next. After a while that wore off and they acted just like the rest of them. We believe, by their unusual attachment to us, that they knew that they had been rescued.

*       *       *

Our neighbors had a farm auction and sold everything they had before they moved out. After the auctioneer, bidders and neighbors had left, Wayne Birch said, "Oh, Lloyd, we forgot the chickens and geese. Why don't you just take them?" We had been feeding and watering them while Birches were looking for a house. We caught the six geese and took the two dozen chickens from an eight by eight foot shed, where they had been so crowded that they had pecked the combs off of each other. They'd just pecked the heck out of each other's heads. Just like hoodlums in a city—too crowded with nothing to do—turned them mean. It wasn't but three or four days loose in our yard that they quit all that pecking and bothering each other and started acting normal. In a little time their combs grew back, too.

The four or five geese we got from Birches were African. They were gray with a big hump on their black beaks. About the same time the resort wanted to get rid of their three or four white China and gray Toulouse geese. These had yellow noses. Well, once we got all these geese home we had goose wars for two months between the yellow-nosed and the black-nosed—regular battles! Finally things subsided and they got along fine. They interbred and produced lots of goslings every spring.

Needless to say, all these fowl have given us lots of entertainment, meat and eggs over the years.

With them to watch instead of a television, we can truthfully say that chickens have plenty of intelligence, vocabulary, brains and memory.

# The 1996 Flood and Slide
## on the Umpqua River
### As Told by Tom Carley

It was November of 1996 and she'd been raining for gosh, I guess a month or more, and the last two days seventeen inches of rain had fallen. On Highway 38, from our house to Reedsport, all those waterfalls were running full speed—the ground was saturated! I had taken my wife to work the morning of November 18th so in case she had any trouble, I'd at least be with her. That evening I picked her up at work (she's secretary to the Administrator of the Lower Umpqua Hospital in Reedsport), and she told me there had been a slide. Now we live on Oregon State Highway 38, near Scottsburg, at the fourteen mile marker, and she said there'd been a slide at the fifteen mile marker, a mile above us.

We drove home and as we came to our house, the lights were still on in the kitchen, and she wanted to go on past and see what the slide was like. Half the road was plugged off; cars were going on by in both directions you know, so there was not much to it. We drove on by, turned around and got back to home—the lights were off—the storm blew a tree down across a power line somewhere. I went in and lit a couple of Coleman lanterns (we had a big supply of Coleman fuel in the garage). We got flashlights going and a bag of batteries; and so we're usually pretty well fixed.

About seven o'clock we noticed cars were stopping up on the highway in front of our house. From the lights we could tell they were all pulling in behind each other. We later found out that a slide consisting of logs, rock and mud had blocked both lanes up from Mill Creek junction, a half mile from the house. That plugged the road so no one could get through coming from the west. After there got to be fifty, sixty, I don't know how many cars in there, another slide came down at the fifteen mile marker—a big one. And that blocked the road there—so those cars were IN there. I went up and talked with some of the people and told them they'd better get out of their cars and come to the house because there's going to be slides. I know this mountain! I just pleaded with these people. Everybody said they'd be all right. Did I look that bad? None of them wanted to get out of their vehicles, but after a lot of prodding, two women did come with us; one of them wanted to use the phone. They were Janice Polly and Mildred Crookshank of Coos Bay.

They no more got in the door and were taking off their coats, when one of them said, "My name is Janice. . . ."

And Ka-boom! Just like a clap of thunder. One of the women let out a blood-curdling scream. She started to scream more and Glenda told her to hush up. The house shook and pictures fell off the wall, and it sounded like a freight train running through lumber yards for about ten seconds. Then it sounded like hail hitting the house and windows—I was surprised they didn't break.

But nothing broke, and all you heard was rain and the roaring and stuff moving. I looked out the back door and the mud and rubble was as high as the deck, which is off the ground seven feet at the house and ten feet at the railing. Just logs and boulders and sitting up, oh, six, eight feet above the rubble was my truck and my wife's car! They weren't hurt or damaged too badly; had just been carried along with the mud and rubble. The mud and rubble— Gad! We figured it was nineteen feet deep in one place; it was level from the hill above us, clear to the bank of the river. And it took *every* building we had on the place except for the house, and it knocked that a little off the foundation; but that was correctable. A big log about four feet at the butt hit the end of the house and knocked the water faucet off, dented the T-1-11 paneling, and knocked

349

out a post from under the deck and took that almost to the river. A huge supply of good fir logs came out of the canyon and went past the house and expanded out in the pasture in all directions—that supply made me two winters of wood.

I looked up towards the road and said to my wife, "The garage is gone." Everything in line with it was too—the barn, the metal machine shed, the workshop, three boats, the well-house, the woodshed, the chicken coop, the dog pen and houses—all gone! I yelled for my two Airedales and they came out snarling from under the deck. They were scared and ready to fight something, but they were all right.

My wife said, "Tom, I can hear somebody hollering for help!"

She went to the front door and opened it and mud started oozing in, so she got that back shut. The mud was up within inches of the windows all around the house—four to five feet of mud.

I said, "I'd better go out there," and put on my coat and rubber boots.

"I'm going with you," she told me. Well, there's no arguing with Glenda, so away we went, out the back door where the mud was level with the porch. I was carrying a lantern and she was carrying two flashlights, but we still couldn't see anything.

"Keep hollering!" I was yelling to the guy.

"Help! Help!" the voice came back.

It was scary. I thought, "What the hell—has he got a log on top of him or something?" We crawled over logs, we sank in the mud, we came against huge walls of debris and logs and boulders and had to turn around and go back and find other routes, it was *hell* trying to get over to him! We finally went up closer to the road where the knoll had been, and it wasn't as deep there. It was a half-way decent walk except for climbing through limbs—it took us forty-five minutes to go 100 feet. I finally saw this pick-up truck tipped over on its right side, the passenger side; mud nearly up to the windows. Ahead of the steering wheel, the windshield was broken out and also the driver's side window. I got over, bent down—that's how high the rock and mud was. My feet were at the window level; the mud and rock were solid there. I looked through the window and there's this guy in there with mud clear up to his neck, only his left arm was sticking out. Of course, I was shining a light in his eye, the poor devil, couldn't see who was there, maybe it was Ol' St. Peter, or the devil, you never know who come to get him, you know.

He said, "If you don't get me out of here, I'm going to die."

I said, "Looks like it, don't it?"

Glenda told me afterwards, "That was a terrible thing to say to him." Well, the mud was coming up and he only had a couple of inches to go. What are you going to say to the fella, "Let me get you out of here," that's about all you can tell him, but maybe that's wishful thinking.

I got around to the front and crumbled up the rest of the windshield and allowed some of the mud to come out— it was just running in the car and running out. One of our Airedales squeezed in there beside me and licked his face. Found out later this guy was Glen Bales, son of an Oregon State police officer. I came around to where Glenda was holding the two flashlights, and started digging his feet out and untangled his legs. I don't know how in the heck they were twisted around the wheel, but a stick was through them, holding them both; he couldn't move his legs. One of his legs was broken, and he had a really nasty-looking cut on it with a muscle protruding. So I went around to the windshield again, dug out some more mud, got ahold of him under his shoulders and said, "This is going to hurt ya!"

"Can't do any worse than it's doing," he bravely said, "Pull away!"

I remember saying out loud to myself, "Come on adrenaline!" and with him kicking his legs, I snaked him out of the car.

He asked, "Can you get me a stick I can use as a cane?"

"Where in the name of hell am I going to get a stick around here?" and we both laughed like damned fools, with a hundred million of them at our feet, you know. Rain was pouring down, he was shaking pretty badly yet. My wife got under one arm of him and I got under the other, and we were just going to take off, when somebody hollered, "Anybody got a cigarette?"

"Where are YOU?"

"I'm behind the truck here." Here was this guy curled up behind Bales' truck. If he hadn't asked for a cigarette, we'd have left him there. And I'm sure he'd have died because he had come up out of the river and not being able to swim, he got pretty wet. He and his car had gotten carried into the river by the mudslide and his car was floating but held close to the bank by an eddy swirling there. He had gotten out of the car and pulled himself on to a log which had hit the car and the bank, and as soon as he crawled up the length of the log to the bank, the log shot away in the river's current. He just escaped death there. I don't know how he climbed the bank because there were boulders and trees and buildings and everything, but he got through there and he could see the dome light of Bales' truck and he went for that light. He got behind the truck and there he was.

Later he told me he was trying to help Bales, but I don't think he knew where he was; he had the life scared out of him, he was hitting the panic button, he'd been in that cold water. I told him, "Come on, you've got to help us get this guy over to the house." But he didn't want to get up or go anywhere, so I got ahold of his pigtail and gave him a little help to his feet that way.

He got under where I had been and I went ahead with the lantern throwing stuff out of the road. Ol' Bales was hobbling along with this crooked stick. We got almost to the house and there was two crutches standing up right in the mud where the garage had been. They used to be stored above the workshop. They were standing right up in plain sight and we'd walked right by them, never thinking we would be walking someone back with a broken leg and needing them.

When we were getting Bales out, I could hear a bumping and crashing somewhere near me. Thinking it was someone hurt, I said, "What's that?"

Bales said, "I think that's a cow, I can hear her bellowing."

So I walked over a little and there was one of my cows pinned under a big beam from the barn. I don't know if they'd been in the barn or if they were standing behind it or what, but she had a heavy beam over the top of her. She was hurt badly, her front leg was torn off at a joint; blood was pumping out of that. So when we got back to the house I said, "Glenda, can you handle Glen here?"

She said, "Yes, do what you got to do." She had stripped him of his clothes outside, wrapped him in a sleeping bag and laid him down on the living room floor.

I had a rifle right next to the door, and I got the rifle and I went back down and the cow was still alive yet. So I shot her, that was Britches. Then there was another one laying a little ways from there and I think—"Hellbitch" I called her—was dead. So I shot her, too. I don't know where any of the others were. Three days later I found the bull standing on a knoll. Remember Ol' Dandy? About an 1800 lb. Hereford? I looked him all over and he was all right. But he was looking for his cows. But they were all under the buildings. The young bull we had and two young heifers were gone. We never did find the heifers. I suspect they went down the river, but three days afterwards the young bull came walking back up the highway. And I said to my wife, "I wonder where he's been?"

"It probably took him three days to walk back from where he quit running."

But I think he had gotten swept down to the river with the mudslide and carried away downstream because he came a-walking back and then the Airedales took out after him—I COULDN'T call them off—they were going to kill anything that was around, the yard was so different. He went right through a barbed wire fence to get to his pasture. So he and Dandy were the only ones I saved.

Anyway, when I fired the second shot, I heard somebody whistling. And so I hollered, "Where are you at? Can you tell me any idea which way you are? Can you holler?" He had hollered so much, he told me afterwards, that all he could do was whistle. And I could hear that sharp whistle. I looked and I looked. I couldn't get across the little creek that was six to eight feet deep, so I slugged around in the swale where the barn and machine shed used to be for an hour and a half in the oozing mud. (I'd only had my knee replaced a few months before.) I started across the swale—I didn't cover much ground because it was so bad, I was crawling over logs and around boulders. My wife was waving the flashlight and hollering at me to come back in the house. It was like you had bulldozed all this stuff in a pile—well, you know what it looks like in the woods—anyway, I was down almost to my knees in this mud and I was sinking, so I threw myself down flat, and I remember thinking to myself, "Is this the way you're going to let me down easy, God? Just get sucked down in this mud?"

About then a tree came moving down—I had my flashlight yet—and this tree had a root system on it and the root system and the whole ground was moving.

I put my gun up in the roots and I said, "I hope my kids find this rifle and that it doesn't go into the river because I

354

sure wasn't going to get out of here." And I grabbed ahold of the root on the tree and it tightened up on me and started moving. I did the hula, stuck with the tree as it slid on down and it pulled me right out of the mud and back onto my feet! I'd lost one of my boots, they were so full of stones you couldn't tell whether you were barefooted or had boots on. But I had one sock on and walked around more looking for the guy. Finally, I thought I was going to die; my heart was pounding, and I was completely wore out, exhausted. I went back into the house. That's when I noticed my boot was gone.

Now I have always considered myself as a tough man—I *am* tough, physically and mentally and I never cried when my Mom and Dad died; I cried over a puppy, but everybody does. But I went into the house and I started to cry. I said, "Glenda, there's a man out there somewhere and I can't find him and I can't go any more."

She said, "You just drink a cup of coffee and change your clothes and you'll feel better, then you'll be able to go out again."

Well, I got new clothes on—oh God, it was pouring drops as big as your thumb and just a steady roaring of water. There was waterfalls all over and I got ready to go out again. Two Mexican guys came to the window and hollered. They wanted something to eat.

My wife said, "Well, I've got some bananas. We've got a fruit bowl sitting there and apples," but I said, "You get nothing to eat until you help me find a man!"

"Oh? Somebody out here?" he said, "Okay, we look!"

And away they went and away I went down where I'd been. In about fifteen minutes they were back. They said, "We find him! We find him!"

One of them went up the road to get help, the other one stayed there; some truck drivers who hadn't got hit with the slide came down and they got the guy out of the log truck.

355

He'd been hanging there upside down four hours. That was Jack Gillem. They got him out and broke the windows in the neighbor's house and got him in there. The other one came back with the Fire Department, Leo and Steve, they took care of him 'til morning. Leo and Steve had hiked in over the slides from Scottsburg. Leo was able to get out with his radio. Jack Gillem's father, Ted, heard his son was hurt and walked all night clear from Reedsport to get to him, over twelve to fourteen miles of slides. There were 138 slides on the highway that night from Reedsport to Drain.

The next day about nine or ten o'clock in the morning, it was still raining, and the Coast Guard came up and got the wounded out by boat. That was a hell of a thing, too. Because they got them loaded and we started taking movies of them taking out our guys— Gillem and Bales. My wife had packed Bales' broken leg in frozen vegetables and turkeys all night long. Until the EMT's came to relieve her, she was up all night taking care of everybody. We ran out of Coleman fuel, all we had was flashlights. I had a couple of gallons of Coleman fuel in the garage, but the garage was spread from the highway to the river. All my fishing tackle went—thirty-two rods and reels went and every tool that I owned!

But anyway, they came up and they carried our guy up to the highway and then down, to the river and one fella sunk in way up to his waist right on the highway. It was ten, twelve feet of debris on the highway. And at eleven o'clock they got him out and they started downstream and one motor conked out. They were in a big rubber raft. And that must have been hairy laying in that thing with these long, skinny Coast Guard guys running it. After a while the second motor conked out. I suppose the outboard motors filled up with mud, you know; the Umpqua River was flowing hard and the mud in the water wouldn't go through the cooling system and they seized up. I've had 'em do that to me, but then they start up again afterwards. They don't stay seized up, they cool off

356

and start up. But anyway, they radioed ahead and a boat waited for them coming down the river at Unger's Landing and pulled them in and away they went to the hospital and that's the end of those two guys as far as I knew.

The two women, Janice Polly and Mildred Crookshank, had been shopping in Portland and they had $1700 worth of new clothes in their car. And we had got them out of their car to come into the house. They had just got in the house when the slide hit and their car got carried about 150 feet and it was about three feet high with the steering wheel sticking out through the roof. If they would have stayed in it, they would have been deader'n a rock.

Those women, after the slide hit and the one let out that long screech, the two of them stood for two hours in the foyer; just stood there in shock. Now my wife does not hit the panic button; let's see what we can do, that's her motto. They called me a hero—I was on the television and newspapers, but the real hero of that whole night at our place was that ninety-three pound wife of mine, who packed Glen's broken knee and leg to keep the swelling down and fed him soup and took care of everyone. Anybody that came along she fed. She gave them all my clothes, which I've never gotten back. Ten people stayed in our house that night, and they were all soaking wet. She had four pairs of muddy trousers hanging on the railing off the deck. The Mexicans came back and got their own clothes but never brought mine back, including my good boots—a fifty dollar pair of Redwing boots. I never got anything back except a shirt from the wife of the guy who had been laying behind the truck and wanted a cigarette. His wife returned the shirt.

Ah! Jesus Christ she scared me. I was outside doing something and all of a sudden I see these feet by mine. I look up and there was one of these really grim-looking women with hair in all directions, no teeth in her mouth, she was gummin' at me but no words coming out, and I, by

357

golly, near jumped over the log I was monkeying with. She said, "I'm bringing back your shirt."

This was three months after the slide, she hadn't gotten around to washing my sweatshirt that he had. He's the one whose car had gone into the river and later I saw a little corner of it sticking out of the water about thirty feet out in the river, and I thought maybe it was my stock trailer; but then I realized it was a muffler I was seeing. The water went down, and Mast Brothers Towing came and towed it out of there. Towed my vehicles out too. They weren't drivable and I had no way of getting around. One guy came and let me use his truck. He brought his truck when one lane of the road got open in three days, brought it right up, said, "There's that truck, you've got it as long as you need it. We've got another car—you take it." And I've never forgotten him—he got a fishing pole, he got a fishing reel, and I took him fishing. I give him birthday presents—*I talk with that guy!*

Anyway, the next morning after the slide we saw one of the cows standing in the pasture with the water way up on her sides. The river was still coming up from rainfall and about ten feet from the house. Ginger, Ol' Ginger, she was standing on the bottom all right, but she just couldn't walk so good, really having troubles, she was hurt, and God! I didn't want to shoot her; she had a great lump on her side where her hip was—I think she had dislocated her hip. Every time the water would come up on her she'd move a little closer and look up at the house and beller— she was asking for help. She finally got up against a pile of logs and she couldn't go anywhere, soon she'd be floating.

About then two bulldozers and two 4-wheel drive pick- ups from Umpqua River Navigation Company came to evacu- ate us and take us to Reedsport, where a school was set up for the flood and slide victims. Ron Lewis and Richard Terra, operators; Chuck Bither and Tom Plagman, cutters; and

John Joy and Brian Clugston, dump truck drivers, had already seen a light over the edge and pulled the Hausmann's out of their demolished house. All slept overnight in pickups and equipment trapped between slides as more came down. By daybreak they, along with fifteen to twenty bulldozers were clearing the road. By eleven o'clock in the morning they cleared as far as our house.

Two bulldozers made a big U-turn with pickups right behind them before the mud could fill in again. One of the men said, "Tom, you got ten minutes to gather up whatever you want and get out of here!"

We had to leave home and go to Reedsport, so I went out with the rifle and I just said, "Goodbye, Ginger."

One of the guys from Umpqua Navigation said, "You want me to shoot her for you?"

Well, that's the last thing I wanted. I am a deadly shot, and boy, I put that ol' cross-hair on her forehead and, "So long, Sweetheart," and "Ka-boom!" and down she went. We didn't have time to save her and we were afraid more slides would come down, so we went.

I thought I'd have a fight on my hands, but they let me take my two dogs, and I rode in the back of one crew-cab pickup with them. Glenda was in the front with a salesman, the driver, and I don't know how many others packed in there. The two 4-wheel drive pickups followed the two Caterpillar tractors back through the oozing slides to town. I tell ya, that was some ride—those drivers had more guts than can be strung on six miles of fence. And all the cars followed up.

Now, I have never taken any welfare in my life, but we took the government disaster assistance available, and that's how the big job of cleanup was done—by the boys on their Caterpillars from Umpqua Navigation Sand and Gravel Company and the convicts. We never could have afforded it ourselves. I'm still working on it a year and a half later; it's not back to where it was yet, it'll be a long time. You know, you always see this sign, "Where will you spend eternity?" I'll spend eternity in that yard raking and wheeling rock; tons and tons and tons of pebbles, rock and boulders heaped here, scattered there and coming to the surface.

People in their cars later recalled a man who warned them to get out of their cars and come in the house but didn't know who it was—it must have been me—a lot of them stayed in their cars.

I don't know how many people were hurt that night, but one woman was dead in the yard in her car under the mud. I was within twenty feet of her and I didn't know she was there. The officer said she had got killed upon impact when the log hit her car, then it was buried in mud. When we were leaving we saw part of a car sticking out of the rubble in the yard and they dug around and pulled her out.

Jack Gillem—they got him out and his kidneys were shot, quit functioning from hanging upside down four hours, and he was in bad shape for quite a while, but he's back working again; sees me and grins 'n stuff. I didn't know him until they introduced him at a party they were having for Leo Black and Steve Rose. I went up to him and I says, "Do you remember I was yelling at you when you were whistling?"

He says, "You the fella that fired the gun shots?"

I says, "Yes!"

"By God!" he said, "I owe you a lot—that gave me help and heart. I was about ready to give up and when I heard those shots I knew somebody was out there. And they wouldn't be committing suicide; they were out looking; they were killing something."

Bill Otis sent the convicts over, you know, fifteen of them. They dug out all eight cords of wood for me and put it under the deck. And they forgot that it was all water soaked, you know it was under mud, they had to dig it out with a pick and shovel, and boy you ought to have heard them cussing. The women were worse than the men. They were cussing at the guys and smiling at me, and I wouldn't have wanted to have gotten tangled up with them, they'd have punched my lights out.

The convicts worked hard because they get time off for working, they volunteer for this. They've got an overseer, and if you ever get in trouble like that again, ask for them, maybe they'll bring them to your place. They're not allowed to come in the house; strict discipline prevailed.

One of them said, "Sir, permission requested to speak."

"Granted," the overseer said, who was standing there watching them, a big Irishman named Mike Murphy.

The prisoner continued, "Permission requested to talk to the owner."

"Granted."

"Permission to speak to you?" he said to me.

"Go ahead!" I told him.

"What's under this dirt, here?"

I said, "A two-by-four."

"Oh. Sir, permission to ask a question of the owner."

"Granted."

"What is a two-by-four?"

Shoot, I thought everybody knew what a two-by-four was; I got hit by a few of them when I was a kid, didn't you?

But green or not, these prisoners worked in the rain with Umpqua Navigation, my wife and myself to remove the slide of 1996.

*A month after telling his account of the '96 flood, Tom Carley drowned at age seventy-seven in Canada while visiting the old hunting and fishing resort he had owned many years before.*

# Elk Creek Tunnel

During the widening of the Elk Creek Tunnel between Elkton and Drain on Oregon State Highway 38 in 1997, the brush was removed on both ends. Nobody had noticed for years the large squarish caves blasted and carved out of the face of the rock above the tunnel.

During the war these caves had explosives in them in case the Japanese attacked. If a landing was made and troops were invading, someone could run up there into that hollowed-out room and blow the tunnel. No one would get any further up Highway 38. These charges were set so that lots of rock would fall down and block the entrance, similarly the exit; they wouldn't destroy the whole tunnel.

During the war there was also a machine gun nest at the bridge in Elkton. A machine gun was placed in a foxhole in the rock. Anybody coming across the bridge could be stopped right there.

There were also machine gun nests placed along the beach during those four years of war.

# Coming Home From Hunting

As a seventy-year-old hunter, I was returning home after my successful deer hunting trip from the Bald Mountain area in central Oregon. I was driving the motor home, pulling the Ford Bronco. My dog, Bear, a blue heeler-type cattle dog, was with me as we wound along the crooked North Umpqua Highway.

I noticed a loaded log truck behind me; he had caught up with me and was pulling on his air horn. I thought there was something wrong with the Bronco. I was blinded in my rear-view mirrors with that big motor home. I couldn't see the Bronco all the time.

"Boomp, boomp, boomp!" he was blowing his damned horn. Finally I got him on the CB radio and I asked him if something was wrong back there. And he says, "Yeah, I want by."

Well, we talked back and forth on the CB radio and that's when a few choice words and names were exchanged. I told him as quick as I found a wide spot, I'd let him by. And I done that. Down the road a little ways I pulled over and instead of passing me, he pulled up right in back of me.

I had the window down and was starting to open the door when the next thing I know, here he was standing right beside me, about a thirty-five- to forty-year-old man.

At that point he wasn't wanting to get to town as bad as he thought he was. He yells at me, "You miserable damned tourists and hunters in our country! We can't make a living for you obstructing and slowing down traffic!"

I told him, "You guys quit cutting each other's throat and hauling so cheap, you wouldn't be starvin' to death!"

The son-of-a-bitch reached right through the window and hit me right on the side of the brow with his fist. He

363

broke my glasses and bent my nose over. That was my blind side, and I didn't see him coming there. When he smacked me he was right behind the door so I just gave the damned door a hell of a push and sent him reeling backwards and I was out there on him. I grabbed him with both hands and got my back against the motor home where he couldn't pull me over. He could have done me some damage where I had to get around. I'm not too steady on my legs with these replaced knee joints. I pulled him back with me where he wasn't going to get loose and that's when he got the knee. I still had one pretty good leg and just used it. Then I smacked him in the gut about twice and then I landed him a right and then a left to his jaws either side. And that was it. That took care of the smart ass.

Bear dog had been blue heeling him. He was biting on his ankles and legs, nipping on him from down below while I was pounding on him from up above. The truck driver was hurtin' and on his way out. After he was down I kicked him in the ribs a couple of times—hell with him; the son-of-a-bitch wanted to play like that. When I left he was kicking around there trying to get up. That was the last I ever seen of him.

That guy wasn't very smart to start with, shoot, during hunting season like that. Pull a stunt like that, some guy might have had a pistol right beside the seat and pulled that out and shot the bastard. He was lucky mine was back in the house part. I don't think that guy had been hauling logs too long. An old logger wouldn't pull a trick like that—a guy pull over, they'd just pass him and go on by; must have been a hot head.

I figured I wouldn't get too far, shoot, they must have radios. When I got to Wilbur a deputy sheriff was setting up there by the Post Office. He followed me clear through out to Highway 138, then clear out to that truck scales where he turned around.

He had to be looking for something I would think. But I never got pulled aside and made it safely home without further incident.

The log truck driver will probably give it a second thought before stepping out of his truck next time. And if the man was in a hurry to make his extra trip that day he was detained. That North Umpqua Highway ain't so bad any more. They've put some passing lanes in it and widened it. It's lots better than it used to be.

# Sailing Out the Window

I went into the Perry Electric store today and there's a counter there, you know, and there's always a bunch of employees standing behind it and a man was on the other side of it.

He saw me and said, "Hey, there's that guy from Loon Lake! Man, I'll never forget, I walked in his store one day just in time to see a guy sailing out the window. I asked him, 'What the hell's going on? What are you throwing that guy out for?'

"He said, 'The customer shit in his pants. I pleaded with him and I pleaded with him, and he wouldn't leave, so I opened up the window and threw him out.'"

This guy was telling this to the clerks, who were looking at me like I was crazy and then he adds something to the effect of, "Boy, you don't cross that store owner in Loon Lake." He remembered me; he remembered the shit detail. By God, I don't know who he was. I know he has a great big ranch up Sutter's Arm off the Coos Bay, I just can't remember his name.

So I explained to the Perry Electric employees and the man what happened:

"We had a customer named Bob Evans in the back bar. He'd wandered in there. He shouldn't even have been in there drunk as he was. If Althea, my wife, had seen him coming, he'd never even have gotten in the door, I can tell you that. Drunken fellers. Joker like that could jeopardize your livelihood. Liquor inspector see something like that they could shut you down. Althea had been trying to get him out of the store by talking to him and couldn't convince him to leave. So she came and got me to get him out of there. I came out from the walk-in cooler and he was stinking; that's why I asked him,

"'Bob, why don't we go on out of here? Why in the hell don't you get yourself cleaned up?'

"'Naw,' he says, 'I ain't finished yet.'

"That's when I got mad and threw that bastard right out the window by the toilet. I didn't want him in *there* messing things up. Shitty as he was I wanted to get him out. If I'd threw him out the door I'd been covered with it. He'd been drinking that ol' wine. That's all he drank, wine. 'I ain't finished yet.' I finished him, alright, right outside onto the rose bush."

# Photographs

Mary and I right after the war in 1946.
This was when I had that d____d Malaria; about melted
away—down to 145 pounds. That was one of the worse
malaria attacks I ever had.

*Gathered on the Duckett's steps.*
*Pierce and Althea Duckett on bottom step; Bert Shippey, hired*
*man, top right; others unidentified.*

*Althea and one of her customers, "Gordo,"*
*in the Duckett's Store—1974.*

*Marvin Haskell (front) with Ron Robinson and work horses, Rosie and Tillie, logging in 1977.*

*Kenny Winslow and Midnight*

*We've been fishing—Frank Kallinger and I.*
*He was crippled up the rest of his life from*
*grabbing the Samarai sword.*

*Think of the stories this Samarai sword could tell.*

*Me in front of the resort in 1959.*

*Glen Smith helping me make a road.*
*We sprung two sixteen-inch blocks moving this "riggin' buster."*

*Swimming near the boat dock in 1959.*

*Picnickers and boaters in 1969.*

# Glossary

**Barber-Chaired** — When a tree being felled splits up itself, breaks off somewhere up there, kicks back and returns butt first to the ground with lightning speed. Where the butt hits is unpredictable except that it is back of the stump where the cutter is. Usually performed by an inexperienced man, there is little time to get out of the way. Good way to get killed. The stump is left with a great big slab standing straight up on it, resembling the high back of a barber's chair.

**Basko** — Basque people from northern Spain, noted for animal husbandry and hard work.

**Boomsticks** — Long slim poles that hold log rafts together.

**Bronze bushing** — Owner, superintendent, big boss.

**Brush hog** — Tractor implement with lawn mower-like blades that mows heavy brush or fields. Powered by the tractor and pulled behind it.

**Bullbuck** — Man in charge of the cutting crew of fallers and buckers.

**Bucking** — Cutting tree-length logs into mill logs or lengths desired by the lumber mills.

**Camp Push** — Superintendent, bronze bushing.

**Cat** — Bulldozer.

**Choker** — Short steel cable put around logs for yarding them in. A nubbin on the end fits into a sliding bell on the cable so when pulled, cinches up tight.

**Cletrac** — Manufacturer's name for a bulldozer.

**Cold Deck** — Logs that have been yarded and piled up to be moved later.

**Crummy** — Vehicle in which loggers go back and forth to work.

**Duff** — Decomposed bark and woody material.

**Face** — "V" shaped notch made in the direction you want the tree to fall.

**Freshet** — Big, big, horrible rainstorm, which afterwards swells the creeks out of their banks.

**Gypo** — Small logging outfit usually working on a shoestring budget.

**Landing** — Piece of ground, usually flat, to where logs are brought in, whether by horse, Cat, skidder, yarder or high-lead. Here the logs are stacked until loaded on log trucks and hauled out for their trip to the mills.

**Loading Bitch** — Diesel or gasoline-powered cable and drum apparatus mounted on skids made from big logs. Lifts logs by way of the boom or cables being in trees.

**Misery Whip** — Man-powered crosscut saw.

**PTO** — The spinning shaft off the back of a vehicle, usually a tractor, which runs numerous pieces of equipment. The Power Take Off works off the gears of the tractor's transmission.

**Pike pole** — Long, light-weight pole with a hook and a sharp point.

**Potlicker** — A dog, an S.O.B.

**Side Rod** — One who looks after the whole logging operation and keeps his eye on things.
Often this job is wisely filled by a good hook tender.

**Siwash** — When a cable has gotten behind an object so it is not in a straight line.

**Spar Tree** — A delimbed and topped tree that has been rigged with all the blocks, lines and boom for yarding logs and loading trucks.

**Splice** — When you weave an eye or weave two lines together.

**Timber Faller** — Feller that fells trees.

**Yarder** — Machine with hoists that pulls in the logs. Nowadays on tracks with steel towers, some even on rubber. In the olden days, on steam-powered donkeys.

378

# Index of Stories

TO ORDER, WRITE KEELAND
9556 LOON LAKE ROAD
REEDSPORT, OR 97467
$15/BOOK INCLUDES S & H

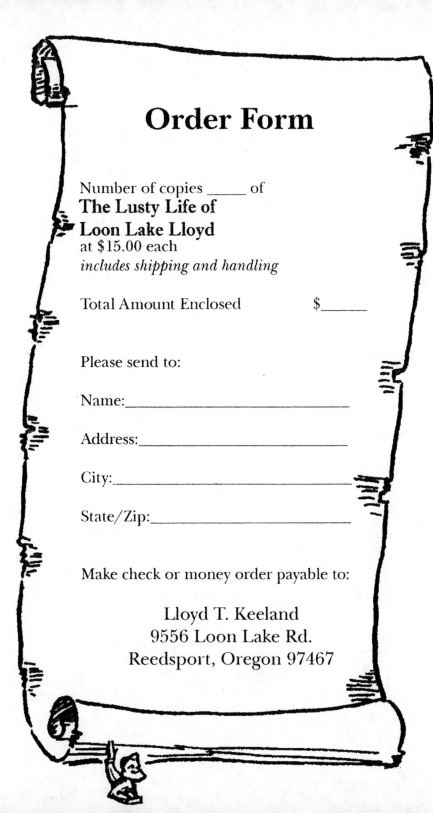

# Order Form

Number of copies _____ of
**The Lusty Life of**
**Loon Lake Lloyd**
at $15.00 each
*includes shipping and handling*

Total Amount Enclosed          $_____

Please send to:

Name:_____

Address:_____

City:_____

State/Zip:_____

Make check or money order payable to:

Lloyd T. Keeland
9556 Loon Lake Rd.
Reedsport, Oregon 97467